# RULE OF LAW INTERMEDIARIES

Scholars puzzle over the conditions that make rule of law development in authoritarian settings successful. In this significant contribution, focusing on the decade of Myanmar's political transformation, Kristina Simion explores rule of law assistance through the practice and experience of intermediaries, their capital, strategies and challenges. How do intermediaries influence the field, and the ways in which the rule of law is brokered transnationally? And why do they matter? Simion relates her research to law and sociology to bring to light these neglected players, focusing on who they are, the influence they have, their double agency and their crucial importance in establishing trust and translating rule of law. Relying on rich empirical data collected in Myanmar, the book shares the voices of the individuals that help to steer societal change within authoritarian confines. This socio-legal work offers some insights into why rule of law change in authoritarian settings often does not go expected ways, one of the development field's long unresolved issues.

KRISTINA SIMION works as a government specialist at the Swedish Agency for Peace, Security and Development (Folke Bernadotte Academy), focusing on rule of law development and Myanmar. She is a Visiting Fellow in the Department of Political and Social Change at the ANU College of Asia and the Pacific, Canberra.

T0382261

CAMBRIDGE STUDIES IN LAW AND SOCIETY

Founded in 1997, Cambridge Studies in Law and Society is a hub for leading scholarship in socio-legal studies. Located at the intersection of law, the humanities, and the social sciences, it publishes empirically innovative and theoretically sophisticated work on law's manifestations in everyday life: from discourses to practices, and from institutions to cultures. The series editors have longstanding expertise in the interdisciplinary study of law, and welcome contributions that place legal phenomena in national, comparative, or international perspective. Series authors come from a range of disciplines, including anthropology, history, law, literature, political science, and sociology.

*Series Editors*

Mark Fathi Massoud, *University of California, Santa Cruz*

Jens Meierhenrich, *London School of Economics and Political Science*

Rachel E. Stern, *University of California, Berkeley*

*A list of books in the series can be found at the back of this book.*

# RULE OF LAW INTERMEDIARIES

## Brokering Influence in Myanmar

*Kristina Simion*

*Australian National University*

CAMBRIDGE
UNIVERSITY PRESS

Shaftesbury Road, Cambridge CB2 8EA, United Kingdom

One Liberty Plaza, 20th Floor, New York, NY 10006, USA

477 Williamstown Road, Port Melbourne, VIC 3207, Australia

314–321, 3rd Floor, Plot 3, Splendor Forum, Jasola District Centre, New Delhi – 110025, India

103 Penang Road, #05–06/07, Visioncrest Commercial, Singapore 238467

Cambridge University Press is part of Cambridge University Press & Assessment, a department of the University of Cambridge.

We share the University's mission to contribute to society through the pursuit of education, learning and research at the highest international levels of excellence.

www.cambridge.org
Information on this title: www.cambridge.org/9781108829854

DOI: 10.1017/9781108914345

First published 2021
First paperback edition 2023

A catalogue record for this publication is available from the British Library

ISBN    978-1-108-83086-7    Hardback
ISBN    978-1-108-82985-4    Paperback

*For Mattias, Carl, August, and Ingrid*

# CONTENTS

# TABLES

# PREFACE

This book was researched during a time of optimism. As one of the 'last frontiers', Myanmar underwent a transition after elections in 2010 that came to excite investors and development practitioners from all over the world: 'internationals' who travelled across the globe to offer their services to a military-led authoritarian government transitioning to democracy. Yangon circa 2014 was a town where new met old. Small trendy cafés and hidden bars were popping up in the most unexpected locations. Young and eager development practitioners were confident about their possibility to contribute, businesspeople were certain about the economic return on their investments in a new emerging market, and local activists were hopeful about development potentials finally brought to their country. As I experienced the year leading up to elections in 2015, optimism about the future was especially vibrant.

When I return to Yangon in early 2020, I stroll through new, luxurious shopping malls and walk past KFC outlets. I have fresh doughnuts at Krispy Kreme during a visit to the re-opened Secretariat building, a place that once housed the parliament dissolved by former military leader Ne Win and where national hero General Aung San was brutally murdered, now a definite stop for tour buses, although still partly a construction site. I stay at what used to be the sleepy old Thammada hotel, now renovated beyond recognition into a trendy boutique chain with a gym and a French restaurant.

I am eager to catch up with local friends and leaders in the rule of law development field with whom I spent time during the transition period (most foreigners I knew back in 2014 have long since left for other places) to get an update of the situation today. I quickly get a sense of their despair and lack of optimism about the future. By now, friendships have ended, well-known rule of law organisations have been dissolved, and new factions have been created. Improvement in rule of law then? My friend, a local lawyer, shakes his head: only on paper but nothing new in practice.

Democracy icon, Nobel laureate, and de facto head of government Aung San Suu Kyi has recently appeared before the International Court of Justice in the Hague to testify in defence of her country facing charges of genocide committed against the mainly Muslim Rohingya minority group. Across town, a huge billboard bears Aung San Suu Kyi's picture accompanied by the message 'We stand with you'. Although by now, notably, not the democratic leader previously expected, Aung San Suu Kyi and her National League for Democracy are still considered by many to be the only alternative to authoritarian rule under military control.

Before she became the de facto head of a civilian government in 2015, Aung San Suu Kyi was the main advocate for rule of law. Yet, although she threw the term around during the early transition period as though it were a panacea for everything problematic in the country, since her own coming to office after elections in 2015, her uses of the term lack the substantive aspects one would expect. A repeated mantra towards rebels and trouble-makers breaking 'the law of the land' is that they will be dealt with by a political leadership that is committed to restoring peace, stability, and rule of law. When Aung San Suu Kyi appeared before the International Court of Justice, her statements on rule of law, described as practical measures to end violence, were mixed with the latest global discourse on sustainable development; she described Myanmar as a peaceful country nourishing a spiritual mindset of unity, harmony, and peace to end cycles of inter-communal violence.

During my visit in 2020, the newspaper reports that the new home minister, a lieutenant general and former head of the Office of Military Security Affairs, pledges rule of law in the country as a tool for combating crime in relation to conflicts with ethnic armed groups and drugs. As the Home Affairs Ministry oversees the country's police force, the minister stresses the need for people's co-operation in solving crimes to ensure the rule of law together with the police. Rule of law as a concept that embraces substantive rights, rather than a tool for upholding law and order, still seems a hope for an uncertain future for the countless donors from abroad that spend big money on projects and programmes to its end and local activists who make their living as development partners and implementers on the ground.

The current rule of law position in Myanmar is considerably more pessimistic than many donors would have hoped for in the transition period when the empirical material for this book was collected. It is not yet a country where the rule of law is flourishing nor where it is a concept understood with reference to its substantive features. Endless foreign funding and initiatives for legal and institutional reform have highlighted problems of access to justice, corruption, and institutional constraints, and still everyday experiences of rule of law and justice remain much alike. Foreign promoters expected an increased understanding of substantive justice and human rights expressed in real change, while activities instead came to focus on planning, with few results in practice. When state counterparts have seemed unwilling, the focus has shifted towards regional solutions, where customary and informal justice systems have been mapped and analysed in ways that are reminiscent of colonial practices. The most contrasting aspect of rule of law development in the country remains that of a perhaps general increase in justice provisions for the ordinary citizen, while some areas of the country are still undergoing heavily armed violence, ethnic discrimination, and crimes against international law. Knowing what we now know about the country (and particularly the backlash against Aung San Suu Kyi's approach to the Rohingya question), Myanmar's 'transition' is looking more and more delayed.

This book is about a time in history that has vanished, a time of unprecedented optimism in the era of liberalisation after the 2010 elections up to those of 2015 when large parts of the population and an elected government struggled to leave its authoritarian past. Its main findings of how rule of law intermediaries broker influence remain relevant for any setting where foreign aid has become an ingrained way of life. Today, intermediaries may come in wider varieties as more people have learned how to capitalise on opportunities to promote change and about the benefits involved in work supported by foreign funding, though they remain a central feature of rule of law development assistance.

Since finishing the bulk of the research for this book, I returned to working on bilateral rule of law development in Myanmar. Similar to the topics discussed in this book, I got to experience, from the inside and not just as an outside observer, the challenges of identifying partner organisations, local beneficiaries, intermediaries, and translators. I have felt the frustration of colleagues struggling over what terminology to use and who have a hard time grasping why local partners refrain from direct critique or voicing an opinion and why one translator interprets sentences differently from another. In the middle of this, I find myself clarifying messages between counterparts, suggesting answers when local facilitators are shy for fear of stepping on somebody's toes, and outlining aspects of culture and history that suggest a need to switch approaches. Amidst all, there are also issues of Covid-19, travel restrictions, and closed borders, internet connections, Facebook, Viber and data security, and ultimately problems with Unicode and Zawgyi conversions that make messages indecipherable. While this book was researched during the transition period, in many ways, it presents an extended case study from then to the challenges of today.

Two days after I receive the proofs for this book, I am struck by news that the Myanmar military have once again ended civilian rule as it arrests Aung San Suu Kyi, the President and other Union-level and state/regional level political leaders, declaring a State of Emergency, purporting to be acting consistently with the 2008 Constitution. The number of arrests increases in parallel to a growing civil disobedience movement that gathers people on the streets across the country. People go into hiding and delete NLD party affiliations from their Facebook accounts and try to stay connected amidst repeated shut downs of the internet and social media.

The way the military throw the term 'rule of law' around to justify their actions, amend legislation, and bend the Constitution to their benefit is an absurd spectacle to follow. Deterioration into lawlessness is frantically ongoing as I have to submit my manuscript.

Once again, we face men in power that dramatically worsen the protection of human rights, potentially throwing the country back into its 'dark ages'. If the military tries to go into isolation again, what they forget is the power of the transnational relationships that were formed with people in Myanmar during its decade of transition. In many ways, this book offers insights as to how large the gap between rule of law and local realities actually was: relationships through intermediaries will become ever so influential as they maintain and strengthen the linkages from the outside-in during the continued struggle for rule of law in Myanmar.

# ACKNOWLEDGEMENTS

The idea for this book started as I was working in the field of rule of law assistance. During a training course at a run-down conference hotel in Berlin's southernmost locality, the city of Schmöckwitz, I chatted with a lawyer from Uzbekistan about his work challenges. The lawyer worked on a large European Union funded rule of law project and told me how he often felt stuck with important information between the project counterparts – the national government and the large foreign donor. He said with frustration: 'One part says it means this, and that, and the international part says, "In our practice it means this ...." ... It's a very small thing but it is so important to get it right. ... I hear both sides and they are very frank to me but not to each other.' The lawyer's story sparked my interest in the topic of this book: the intermediary, a person or organisation positioned in a middle space or place, between international and national norms, ideas, and development objectives. This book is the result of that conversation.

I continued to research and write the book at the School of Regulation and Global Governance (RegNet) at the Australian National University (ANU) where I was generously supported by an International Student PhD Scholarship and an HDR Merit Scholarship. I am deeply grateful for the opportunity that such generous funding gave me. I was fortunate enough to get to know many inspiring scholars during my years at the ANU. Robyn Holder, Therese Pearce Laanela, Imelda Deinla, Ben Authers, Emma Larkin, and Kate Henne provided advice when I needed it the most.

At RegNet, I was introduced to the idea of studying the work of intermediaries during Myanmar's ongoing transition, which pretty much coincided with my candidature. Ma Khin Mar Mar Kyi, Chit Win, Naing Ko Ko, Oo Kyaw Maung, and Jaqueline Menager provided me with excellent introductions to the country and offered me great support ahead of the fieldwork that was an integral part of my research. To my research participants in Myanmar, I am humbled by the fact that you took time to take part in my project. This book would not have been possible without your openness and generous contributions. Friends in Yangon provided invaluable advice and support and made this project a truly memorable experience.

From my supervisors, I got all the support I needed. Martin Krygier, thanks for always showing interest and positive support throughout. Morten Pedersen, I enjoyed our talks and drinks in Yangon when I was frustrated with everyone and everything. Without Veronica Taylor's demanding supervisions my work would not have been as polished and well prepared for future publication. Thanks to Nick Cheesman for remaining a mentor and friend after the formal supervision ended and for pushing me to think of my research from new perspectives.

Thanks to Terry Halliday for advice that helped move my research forward. A heartfelt thanks to Mary Callahan and Bryant Garth who provided great advice, excellent reviews, and encouragement to move my project towards publication.

I am grateful to Thomas Bierschenk for inviting me to the 2014 Summer School on 'Conceptualising Brokers Engaged in Translation' in Halle, Germany, where I got the chance to engage in fruitful discussions about my project. The opportunities I had to present my work at the Law and Society Association's annual meeting in Seattle in 2015 and in Mexico City in 2017, at Harvard Law School's Institute for Global Law and Policy Conference in Boston 2015, and at the Australasian Aid Conference in Canberra in 2015 and 2017 greatly enriched my project. I also benefited greatly from discussions with peers at the 2017 Asian Regional Graduate Student Workshop organised in Bangkok by the Harvard Law School's Institute for Global Law and Policy.

I enjoyed invitations from Mana Takahashi and Maj Grasten to discuss my research in Nagoya and Copenhagen. At Stockholm University, Johan Lindquist and the Forum for Asian Studies provided generous funding and support that enabled a space for discussions about law, society, and culture in South East Asia. Thanks to Lynette Chua and David Engel for showing interest in my research and letting me join the Training Initiative for Asian Law and Society Scholars (TRIALS).

My colleagues at the International Network to Promote the Rule of Law helped me stay connected to rule of law practice throughout my years of research. My employer and colleagues at the Folke Bernadotte Academy showed great patience and support during several years of leave to work on this project.

I am grateful to the Department of Political and Social Change, ANU College of Asia and the Pacific, for hosting me as a visiting fellow while I finished this book. Special thanks to Paul Kenny, Helen McMartin, and Maxine McArthur for assistance and support during my fellowship.

My interactions with Cambridge University Press were nothing but positive from start to end. My first email to the series editors was answered within hours, if not minutes, and I was instantly met with encouragement and great advice. My greatest thanks to Mark Fathi Massoud and Jens Meierhenrich for helping me to navigate the world of academic publishing and to Rachel E. Stern, Finola O'Sullivan, and Joe Ng for supporting me in following through on this project. The anonymous readers of initial drafts of this book provided great support and suggestions that helped with its improvement. A heartfelt thanks for your kind and constructive comments.

Copyright acknowledgements are as follows: Chapter 1 contains parts from 'Research Access and Ethics in Myanmar', first published in the *Journal of the Oxford Centre for Socio-Legal Studies*, Issue 2, 2018; Chapter 3 builds on 'Bottom-Up Explorations: Locating Rule of Law Intermediaries after Transition in Myanmar', which first appeared in the June 2019 issue (Volume 23, Number 1) of the *Journal of Burma Studies* published by the University of Hawai'i Press for the Center for Burma Studies.

# ABBREVIATIONS

| | |
|---|---|
| AFPFL | The Anti-Fascist People's Freedom League |
| ANU | Australian National University |
| BABSEACLE | Bridges Across Borders Southeast Asia Community/ Clinical Legal Education |
| BC | British Council |
| BIA | Burma Independence Army |
| CEELI | Central and East European Law Initiative Institute |
| DFID | UK Department for International Development |
| DPKO | United Nations Department of Peacekeeping Operations |
| EU | European Union |
| FNF | Friedrich Naumann Foundation |
| HD Centre | Centre for Humanitarian Dialogue |
| IBA | International Bar Association |
| IBAHRI | International Bar Association's Human Rights Institute |
| ICC | International Criminal Court |
| ICJ | International Commission of Jurists |
| ICTJ | International Centre for Transitional Justice |
| IDLO | International Development Law Organization |
| ILAM | Independent Lawyers' Association of Myanmar |
| ILO | International Labour Organization |
| INGO | international non-governmental organisation |
| ISLP | International Senior Lawyers Project |
| JICA | Japan International Cooperation Agency |
| MLA | Myanmar Lawyer's Association |
| MLAW | Myanmar Legal Aid Network |
| NGO | non-governmental organisation |
| NLD | National League for Democracy |
| OHCHR | Office of the United Nations High Commissioner for Human Rights |

| | |
|---|---|
| OSCE | Organization for Security and Co-operation in Europe |
| PILPG | Public International Law and Policy Group |
| SC | The Supreme Court of the Union |
| SDGs | Sustainable Development Goals |
| SLORC | State Law and Order Restoration Council |
| UAGO | Union Attorney General's Office |
| UN | United Nations |
| UNDP | United Nations Development Programme |
| UNHCR | United Nations High Commissioner for Refugees |
| UNICEF | United Nations Children's Fund |
| UNODC | United Nations Office on Drugs and Crime |
| USAID | United States Agency for International Development |
| USIP | United States Institute of Peace |
| WB | World Bank |

# CHAPTER ONE

# INTRODUCTION

I had travelled to *Hpa-an*, the capital of Myanmar's[1] eastern Karen state, for a chance to meet with a local lawyer who worked for several of the foreign-funded initiatives of rule of law assistance – defined here as foreign actors' transnational 'project' of supporting legal systems in fragile settings – that were initiated in the country after its political opening in 2011. While usually based in Yangon, the lawyer was in *Hpa-an* for one of his regular training sessions with local activists and lawyers. On my way to our meeting, I walked through the pitch-black streets of the small town in a country I still did not know much about to meet a person whom I imagined would have little patience with a foreign researcher asking questions about his work. As I walked into the tiny shed of a restaurant where we were meeting, I saw Zaw Win Thein's[2] dazzling smile, and I felt a sense of instant relief. His personality was inviting and friendly.

Zaw Win Thein is a fluent English speaker with definite views on human rights and what is needed for rule of law development in his country. He was one of the most sought-after persons when representatives from foreign organisations came to Myanmar to assess the rule of law situation and plan activities as part of new assistance packages in the donor frenzy that emerged as the military-led country opened up to

---

[1] I use the official name of the country, which was changed to 'Myanmar' after 1989, unless writing about the period before that when the official name was 'Burma'.

[2] All names used in this book have been modified to protect the identity of my research participants. Myanmar names (except those of some ethnic minorities, see Skidmore 2003:6) often consist of several syllables, none of which would be classified as a 'surname' as in naming structures found in some other countries.

political change in the aftermaths of elections in 2010. Zaw Win Thein also ran his own non-governmental organisation (NGO) and worked to attract funding to local rule of law projects in his home town. His role changed depending on the task he was faced with: sometimes he did 'lawyer work', which he preferred to 'handling money matters'. He needed to translate foreign concepts and terms so that they made sense to national and local counterparts. Often, he found himself in situations where he needed to mediate when the involved actors did not share the same values and understandings (or worldviews) – a position he was not comfortable with. Sometimes, Zaw Win Thein confused the foreign organisations he was contracted by, who were puzzled as to why certain people were invited to the development activities they funded while others were not. Donors also felt as if peculiar translations took place during meetings. At the same time, these development actors from abroad confessed that they were wholly reliant on people like Zaw Win Thein to carry out their rule of law assistance activities. Zaw Win Thein would also upset local counterparts, who believed that he distorted messages and kept information from them. They claimed that he did not have any real influence but still got much attraction from, and was loyal to, the 'internationals'. Zaw Win Thein, on the other hand, explained that the upset feelings were due to the distrust local actors had towards international law and foreign interests and that he was just trying to explain the international framework as part of his work on translating rule of law to the local level.

Local lawyer Zaw Win Thein illustrates the role of rule of law intermediaries – actors (individual or collective) who play a critical function as mediators, translators, or brokers 'in between' counterparts – in the field of rule of law assistance. In general terms, they are persons who occupy ground from where they broker ideas, models, and templates for change. They oscillate between different roles, depending upon what the circumstances call for. More particularly, rule of law intermediaries work as interlocutors between foreign donors and domestic institutions (see Nicholson and Low 2013). They are not neutral go-betweens but people who stand to gain or lose from different transactions and capital (see Long 1975; Silverman 1965).

Intermediaries matter because they appropriate and adapt ostensibly global ideas and strategies by vernacularising them (Levitt and Merry 2009). They are influential when they successfully navigate struggles that accompany transnational development, where multiple forms of power and influence overlap (Koster and van Leynseele 2018). They also shape transnational law through their understanding of how institutional conventions, knowledge, and practices diverge from conditions where they work (see Berger 2017; Berger and Esguerra 2017; Zimmermann 2017).

While intermediaries are a known feature of development practice, for long they remained silenced in the scholarship that analyses such activities (Bierschenk, Chauveau, and de Sardan 2002; Halliday and Carruthers 2009; Lewis 2005). Intermediaries' role in brokering, making and remaking, rule of law tends to be occluded (Zürn, Nollkaemper, and Peerenboom 2012). Legal scholars who write about rule of law as a field of development sometimes mention that intermediaries are indeed playing their part in transnational relationships; however, they single them out as methodological entry points from which to understand that the interaction between global and local law is yet to be seen (cf. Gillespie 2017). Practitioners who work on rule of law assistance have attended to inputs and outputs, rather than to how projects in its name are intermediated and translated. Official discourse privileges international expertise and elides the parts that intermediaries play. Yet, in brokering the rule of law, intermediaries are also producing some version of it, or at least trading in knowledge about it. By concentrating on them, not only do we get a better sense of how rule of law projects rise or fall but we can also illuminate facets of transnationalism that ordinarily are obscured from view (see Lindquist 2015a).

The intermediary as an agent, occupying Merry's (2006a) amorphous middle space between the global and the local, embodies the interplay between the universal and the particular, the tensions between rule of law as a pre-eminent political ideal versus the vernacularised knowledge necessary for its reception in conditions that are often hostile and always linguistically unique, culturally relative, and historically contingent. If the question is how to build rule of law abroad, then the answers in no small part lie in who these intermediaries are, what they do, and how and why they do it. Intermediaries occupy positions between parties through which others desire to pass, but most cannot. Instead, they have to rely on the intermediaries to smile or frown upon their ideas and make them happen, along with other things that might be incidental to transnational organisations' goals but sometimes also contrary to them.

Exploring the work of intermediaries casts light on some of the relationships that official donor reports seldom mention (see Hancock 1989). Unlocking intermediaries' knowledge and the 'black-boxes', as per science and technology studies (e.g., Kuhn 2012), of rule of law 'making' in illiberal societies provides insights into how foreign-led interventions can be conducted more effectively and without risking the further strengthening of authoritarian systems of law and order. If the donor community is willing to move away from the predominant tendency to listen to international 'expertise' and knowledge (Crewe and Harrison 1998) and also take into account intermediaries' accounts, interventions may be designed that better benefit people who live in societies where a well-functioning system of rule of law is lacking.

This book moves beyond top-down explorations of the impact of rule of law assistance on Myanmar actors by following a law and society tradition of nuanced and contextual analyses (see, e.g., Chua 2014) of the ways in which intermediaries broker influence, which in turn contributes to a socio-legal framework that can be applied in other settings where development assistance takes place, to explain how rule of law making at new sites involves and requires contestation and adaptation.

## 1.1 A LAW AND SOCIETY APPROACH TO THE STUDY OF RULE OF LAW INTERMEDIARIES

Rule of law intermediaries are found across various institutional roles; some are lawyers, some are not. They move within central and peripheral domains of the law while drawing on various forms of capital in a dynamic yet problematic struggle of allegiance and distrust. While some intermediaries are connected to the government, others are closer to local communities and build on their work as activists. They may represent themselves as individual consultants or as leaders of NGOs and be both an intermediary and a counterpart to a foreign development organisation at the same time. These are not fixed roles because intermediaries wear different hats and oscillate between assignments and institutions which enable them to obtain multiple influences at different levels. Most are engaged in intricate networks and embody various forms of expertise. Some have actively sought out a position as an intermediary; others have become involved by chance or as a consequence of their social position.

The myriad of agents that translate global ideas to local levels within the field of rule of law assistance suggests that the lines between global and local processes and the roles individuals have that inhabit these spaces often blur. A law and society approach – which emphasises the social and cultural contexts in which law operates in practice between places, peoples, institutions, and histories to tell us the full story about how and under what conditions law is produced and reformed (Darian-Smith 2013; Ewick and Silbey 1998) – to studying intermediaries invites us to think broadly about law in society and the agents that make it meaningful. To give a practice example, rule of law actors typically look to lawyers as counterparts or beneficiaries of their work. One reason is that their own staff often have expertise in law – though not so often in the law of the place where they are sent to work, or on the relationship between law and development generally (Nader 2007; Simion and Taylor 2015). Another reason is that, since the early days of the law and development movement, practitioners saw law as an instrument for development, and those who were expert with that instrument became the practitioners of choice, their own progress symbolic of general advancement (see Trubek 2006). Krygier (2017b:135) has observed that rule of law promotion continues to be premised on the (wrongheaded) notion that 'if the rule of law is what you want, it seems obvious that it is lawyers, with their insider know-ledge[,] who best understand it and seem best placed to deliver it'. And, in many places, lawyers are indeed important drivers of political and social reform (see, e.g., Cheesman and Kyaw Min San 2014; Dezalay and Garth 2012; Munger 2012a). However, conditions in Myanmar circa 2014 were not amenable to transnational organisations' goals of getting for themselves a local lawyer who could pretty much speak, think, and act the way foreign actors expected. For one thing, legal education had badly deteriorated under military rule (see Khan and Cheesman 2020; Myint Zan 2000a). Lawyers had not had the kind of formal training that transnational organisations were after. For another, successive governments subordinated the legal profession (see Crouch 2020), which had been politically active in the first decade after independence, when law had been a path to a career in politics. The army pulled lawyers from their pedestals. Already by the 1970s there was no longer any such thing as an elite lawyer under its watch (see Dawkins and Cheesman 2021; International Commission of Jurists 2013). So the lawyer-intermediaries whom people from abroad met in the transition period, for the most part, had come from underground political struggles and local-level activism. They were not so much formal legal practitioners as they were informal brokers of law: manipulators and strategists adept at working with law but not working within it (Batesmith and Stevens 2019; Prasse-Freeman 2015); and for good reason, since only a fool, or someone with no expectation of winning a dispute, would have tried to work strictly within the law under the country's successive military rule. Yet it was this very thing, which made lawyering viable under those days, that now diminished it in the eyes of newly arrived advisers to foreign organisations and corporations (see Tungnirun 2018). All they saw was an unusually low-quality legal community over which they could claim superiority by emphasising formal training and doctrinal knowledge of rule of law. On the transnational hierarchy of legal credibility, a lack of country-specific expertise or relevant language skills was no obstacle to their professional superiority (see Simion and Taylor 2015). We see from this example that foreign development actors seek to work with local lawyers, regardless of the role being significantly different from what foreign practitioners are used to, which is suggestive of their attempt to replicate institutions as they know them through 'isomorphic mimicry' (Andrews, Pritchett, and Woolcock 2013; DiMaggio and Powell 1983; Pritchett, Woolcock, and Andrews 2012). Such mimicry is a typical example of how forces outside the formal legal sphere are ignored when lawyers put on their formalist glasses as they try to access the legal systems in the countries where they work but remain much excluded from them (Chesterman 2008). If we scratch the surface, we see that lawyers in Myanmar are busy navigating a marketplace of bribes rather than trying to advocate ideas of rule of law development (Batesmith and Stevens 2019).

While I situate the focus on intermediaries within the voluminous literature on rule of law assistance, this is not a study of what happens in the form of rule of law projects and programmes. Following a law and society ideal, the enquiry is based on the assumption that the interface between development actors from various arenas (international, national, local) is the key 'technique' for rule of law making through development assistance. A language that situates actors as local, national, or global and international is uneasy. Often these locations and cultures are overlapping, interrelated, and difficult to distinguish. For example, local actors also operate in global arenas and thus come to apply international discourses in national settings. The inherent bias in such terminology is problematic because international knowledge is often perceived as superior to local. Following Rossi (2006:29), I recognise that there are problems 'raised by analyses relying, even figuratively, on the notions of donor and recipient "cultures," or on the opposition between "local" or "indigenous" knowledge and "Western scientific knowledge"'. This book makes a repeated argument for the importance of localised knowledge as opposed to that brought in by foreign promoters. Nevertheless, to completely deconstruct the language of development would not serve the purpose of identifying the key gaps between these distinct worldviews – as my book sets out to do. Rather, the discourse of development can be enriched by adding analysis of processes in the middle of the spectra. Thus, while tending to the technique of construction of development, I am addressing a specific point at which development agents connect: the interfaces. Unlike much scholarship within the field of rule of law assistance, this is an actor-oriented approach (Long 2001) to the study of a phenomenon. Consequently, this is a study not of 'rule of law' (or law) in Myanmar but of the people who, as agents, populate and translate 'technologies of social ordering'; it requires in-depth explorations of linkages and objectives as well as the translation chains that modify the rule of law as it travels in the hands of numerous actors (Behrends, Park, and Rottenburg 2014).

## 1.2 BROKERING INFLUENCE: CENTRAL ARGUMENTS

How do intermediaries broker influence in the rule of law assistance field? As the example of Zaw Win Thein suggested, intermediaries exert influence by acting as translators of global concepts that sometimes blend uneasily with the political reality faced by foreign promoters on the ground in authoritarian settings, and sometimes with the effect of angering local counterparts, which in turn can lead to greater resentment of foreign interests, especially in settings where trust is low (Latusek and Olejniczak 2016). They mediate conflicts between development counterparts that do not share the same values and understandings in situations where foreign donors resort to simplified storylines in lieu of detailed and nuanced information of the situation on the ground (Autesserre 2012). Intermediaries help assess legitimate partners of foreign aid as they decide where rule of law activities should be allocated and select who is invited to participate in development activities. Their influence springs from a combination of personal charisma, the possession of large networks, and the control of knowledge.

This book provides a detailed exploration of those individuals and organisations who sprang up as intermediaries in a moment of optimism that surrounded the rule of law activities that were initiated in Myanmar's transition period after decades of aid that was low in intensity and focused on humanitarian and health needs rather than governance and the law (Décobert and Wells 2020). Several sub-questions focus on the way intermediaries came to engage themselves in the development aid field and asks about their backgrounds, motives, methods, and activities. For example: What is the profile of intermediaries? As the example of Zaw Win Thein illustrates, intermediaries have large networks, are charismatic, fluent in English, and have been educated abroad. In addition, many have a background of social or political engagements and experience of working for foreign development actors. How did they come to possess such experience and skills in a country that for decades has been described as isolated from foreign influence and knowledge?

What social processes transform certain actors into intermediaries, and why do foreign promoters seek them out? By highlighting the effect of intermediaries' activities during a historical moment of political transition, this book provides empirical insights into the particular challenges of entering unknown terrain, lacking nuanced and detailed information, as a foreign intervener, which 'is especially the case in closed, authoritarian regimes' (Décobert and Wells 2020:296). Here, donor discourses and global regulatory instruments that stress local ownership and participation are disregarded in practice as foreign actors quite deliberately screen the group that they regard as legitimate partners as well as local owners: donors are particularly cautious not to engage actors too closely connected to the military, or those who do not share their ideas of what human rights constitute (see also ibid.).

Whose expectations and priorities do intermediaries serve, and what are their motives and goals? The answer to these questions also runs throughout this book. In essence, intermediaries have motives, which involve fostering their own networks and transforming the environment, which stretch beyond the work they do for their foreign employers. Intermediaries' personal intentions have implications for how rule of law project activities are steered, how rule of law is translated, and ultimately for development sustainability.

## 1.3 STATUS QUO AND SHORTCOMINGS: RULE OF LAW AS DEVELOPMENT ASSISTANCE

From a narrow transnational field addressing development, after the end of the Cold War rule of law assistance witnessed 'a tremendous growth in "rule doctors" armed with their own competing prescriptions for legal reforms and new legal institutions' (Dezalay and Garth 2002:1). '[T]he intensive exportation of laws and institutional models around the world' (Humphreys 2010:6) amplified to the extent that it is now referred to as a 'rule-of-law industry' (Taylor 2016). Not only development agencies but also transnational and domestic NGOs, consultants, lawyers, judges and prosecutors are key facilitators of transnational flows of rule of law models, legal institutions, principles, and procedures. A dense network of transnational 'in-between' actors has resulted from this functional expansion.

The field of scholarly enquiry into rule of law assistance has remained largely dominated by legal scholars and practitioners with little recourse to interdisciplinary and socio-legal methods for analysing the field's impact on local and global societies. Although critique and a need for reinvention have repeatedly been voiced, an examination of the field's ideological underpinnings has remained relatively static. It is a field that continues to favour debates and ideas derived from the West while constructing superficial regulatory instruments that stress a need for ownership, partnership, and participation (Bosch 2016). In addition, the results of rule of law assistance efforts have often been deemed disappointing (Taylor, V. L. 2009). The reasons for failure have been explained with reference to the practice of development agencies basing their work on simple models and 'off-the-shelf toolkits' believed to work in all sorts of settings (Peerenboom 2009). Such formalist approaches to rule of law assistance see law as a technology rather than a politics or sociology (Upham 2006) and they miss the mark in terms of conducting reforms that take into account local processes, actors, and plurality (Channell 2006).

The repeated lack of success in supporting improvements in rule of law globally has led to various attempts at repositioning through new 'movements' (Trubek 2006) but often without genuine recognition of the particulars of processes and agents on the ground. Van Rooij (2009) calls the field one of 'trends' because it hastily adopts new approaches and paradigms while dismissing the old, all under the umbrella of doubting the industry's effectiveness. Organisational theorists such as

Meyer (1996:246) explain this phenomenon as attempts to swiftly turn around 'inefficient mechanisms'. What these attempts at improving operations lack are Western actors taking responsibility for the failures. Instead, it is more often the case that 'Third World' people are blamed 'because something is the matter with them' (de Soto 2001:4) and especially because they lack a 'will to reform' (as suggested by Carothers (1998); for a critique, see Beard 2006).

The founding story, then, of rule of law assistance that scholars tend to reinforce started in the USA in the 1960s with the 'law and development movement' (see, e.g., Trubek 2006). However, as Humphreys (2010) points out, and Massoud (2013) convincingly illustrates, historicising the initiation of rule of law assistance to this 'movement' is not a sufficient narrative because such reform activities were extensively pursued by colonial administrations as a mode of governance. In colonial Burma, the scale of the colonial legal and regulatory intervention was significant and has come to influence the way rule of law, the central ideology of contemporary reforms, is understood and remembered (Callahan 2004). And, as Veronica Taylor shows (2010b), the American-centricity of historicising rule of law assistance (of which, e.g., Kleinfeld 2012 and Carothers 2006a are illustrative) is bolstered by remarkable silence when it comes to recognising the influence of non-Western donors, like Japan and China, that are prominent in Myanmar. In today's aid landscape, non-Western donors are increasingly influential in promoting alternative values and ideas. This is especially the case when aid is blended with economic incentives and foreign direct investment from countries like China that may be able to provide ideals that are more apt to authoritarian rulers and geopolitical reality but that make little demands about human rights, substantive rule of law, or democratisation (Nicholson and Kuong 2014; Reilly 2013).

These relative newcomers in the field of rule of law aid share more similarities with the historical thinking that influenced the law and development movement, including the perceived link between law and economic growth and the belief that other goods (e.g., social development or democracy) would follow once economic growth was a fact. Having defined such evolution as development, an authoritarian rule could be accepted by liberal actors as a stage in the process that would eventually vanish (Trubek 2006). The leading 'technologies' (Behrends et al. 2014) of this movement included legal education and institutional transplants that legally skilled individuals channelled.

By seeing law as a tool, lawyers defined what best symbolised progress: modern lawyers skilled in law's instrumental culture (Trubek 2006).

The law and development movement was criticised for being dominated by American-style thinking and legal models, imposed on societies by experts without an understanding of local culture or political theory (Merryman 1977). Lack of success led to a critical moment because legal transplants did not end up functioning the way that was planned; they were often ignored or rejected, and legal education efforts proved to have only minor impact (see, e.g., DeLisle 1999; Gardner 1980; Trubek 1972; Trubek and Galanter 1974; Upham 2002). When changes did occur in the economic sphere, the anticipated spillover effects on individual rights and democracy were nowhere to be seen. Similar to what Moustafa (2008, 2014) later cautioned, Trubek (2006:79) recalls that the 'reformers' involved in the law and development movement in the 1960s 'found themselves facing the frightening possibility . . . that their efforts to improve economic law and lawyering could strengthen authoritarian rule'.

Nevertheless, the idea of law's role in development was not abandoned. Instead, rule of law practitioners and scholars focused their attention on the challenges of democratisation and constitutional reform after the fall of the Berlin wall in 1989. A new moment of reforming political and economic systems accelerated into what has been described as a 'rule of law revival' (Carothers 2006b) that led to a capacious political and ideological use of rule of law by Western European and North American donors and governments, to champion preferred forms of legal or institutional reform in target countries (see, e.g., Tamanaha 2004; on the revival, see also Carothers 1998). The role of law in supporting constitutional reform and democratisation in post-communist states became a key focus (Carothers 2009; Czarnota, Krygier, and Sadurski 2005; Krygier and Czarnota 1999; Trubek and Galanter 1974). While socio-legal scholars stressed the importance of sociological dimensions for rule of law development (Krygier 2009a, 2009b), the post-Soviet experience provided a playground for testing new models of law and economic development. Now, actors who traditionally had not been involved in law and development, for example the IMF (International Monetary Fund) and the World Bank (WB), started to incorporate legal reform in their programming (Newton 2006) as the Washington Consensus established a link between legal reform and neo-liberalism for the efficient distribution of economic resources: a functioning legal system on the one hand and privatisation, foreign direct investment, open trade, and marked deregulation and macroeconomic stability on the other (Trebilcock and Prado 2011). This idea of rule of law as necessary for economic growth and poverty alleviation has been prevalent ever since and is still one of the industry's driving ideas (Crouch 2017). Such prescriptions, however, did not always deliver their intended consequences and the limits of the market were increasingly recognised by both practitioners and scholars (see, e.g., Trubek and Santos 2006). The Asian financial crisis in 1997 and the failure to support post-Soviet states in transitioning further contributed to such questioning (Newton 2006). The complexities of a perceived link between law (in this case property rights) and economic development were also replicated in Myanmar. For example, one foreign lawyer who worked on land rights (Interviewee #4, 15 May 2014) explained how, after the introduction of formal land titles, people were questioning why they would need a piece of paper when they had been farming land for years. The procedures also include the possibility of filing an objection to the registration through the administrative system. Still, people would take matters to court and sue for trespass as a means to clear the disputed land. The result was that instead of introducing a simplified system, people chose to take a lengthier and more costly road through court and continued to rely on customary regulation of land (see de Soto 2001 for an in-depth analysis of why Western transplants of property law fail). Such failure to grasp the reality and resilience of legal pluralism is not limited to legal reforms in Myanmar (Merry 1988; Tamanaha 2008, 2011; von Benda-Beckmann 2002).

The idea of rule of law as necessary for economic development was also questioned when significant economic progress took place in Asian states not considered as rule of law-abiding from a Western perspective (Antons 2003; Jayasuriya 1999; Kamarul and Tomasic 1999; McAlinn and Pejovic 2012). Consequently, the awareness that rule of law might not cause, or even be necessary for, economic development took hold and several scholars embarked upon questioning the existing rule of law orthodoxy (Davis and Trebilcock 2008; Ginsburg 2000).

Again, as a response to the recognition of failure, alternatives to existing approaches were developed. One such shift was seen in the legal empowerment (of the poor) movement that sought to provide a perspective of law and development where law was used to enhance broader goals of socio-economic development and 'rights-based' development by translating ideas from the bottom up (Golub 2006). The movement emphasised the importance of 'local' knowledge and context (van Rooij 2009), legal pluralism (Tamanaha 2011), justice for the poor (see, e.g., Dias and Welch 2009), and access to justice (see, e.g., van de Meene and van Rooij 2008). Economist Hernando de Soto (2001) was especially influential in promoting his ideas relating to legal empowerment and property rights for the world's poor as he suggests that it is crucial to understand local social rules and customs that operate outside the formal law in order to solve the puzzle of economic development. De Soto argues that a shift of focus that could help understand norms and people's law entrenched in local beliefs, was, therefore, necessary, rather than drafting good-looking laws and regulations 'on paper'. Perspectives of law and development were shifted to enhance broader goals of socio-economic development – as an alternative to the state-centric rule of law orthodoxy, to prioritise 'rights-based' civil society support and grass-roots needs.

That expansion of rule of law assistance further increased in quantum and scope after the events of 11 September 2001 (see, e.g., Baylis 2008; Samuels 2006; Stromseth, Wippman, and Brooks 2006). Rule of law came to be seen as important for peace and security, and components were thus incorporated into most peacekeeping and peacebuilding activities (Sannerholm et al. 2012). As a result, rule of law assistance was extended to areas with a clear link to security: criminal law reform, police reform, prison reform, and judicial reform (Call and Wyeth 2008; Sannerholm 2012). Carothers (2006a) describes how such developments helped turn the rule of law field into a global phenomenon that seeks to aid everything from democratisation and economic development to peace and conflict prevention. Kleinfeld (2005) and also Jensen (2003) argue that the effect of such expansion is that rule of law has come to be viewed as different sectors, classified by activities that centre on specific institutions and topical areas of reform, rather than as a coherent concept. A tacit acknowledgement of the conceptual incoherence is also recognised by the practitioners that today populate the field (Desai 2016; Simion and Taylor 2015).

The agenda of rule of law assistance includes topics as diverse as customary and non-state justice, gender equality, economic development, anti-terrorism measures, anti-corruption strategies, access to justice, conflict prevention, and human rights monitoring. Such diversity shows that rule of law assistance encompasses much more than just law. In fact, it appears as if the field includes everything that can cater to the latest development trends, everything 'that sells' as it has been packaged into a 'model' supported by various 'technologies' (Behrends et al. 2014). In the twenty-first century, several international organisations have adopted rule of law assistance components of their work as ends in themselves and the broadening scope is likely to continue with the emphasis of the United Nation's Sustainable Development Goals (SDGs) on 'justice' and 'rule of law' for global peace and institutional development (Bergling and Jin 2015; Arajärvi 2017; Desai and Schomerus 2018), and in light of increased recognition that rule of law is in decline and illiberalism on the rise (see, e.g., Freedom House 2020; Krieger and Nolte 2016).

The overview just given highlights that the ideological underpinnings of the rule of law field's various 'movements' have remained relatively static, although critique and a need for reinvention have been voiced. This book presents a law and society perspective that highlights the actors who operate between global and local norms and meanings and thus theoretical insights that stress the importance of sociological understandings of the law, central dimensions for rule of law development so commonly ignored by rule of law development actors (Krygier 2009a, 2009b).

## 1.4   VERNACULARISING RULE OF LAW AS A SUBSTANTIVE CONCEPT IN AN AUTHORITARIAN SETTING

The site for my enquiry into rule of law intermediation, Myanmar, is a country that has been a fecund place in which to ask questions about the relationship between the rule of law in principle and that in practice. Myanmar has a long history of rule of law intermediation and translation, from British colonial rule, which terminated in 1948, through decades of military dictatorship after 1962, in which the language of the rule of law enfolded with that of law and order (Cheesman 2015, 2016).

The setting in which foreign development actors intervened to promote rule of law after the political transition in 2010 was thus one coloured by decades of rule under one of the most '(brutally) authoritarian' (Steinberg 2001; Turnell 2011) regimes under 'military dictatorship' (Shwe Lu Maung 1989). During such rule, state ideology was dominant, political opposition and ethnic minorities faced serious mistreatment and oppression, people were under intrusive surveillance, economic mismanagement often reached absurd dimensions, and human rights were systematically violated.

While it was tempting to write about the country's authoritarian system as a practice of the past, its residues continued to influence political and social life in the transition period as practices associated with previous military rule remained in place (see also Holliday 2013). For example, judges intimidated lawyers who attempted to observe court hearings (Interviewee #53, 25 September 2015) and Military Intelligence personnel showed up at rule of law training courses for local lawyers and politicians (personal observation, 2014). Nevertheless, in the transition period, rule of law promoters from abroad, filled with the moment of optimism and often as newcomers to the place, believed in the possibility of contributing to the development of rule of law as a substantive ideal that pays regard for human rights and liberal democracy.

Perhaps it was most evident in the incoming rule of law promoters' meeting with local counterparts whose understandings of the concept diverge from the contents of international law, when the challenges of the assignment dawned on them (see Chapter 8). In terms of official discourse, 'rule of law' (*taya-ubade-somoye*) was not a new term in political speech in Myanmar; the term was used for decades to stress and maintain the importance of maintaining 'law and order' (*ngyein-wut-pibyaye*) rather than substantive and procedural rights (Cheesman 2015). These are concepts that are opposed to each other, as the former is based on defined values of procedural justice and rights while the latter is primarily concerned with administrative and coercive measures to keep control in society (Cheesman 2014a).

There is a growing body of literature that analyses legality in these types of setting, especially in relation to authoritarian legality (Chen and Fu 2020; Hurst 2018), the politics of courts and the judiciary (Balasubramaniam 2009; Cheesman 2011; Ginsburg and Moustafa 2008; Gretchen 2005; Hilbink 2007; Moustafa 2014; Ng and He 2017), and the dysfunctional nature of rule of law (e.g., Balasubramaniam 2012; Pereira 2005; Rajah 2012). Rajah's work on 'authoritarian rule of law' in Singapore unpacks regime practices of manipulating rule of law for their (often economic) purposes. While Rajah's work does not address dimensions of foreign intervention, it provides key insights to how an authoritarian regime can progress in economic terms under a 'rule of law' banner while continuing its authoritarian governance and 'rule by law' practices. Also, Meierhenrich's (2008) historical study of the nexus between law and democratic development in South Africa illustrates how the inner life of law, even in illiberal forms, has an important role to play in authoritarian societies. Here, law can bring about solidity drawn from common norms and institutions which eventually help strengthen liberal progress. Rather than disregarding these settings as lacking rule of law, it is fruitful to analyse the variations of law, and the opportunities law brings to a broader change in society (see also Hurst 2018 for a similar argument).

Few studies analyse the dynamics, particular complexities, and parameters for success of foreign assisted rule of law promotion in authoritarian settings (Moustafa 2008). Massoud's (2013) detailed account of such enterprise in Sudan's authoritarian regime is an illustrative exception. He shows how foreign actors have pushed for law as a tool to oppose authoritarianism but with effects that include the regime's strengthened ability to impose law and order. Parallels can be drawn to Myanmar's continued systemic crisis of disregard for human rights and continued authoritarian rule rather than governance. In Sudan, as in Myanmar, as Massoud shows, awareness of local power dynamics and contextual realities were weak. Impacts of initiatives were varied and at times resulted in additional risks, failing to bring about changes. Lessons from Massoud's study highlight the need to be cautious about the enlightened place given to law within development programmes because law also has a dark side and, in authoritarian regimes, it easily becomes another arsenal for the political elite to contain their power (see also Nouwen 2012).

Explorations of how individuals broker influence as intermediaries in illiberal societies amidst development- and rule by law challenges are less pronounced. We need such analyses, as we can hypothesise that intermediaries become extra indispensable as they navigate non-transparent systems of authoritarian governance. Exceptions include Chua's (2015, 2019) in-depth account of how human rights are vernacularised in Myanmar. She shows how human rights activists deploy a strategy of reframing grievances to cultivate opposition and mobilisation for rights under repressive circumstances. Chua argues that international human rights 'lack cultural resonance' in Myanmar and, therefore, an approach that investigates activists' strategies can bring a nuanced picture to the challenges of implementing human rights. She shows that, here, the intermediary role is fluid and open to distrust: '[I]f domestic activists adopt human rights strategies to secure Western funds, they might attract government hostility. In the efforts to render human rights locally palatable, they could also end up undermining the essential ideals of human rights or reinforcing existing power relations and social structure' (Chua 2015:327). Chua illustrates how activists act as norm entrepreneurs as 'they are not simply driven by external funding opportunities but find courage and inspiration in human rights to challenge oppressive social norms and authorities' (Chua 2015:327). Human rights thus move through the hands of activists that act as intermediaries and translators of these norms at local levels, 'who astutely navigate local conditions and global norms to galvanize political action, and who know how to make use of and cultivate social ties' (Chua 2015:328). They are not passive in their actions but take on a role as active agents of the causes they believe in. For development purposes supported by organisations from abroad, as is the focus of this book, intermediaries help suggest what strategies foreign actors can apply and when; sometimes they are listened to, sometimes not.

We know by now that authoritarian settings are challenging in terms of achieving change that is also normative and aligned with human rights (Carothers 2009; Daniels and Trebilcock 2004). A likely outcome of foreign promoters having aims that are unrealistic in relation to the history, values, culture, and institutional traditions of countries embarking upon such reforms, in terms of what they hope to achieve, is foreign assisted rule of law initiatives assisting authoritarian rulers to consolidate rule *by* law regimes (Davis and Trebilcock 2008; Pompe 2005).

In Myanmar in 2020, policy statements continue to convey ideas about the rule of law not as a panacea for arbitrariness but as a mode of social control. The divergence between international and domestic ideas about the rule of law was perhaps thrown into sharpest relief during 2016 when Aung San Suu Kyi, who for years harped on the topic, in her new role as de facto head of state suggested that violence in Myanmar's Rakhine State, which had by then already forced hundreds of thousands to flee to Bangladesh (see Cheesman 2017), was being handled according to 'principles of the rule of law' (Funakoshi 2016). Whatever game Aung San Suu Kyi, whose rhetorical use of the rule of law has varied with time and audience (see Cheesman 2014b), may be playing at here, clearly her reference to principles of the rule of law is a long way removed from those principles that promoters from abroad seek to advance. Events since the widely lauded 2015 elections when Aung San Suu Kyi and her NLD won a landslide victory (BBC News Asia 2015) show how illiberal practices are fully ingrained in the country's political leadership and that authoritarian styles of rule persist. Now a 'political scene filled with anomalies' between Myanmar's proclaimed transition and actions in practice is ever so evident (David and Holliday 2018) as illustrated by the rising prevalence of extremist monks who previously stood up for democracy, the deterioration in interfaith contact, and the extensive intolerance of Muslim minorities. In 2020, in a country where military rule and democracy are 'viewed [not necessarily] as alternatives, but rather as options that can coexist', it is not viable to nominate the country's political transition as successful or its political system as one of democratic liberalism (David and Holliday 2018:59; see also Stokke and Aung 2020).

This book thus provides insights into the enterprise of rule of law assistance in a setting that has been labelled 'authoritarian' (Linz 2000). Previous experience shows that rule of law reform attempts in an authoritarian regime do not guarantee a straight line of development towards the ideal substantive rule of law that foreign promoters propagate. Even when flexible in their approaches and strategies of bottom-up understandings, as one practitioner exclaimed, 'Even if we say we don't want to impose, that's bullshit; we would never accept it if they say they want a Chinese version of rule of law' (personal communication February 2020; see also Wang 2015). However, this is more likely the end product that practitioners from abroad will have to settle for, as in an authoritarian setting the indigenised version of rule of law may well challenge both Western understandings of and normative preferences for the concept.

What we see is that when the whole package of the so-called 'rule of law' is transposed onto pre-existing authoritarian social and political realities, you end up with a stronger system of 'rule by law' or 'law and order' – the powerful drafting and applying of more and more laws by which to control, not protect, the mistrusted masses. In other words, strengthening an institution like the judiciary (the focus of many foreign-supported reform initiatives) may simply consolidate authoritarianism rather than bring about a shift towards liberal democratic values and guaranteeing equal rights. Terms like the 'rule of law' may sit comfortably in the international forum (from which NGOs get their funding), and with Burmese elites, who read it as 'law and order', but, for the same reason, it is mistrusted by ordinary people who are used to 'law and order' being used to coerce rather than represent them.

## 1.5   DATA COLLECTION AND ANALYSIS

This book presents an interdisciplinary dialogue among law, sociology, and ethnography (Flood 2005) through a qualitative methodological framework that seeks understanding of experiences, characteristics, descriptions, and the meanings given to them (Berg 1989). Intermediaries in the rule of law field are the 'social phenomena' (Yin 2003) of study. I adopted a qualitative case study approach (focused on the experiences of a single country) to develop nuanced and grounded understandings of how rule of law assistance is given meaning in specific contexts, to draw conclusions about larger processes of transnational interaction.

### 1.5.1   Studying Rule of Law Assistance in the Myanmar Context

As the idea of this research developed in late 2011, the prospect of conducting extended empirical field research in Myanmar was still not certain. The country had long been restricted to foreign researchers (except for a few individuals) due to its history of isolation under military rule (Selth 2010). In 2011 Myanmar was a young transitional setting with few rule of law assistance activities taking place. Only in late 2012 and early 2013 did foreign rule of law actors start to conduct assessments and fact-finding missions to identify rule of law deficits and possible solutions (International Bar Association's Human Rights Institute 2012; New Perimeter, Perseus Strategies, and Jacob Blaustein Institute for the Advancement of Human Rights 2013; United States Institute of Peace 2013). An increasing number of foreign organisations thereafter established field presence and initiated activities intended to promote the rule of law. These years leading up to the 2015 election saw a significant surge in official development assistance to Myanmar (Décobert and Wells 2020; Farrelly and Win 2016). In light of the rule of law activities that were accelerating in Myanmar at that time, the location suited my interest in transnational settings where development projects proceed at a frantic pace. The arrival of ideas that accumulated in a field for rule of law development in Myanmar meant that I was able to study a setting where relationships among development counterparts were just emerging, unlike other more established places where rule of law assistance projects have been ongoing for several years.

This book uncovers the effect of intermediaries' activities during a historical moment of political transition, a time in history that passed and that we now know failed to proceed on its expected path (Huang 2020). In Myanmar's immediate transition period, the introduction of global ideas of law and justice was comparatively new (if we think in terms of a law and development trajectory and ignore a past of colonial intervention) because the country had remained largely isolated under military rule while neighbouring countries in Southeast Asia, such as Vietnam, Cambodia, and Indonesia, experienced the trials and lessons of the 'third wave' of democratisation and accompanying foreign assistance efforts (see, e.g., Gillespie 2004; Lindsey 2007).

Studying a transition period provides important insights into just how intermediaries emerge during societal transformation and governance transition (Koster and van Leynseele 2018). The case of Myanmar conforms to observations made by scholars of political anthropology that the emergence of intermediaries follows a process of political change and/or intervention, for example authoritarian regimes transitioning to more democratic systems (Bierschenk et al. 2002). As a result, foreign development aid may increase and lead to new relationships between foreign and local actors that in turn give rise to intermediaries who negotiate between the two parties (Bierschenk et al. 2002; de Sardan 2005). The phenomenon of intermediaries, however, is just as prevalent in Myanmar today as in the transition period, even if in slightly adapted and morphed formations, which is why this study is in many ways an extended case study from the transition period to today.

This book distinguishes itself from other studies of rule of law in Myanmar, where scholars, as is common for the rule of law field, have focused much on legal and institutional reform (Crouch and Lindsey 2014b; Harding 2014) rather than on seeking ethnographic insights into foreign-funded development assistance. Before transition, legal researchers focused on the law and its (im)practical application in Myanmar rather than on foreign actors' attempts to develop it. Huxley's, Myint Zan's, and Cheesman's scholarship provides rich accounts of what law, rule of law, and related concepts meant during the decades in which Myanmar was under regime rule and political transition (e.g., Cheesman 2011; Huxley 1987; Myint Zan 2000b).

After the political transition, scholars have attempted to understand Myanmar's Supreme- (Nardi and Lwin Moe 2014) or Constitutional Court (Khin Khin Oo 2017; Nardi 2014, 2017), economic law reform (Crouch 2017; Tun 2014; Tun Zaw Mra 2014; Turnell 2014), and police reform (Selth 2013). Many took an interest in the problematic

2008 constitution (Harding 2017; Myint Zan 2017; Williams 2017). Scholars also sought to understand ordinary people's perceptions of 'justice' and 'rule of law' in Myanmar's ethnically diverse rural and conflict settings (e.g., Prasse-Freeman 2015). Such analyses were also sought by researchers involved in assistance projects that explored local perceptions of justice (Denney, William, and Khin Thet San 2016; Kyed 2017). Practitioners analysed national failure to achieve rule of law development but for the most part failed to reflect on the activities and engagement of donors involved in rule of law assistance in Myanmar (Booth 2016; Pritchard 2016). Scholarly and policy analyses of the rule of law assistance industry in Myanmar, as well as socio-legal studies of the translation of rule of law to local arenas, remain underexplored.

### 1.5.2 Methods

The primary method of data collection used for this book was in-depth, semi-structured interviews (Edwards and Holland 2013). Document analysis of what included donor reports, an overview of the rule of law assistance actors, minutes of meetings, letters, project proposals, internal records, and news articles was used to inform and understand the research context and highlight questions. While my research draws primarily on the qualitative data I collected in the field, the adoption of a range of methods meant that the data collected for this book was triangulated (Carter et al. 2014). The validity of the data was enhanced through the collection of information from different sources, including general development practitioners, government actors, rule of law development actors, and intermediaries.

Because I sought an in-depth understanding of the daily experiences (Madden 2010) of my research participants, I also employed ethnographic research tools such as accompaniment and observation during field research. Ethnography focuses on 'the shared patterns of behaviours, language, and actions of an intact cultural group in a natural setting over a prolonged period of time' (Creswell 2013:14). My direct interactions with individuals, and particularly with intermediaries in the rule of law community, informed the 'thick descriptions' (Geertz 1973) of participants and their behaviour in the specific context.

My sampling was purposive, and respondents were selected for specific characteristics, such as their occupation or position. There are many different strategies for purposive sampling (Patton 2002); I chose what is often referred to as 'chain referral' or 'snowball sampling' (Noy 2008). Such sampling is useful in settings where it is difficult to locate individuals to study (Atkinson and Flint 2001) as you capitalise on the few you manage to locate and then ask them to refer you to other individuals similar to themselves. When applying purposive sampling, the issue of sample size is not easily determined. The need for a detailed description of a phenomenon (which is the main purpose of qualitative research) makes it necessary for samples to be small, but small samples do not permit generalisation to a larger population. However, the aim of qualitative research is not to generalise but rather to have a complete understanding of a social phenomenon.

Respondents worked for multilateral and bilateral donor agencies, the Myanmar government, and international and national NGOs, as local lawyers and international consultants. The table in the Appendix illustrates a breakdown of research participants. However, reality is not as neat as what is depicted in the table because many of my participants wore multiple hats, which means that they could fall under the categories of local lawyer, rule of law consultant, and development practitioner working for an international NGO (INGO), all at the same time. To add complexity, they are also the ones I identified as intermediaries, and they sometimes described themselves primarily as such, rather than with a professional or institutional label.

I interviewed for this project a total of seventy-seven individuals who work on rule of law assistance-related activities; sixty-four of those interviewees have been included as respondents. Of the sixty-four respondents, thirty-one were foreign practitioners (fifteen male and sixteen female), out of whom twenty-four were lawyers. They had previous experience from development work in Southeast Asia (Thai–Burma border, Thailand, Cambodia, Aceh); the Pacific Islands; Africa (South Sudan, Sierra Leone); and Hong Kong. Ten were European (five British), eleven were North American (nine American, two Canadian), five were Australian, and five were Asian. Three foreign practitioners had one parent who was from Myanmar. Thirty-three respondents were local practitioners (twenty-four male and nine female); out of these, thirteen were lawyers (three judges). Of the thirty-three local respondents, I defined twenty-six as 'intermediaries'. All rule of law intermediaries were bilingual and spoke English; all but four had studied abroad; many identified as belonging to ethnic minority groups; and all but six had worked with development organisations previously. Five were former political prisoners. In addition, although not bilingual, five foreign respondents stood out in their intermediary role. Often, that was the case because of their positioning through their work, for example because they were hired as foreign consultants to be placed as interlocutors within local or national organisations.

Interviews were semi-structured or unstructured (Edwards and Holland 2013). Most semi-structured interviews took place at offices, cafes, hotels, or restaurants. I did not seek to measure the 'truthfulness' of interviewees' accounts; rather, I was interested in the meanings of interview material and the stories they tell rather than 'objective reality' (Elliot 2005:22–7). Semi-structured interviews were based on an interview protocol that listed the questions or topics to be asked (DiCicco-Bloom and Crabtree 2006). Unstructured interviews resemble a conversation rather than the more semi-structured interview situation, and they allow respondents to express themselves more freely (Corbin and Morse 2003); however, the conversation is always 'controlled' because the interviewer steers it towards her interests (Gray 2009). In total, I conducted seventy-four semi-structured interviews and approximately twenty-eight unstructured interviews (low estimate). Out of the seventy-four semi-structured interviews, all but eleven were conducted in Yangon. Other interview locations included Mandalay, Nay Pyi Taw, Europe, Australia, and two via Skype.

I also had the opportunity to engage in informed conversations about the broader development field as well as issues related to local understandings of 'rule of law'. Gray (2009) suggests that unstructured interviews can be of an even more informal, conversational character and based on an unplanned set of questions that is generated during the interview. I had many opportunities to participate in such informal discussions, some that generated quick notes and some that were useful for informing me about the research setting. For example, I attended some infamous boat parties for 'ex-pats' on Yangon River and evening events hosted by the French Institute in Yangon. These types of occasion provided fruitful opportunities to establish contacts, get a deeper insight into ex-pat life and the development community, and get updated on the latest gossip in the rule of law field. During rule of law events in regional areas, I had the opportunity to talk to local lawyers and activists about their understandings of 'rule of law' and the current transition.

Because I conducted interviews with different categories of participants, my interview approaches and questions at times differed. For example, obtaining personal accounts of rule of law intermediaries sometimes presented methodological challenges. Generally, they were willing to talk about rule of law project activities and outputs, or even the lack of rule of law under 'a brutal military regime'. They were also happy to share stories about their childhoods, early political activities, and motivations for working on social causes (their interpretation of their work). However, as my questions turned to the theme of their current motivations and activities in relation to the donors they work with, interviewees were more reluctant to talk. For example, some would not reveal that they worked on several contracts or that they had aspirations to be elected for political office. Corbin and Morse (2003:336) suggest that interviewees might consider topics 'sensitive in nature' because when they are asked to 'tell their stories about some topic, they are sharing personal, often intimate aspects of their lives'.

Also, among my interviewees who were from Myanmar, it proved difficult to encourage interviewees to talk about other people, which was a central aspect of my research. Lee and Renzetti (1990:512) have noted that any topic has the potential of being 'sensitive'. I soon understood that it was problematic for me as an 'outsider' to ask questions about 'insiders'. The sensitivities of an approach that included asking about others can find their explanations in Myanmar's history of intelligence surveillance and culture of informers (see, e.g., Selth 1998) and, as I discuss in more detail in Chapter 7, in its being home to immense distrust generally. On the other hand, it is possible that with greater Burmese language skills, interviewees would have been more suspicious towards me as a foreigner. My approach let me cruise within different spaces: I was a foreigner but not one of the donors; I was culturally adept and showed knowledge of the country, but I was not pushing an agenda or asking questions about everything and everyone. Eventually, when I had built up personal relationships, I managed to obtain accounts about 'other people'; most often, such stories were shared during informal and unstructured conversations rather than in initial semi-formal interview situations.

### 1.5.3 Analysis

Qualitative data analysis involves the interpretation of observations, words, and symbols in the data, which consists of written texts. Upon returning from fieldwork, I reviewed field notes, interviews, and documents, and analysed these through an inductive process that involved a combination of case study analysis and looking for recurring patterns or themes in the data (Patton 2002). An inductive analysis, as opposed to a deductive one, is one in which I develop the findings through my interaction with the data, instead of by looking at the data through a pre-existing framework. During fieldwork, I initiated a preliminary analysis of my data. When reading through my notes, I wrote down comments and follow-up questions (that I was often able to ask at later interviews) about topics I found interesting. When possible, I presented my initial analysis to the intermediaries I had a long-term engagement with. My analysis was often met with a nod of recognition, especially in relation to the way I had captured the experiences of rule of law intermediaries. Foreign practitioners, however, were sometimes less understanding and found my analysis 'too theoretical'. I tried to conduct a follow-up discussion with a foreign consultant about his role as 'embodying' his foreign employers' objectives as he promoted them at the local organisation he was positioned at. His only reply was: 'That sounds very theoretical.' I managed to upset an American INGO representative when I suggested that intermediaries translate the INGO's objectives and that, as foreigners, it may be difficult for us to know exactly what happens 'on the ground'. My data collection confirmed that foreign practitioners and intermediaries often had different understandings of what was going on in the field.

To develop a manageable scheme for analysis, coding, and classification of themes, I was helped by research software. I read through my field notes before inserting them into the software in order to find classifications and coding categories. After coding the data, I turned to a 'thematic' analysis of my data. By applying thematic coding, I connected and clustered the codes into broader themes and patterns (Liamputtong 2009). For example, codes that included labels like 'picked-up' and 'chased me up' were themed around foreign actors' 'enrolment' of intermediaries. Codes that included words like 'translator', 'fixer', and 'go-between' became the theme 'intermediaries'.

## 1.6 OUTLINE OF THE BOOK

This book consists of nine chapters. Chapter 2 presents a macro perspective of the field of rule of law assistance. The chapter contains a contestable assertion regarding the field, which is whether it makes sense to raise the general question of the development of rule of law as if it could be a unified object of observation. To ask this question runs counter to recent approaches which break the concept down into various elements, or activities. But while there are competing definitions and incoherence as to what the rule of law *is*, I argue that we find features of a model among these shattered elements. The chapter draws on a 'travelling models' framework as articulated by scholars of anthropology (Behrends et al. 2014; Rottenburg 2009) to illustrate the authoritative features that rule of law takes on as a model for development intervention. A travelling model's framework emphasises rule of law's mediated necessities rather than its universalities. This framework does not claim that models are coherent and static; rather, it claims that they are fluid but they always present a contrast to domestic worldviews and understandings, and, thus, they are an intervention of some sort. The result of bringing in models in illiberal settings that are accompanied by decades of miscomprehensions and that thus have preconceived meanings in the specific locale is an adapted version of the substantive rule of law that ideal development assistance seeks to propagate. The chapter sets the scene for understanding later ones that present the ambiguous work and influence of rule of law intermediaries as they broker different worldviews and understandings in between development counterparts in an authoritarian setting.

Chapter 3 charts what we know about intermediaries across settings and times in history in order to provide a comparative perspective on their being within fields of development that broadly relate to interventions of law, regulation, rule of law, justice, and institutions. It recognises the utility of classical studies of intermediation and brokerage to analyse current phenomena of transnational rule of law assistance. The chapter highlights the role that intermediaries play, and the challenges they face, at the interfaces of different knowledge and value systems that appear as the development industry intervenes across the globe. The chapter also shows how my use of an inductive approach was key for locating individuals who played an intermediary role in Myanmar's rule of law assistance field across several institutional positions: the local lawyer; the local NGO; the locally employed staff who work for an international organisation; the government employee; and the international consultant. While positioned in different roles and allocated different assignments, what they all have in common is that they perform as brokers, translators, and mediators in order to relate globally oriented ideas to the Myanmar locale, in a middle position among foreign, national, and local actors.

Chapter 4 presents the field of rule of law assistance as it became established in Myanmar after 2011. It introduces common rule of law actors and their technologies and also provides a brief background to the political and legal features of the case study. While doing so, the chapter hints at the frictions of foreign-funded rule of law assistance that emerge because international, national, and local understandings and approaches to rule of law development differ and are challenging to align. It shows how intermediaries emerged to mediate between counterparts regarding issues such as monetary compensation; applications for funding; the best approach to achieve rule of law development; donor involvement in local affairs; and institutional constraints.

Chapter 5 provides an account of the sudden rise in demand for intermediaries in Myanmar after the opening up of the country to foreign aid and influence. It focuses on the competitive 'market' for rule of law intermediaries, showing how individuals have reinvented themselves as consultants, NGO leaders, and employees for international organisations and then how central are personality and linguistic ability to getting selected by foreign actors, and the important difference between often reluctant governmental intermediaries and those operating non-governmentally. This chapter also adds structure to the picture; these questions are important because they reveal structural aspects of development aid as it operates in the rule of law sphere: for example, who gets to be included, who gets to exert influence, and why. The chapter concludes that intermediaries emerge because foreign development actors need the assistance of individuals who understand their aims and objectives, to navigate unfamiliar systems, and to reach out to potential counterparts as intermediaries of rule of law.

Chapter 6 answers a set of central questions that concern intermediaries' backgrounds, profiles, networks, and self-perceptions. It suggests that intermediaries' backgrounds are important to understand as they give an indication of whom they respond to as well as what their strategies and interests are. Chapter 6 also analyses intermediaries' capital (social and foreign) to show how the capital that gave intermediaries local clout came in part from the risks that they took in favour of democratic ideals during the authoritarian period. The chapter shows that while rule of law intermediaries' access to international capital 'amplifies' their work on rights-related issues at home, the use of foreign capital is not solely to intermediaries' benefit because distrust of foreign interests affects the value of their capital. This ambivalence led intermediaries to apply different strategies to hide their connections to foreign actors. Still, they needed to be in a position where they could use their networked resources to channel aid money or development activities to local levels, in order to gain political influence.

Chapter 7 focuses on the important issue of building trust both ways, and the need for many of the intermediaries to behave in a Janus-faced fashion. They have to play up their commitment to the funders and global actors in certain settings while playing down their global connections in local settings where there is a distrust of foreign connections. The chapter concludes that trust and relationship building can be seen as a prerequisite for successful rule of law assistance and is the focus of much donor effort. However, because foreign actors cannot supply prior proof of trust, it is the known actors, such as intermediaries, who instead take on the role of trust builders.

Chapter 8 concerns the translation of the rule of law by and through intermediaries. The intermediaries change and distort the messages from their global employers and funders in order to make them palatable to local and national actors – and also to build their own local career trajectories. The chapter highlights the main translation challenges rule of law practitioners experience and presents intermediaries' insider perspectives of how they translate rule of law. By analysing the strategies that intermediaries use, the chapter concludes that intermediaries become influential in their role as translators. Intermediaries do not just mobilise their contacts and use their local language skills – they also buffer conversations in which the speakers are mutually incomprehensible and substitute content where they consider this necessary. While Myanmar's political history and reality have produced a semi-authoritarian form of rule of law, associations with formal aspects of the concepts were initially enhanced by foreign promoters who brought in their versions of concepts they deemed modelled on international standards that were universal and non-negotiable. The dynamics shown in the chapter are such that intermediaries, on the one hand, broker influence in the authoritarian setting by propagating for terminology that steers away from an often misinterpreted term, when the work of foreign promoters risks support of illiberal versions of rule of law when the political reality is oversimplified, while, on the other hand, they use statements that fit idioms matching foreign donors a bit too well for their liking without revealing their actual values.

The concluding Chapter 9, titled 'Intermediaries' Influence, Foreign Actors' Dependence', summarises the findings on the importance of understanding the role of intermediaries in rule of law assistance. As Myanmar struggled for foreign credibility and investment, the findings are also consistent with the global version – foreign actors' influence, and local dependence in societies where donors become an established but delicate feature of social, political, and economic life that people encounter on a daily basis. In this new landscape, intermediaries become responsible for navigating local and national institutions, values, and people. This book keeps both sides in view while focusing on the intermediaries. It also considers the extent to which the findings could be generalised beyond Myanmar and their practical implications to help advance enquiry into the field of rule of law assistance globally.

# CHAPTER TWO

# BETWEEN UNIVERSALS AND PARTICULARS: RULE OF LAW AS A TRAVELLING MODEL

Shattered elements of the rule of law ideal (Tamanaha 2004), derived from Western-centric ideas of universal international law (Eslava 2015) and washed from their colonial formations (Benton 2018; McBride 2016), travel through intermediaries who operate at the interfaces of different social orders and multiple sites of authority, across dispersed localities. While there are competing definitions and incoherence as to what the rule of law *is*, we find features of a model among these shattered elements that informs the work of rule of law practitioners active in the development field (Gowder 2016) who seldom question 'simple arguments' of the causal connections among rule of law, democracy, and peace (Merry 2016).

This chapter presents a macro perspective of rule of law promotion. The chapter contains a contestable assertion regarding the field, which is that it makes sense to raise the general question of the development of rule of law as though it were a unified object of observation. To do this runs counter to contemporary approaches that break the concept down into various activities.

To further dwell on the idea of rule of law as a model of sorts, in this chapter I draw on a 'travelling models' framework as articulated by scholars of anthropology (Behrends et al. 2014; Rottenburg 2009) to illustrate the authoritative features of the rule of law as a model for purposes of development intervention. A travelling models framework emphasises rule of law's mediated necessities rather than universalities. This framework does not claim that models are coherent and static; rather, that they are fluid but they always present a contrast to domestic worldviews and understandings, and thus they are an intervention of some sort. Even when adapted and adjusted by skilled development workers, models need mediation and translation because they will never be fully promoted from the bottom up. If they were, they would not have a preconceived branding, like 'rule of law' (Taylor 2016), and thus practitioners would be not be promoting anything concrete that motivates the basis for their professional existence.

The travelling models framework illustrates that the rule of law in itself in many ways is authoritative rather than substantive and open to modification (for an example, see the imposition of attempts to create 'global administrative law' (Kingsbury, Krisch, and Stewart 2005; Krisch and Kingsbury 2006) that often become contested in the specific setting (Wiener 2008)). This comes with the consequences of semi-authoritarian understandings of rule of law as a result of the struggle between universals and domestic realities. Here I agree with Chua's (2019) thesis on human rights, which she suggests, when imported in the specificities as universal models, 'could even make things worse' (Chua 2019: 14). Rule of law, as human rights, when promoted, has been shown to help authoritarian rulers further their legislative control (Massoud 2013). The helpful aspect of promoting rule of law, versus human rights, in illiberal regimes is that rule of law is ambiguous enough in its interpretation that authoritarian rulers can adapt its formal aspects for purposes of economic progress (Rajah 2012; Wang 2015).

What then is the 'rule of law model'? When observing the global arena of activities involving 'rule of law', we see that the concept has been elevated by specific elements – for example, the rights to a free and fair trial, to access to justice under laws that are non-discriminatory, and to a government that is bound by law. These shared ideas travel to new settings to be promoted and operationalised, but, in this process, supporting institutional conventions, knowledge, and practices (the model's rationalities) are left behind (Behrends et al. 2014). What rationalities accompany rule of law? Perhaps elements of society such as institutional appointments of judges and epistemic communities such as bar associations. Rationalities are expected to operate according to established rules, but, in practice, they will seldom function the way they did in their original setting because they get entangled into re-inventions when they arrive at illiberal sites where institutional, cul-tural, or economic factors will influence a model's reception (Massoud 2013; Pompe 2005; Remadji and Behrends 2014). One example is the practice by rule of law assistance actors of building courthouses to mimic (justice) institutions (per Pritchett et al. 2012) in settings where justice and conflict resolution are dealt with in other symbolic places (see, e.g., Forsyth 2009). Such actors fail to take into account the realities of the setting into which they are attempting to transport the model. Another example is a national bar association that elects its members democratically and transparently, which, in some places, would be considered a prerequisite of rule of law. In Myanmar, such rationality is difficult to translate because power dynamics that favour values – such as seniority – over democracy and transparency may be considered more suitable for deciding who should be a member of the Bar (Interviewee #14, 5 October 2014; see also Liljeblad 2019).

This chapter sets the scene for later chapters that present the ambiguous work and the influence of rule of law intermediaries as they broker different worldviews and understandings between develop-ment counterparts. With this chapter, I seek to illustrate that rule of law, no matter how fundamental and well-meaning a concept, takes on authoritative features when it is introduced as a travelling model for development progress across the globe. The result of bringing into illiberal settings models that are accompanied by decades of miscom-prehensions and that thus have preconceived meanings in the specific locale (McBride 2016) is an adapted version of the substantive rule of law ideal that development assistance seeks to introduce.

This way of thinking about rule of law as a model that travels allows us to draw on theories and insights from sociology and anthropology with less focus on trying to define what the rule of law *actually is* and more focus on the agents that broker the field's disparate but authorita-tive technologies and ideologies to better understand how such a normative concept intervenes in illiberal or semi-illiberal regimes. Through this approach, we provide some of the improved sociological insights into rule of law assistance that Krygier (e.g., 2009b) unfailingly calls for. This view is supported by Halliday and Shaffer's (2014) concept of a 'transnational legal order', which also shifts focus away from the assumption that international instruments make up authori-tative legal technologies and instead make us aware of what is required for these to settle and align, recursively and dynamically, at trans-national, national, and local levels (see also Rajah 2014).

The analogy of a 'model' does not reduce rule of law to an instrument or an 'off-the-shelf' toolkit (Peerenboom 2009) to be used in the service of a theory or action agenda animated by a particular ideology – all conceptualisations that are themselves heavily critiqued (Carothers 2006b; Taylor, V. L. 2009; Upham 2006). Also, this analogy does not seek to suggest that rule of law practitioners do not hold different and contrasting views as to what rule of law means. This fact has been confirmed by previous research (Evers 2010; Grasten 2016) and it is seen in practice. It is to this topic that I turn next.

## 2.1 INCOHERENT AUTHORITY

There are competing definitions and incoherence as to what rule of law *is*. 'The United Nations Rule of Law Indicators: Implementation Guide and Project Tools' suggests that '[a]lthough the term "rule of law" is widely used and often linked to State-building efforts, there is no single agreed-upon definition' to guide rule of law assistance (United Nations Department of Peacekeeping Operations (DPKO) and the Office of the United Nations High Commissioner for Human Rights (OHCHR) 2011). A survey by Santos (2006) on conceptions of the rule of law within the World Bank (WB) finds that as many as four variations of a definition were being used simultaneously by the bank's staff. Moreover, a 2010 survey of the Organization for Security and Co-operation in Europe (OSCE) field missions concluded:

> The field operations have no recourse to a standardized, conclusive defin-ition of the rule of law or rule-of-law promotion. A number of field operations (30 per cent) work without any definition whatsoever. The majority, however, define the rule of law or rule-of-law promotion, some with reference to Kofi Annan's 2004 report for UN rule-of-law promotion, the Copenhagen Document (1990), or the Ljubljana decision (MC.DEC/12/05), and others according to their own preferences.

One explanation for the conceptual incoherence is found in the exten-sion of rule of law assistance to various sectors closely linked to security concerns: criminal law reform, police reform, prison reform, and judi-cial reform (Call and Wyeth 2008). Yet, though these sectors are combined in the so-called 'justice chain', they each present their specific, sometimes contradictory formula for how to achieve rule of law. Thus, the effect of such an extension of rule of law interventions is that the rule of law has become a less coherent concept (Kleinfeld 2005).

Instead, understandings of rule of law are now fragmented across different transnational fields of practice, operationalised within different institutions the mandates of which often differ, and conceptualised according to particular policy concerns and professional expertise. In the words of Rajagopal (2007: 1348), 'the rule of law has come to be considered the common element that development experts, security analysts and human rights activists agree upon and ... the mechanism that links these disparate areas'.

Moreover, faced with a lack of clear guidance on rule of law assistance, practitioners may also bring their own 'choice of law' to their work and adapt their own particular understandings of the rule of law from their 'home' system (Derks and Price 2010). Different understandings of what the rule of law *means* and what its promotion *entails* are therefore likely to be informed by a range of linguistic, cultural, institutional, and professional priorities and backgrounds. As I have argued elsewhere, rule of law

> is simultaneously a range of normative ideals; a rallying cry for political and policy reforms; and a well-established and expanding domain of transitional policy and practice. ... We do not take the position that rule of law is simply the sum of those policies and practices. We suggest, rather, that rule of law practice and its practitioners are influenced by the theoretical and ideological concepts of rule of law, while also helping to shape them through practical application
> (Simion and Taylor 2015:15).

Nevertheless, we find features of meaning in these disparities derived from Western ideas and systems of governance that are then blended with preconceptions based on experiences from colonial intervention, which was brutal in Myanmar (Callahan 2004) where the rule of law championed legislative drafting with 'no roots in the community' (Furnivall 1948:133–5) as a means to order culture (Cheesman 2015). This means that we find features of a model among the field's disparities that derive from Western-centric ideas of universal law and human rights. And even if practitioners and the field itself perceive that they lack a coherent rule of law definition, there are several dominant technologies that occupy the field. For example, the rule of law-promoting activities of the United Nations (UN) are telling: one focus of such efforts is on seeking to reform the judiciary. Sub-activities include the set-up of mobile courts, ethics training for judges, and introducing computerised case management programmes for courts (Sannerholm et al. 2012). At the start of any reform activities, there will be tools for measuring to what extent a country has a well-functioning judiciary to evaluate whether assistance is needed (United Nations 2011; United Nations Department of Peacekeeping Operations Department of Field Support 2009). The translation of judicial reform will be accompanied by technologies such as guidelines on a normative legal framework for the judiciary (e.g., United Nations Office on Drugs and Crime 2006), guiding principles for judicial conduct (e.g., United Nations 1985), and evaluation tools for judicial reform activities (e.g., United Nations Office on Drugs and Crime 2010/2011). These tools are based on mimicries (DiMaggio and Powell 1983) of what a well-functioning judiciary should look like, with little consideration of local realities in illiberal settings where institutions often function based on a mix of formal and informal rules (Pompe 2005).

It is through technologies like these, and here I use a Latourian viewpoint (Latour 1987), that fact-making is produced and reproduced *in* and *for* the field and its inhabitants. Rule of law's technologies, which I review hereafter, are located in different and often distant sites of governance, such as headquarters and field missions, and different meanings are inscribed into them by various intermediaries along its life cycle (Grasten 2016). This then means that rule of law is translated when it moves between these sites (see also Berger 2017; Berger and Esguerra 2017; Zimmermann 2017). The translation is not ordered because models intervene in established settings that may appear 'complex' for the outside observer, for example, because the new site lacks the institutional channels of a liberal democracy (Elwert and Bierschenk 1988) but may in fact follow their own logic of rules (Schaffer 1998). Translation was also a common feature of the colonial mindset, instrumental in turning indigenous cultures into reproductions of the culture of the coloniser and the 'modern state' (Young 2003). During British rule over Burma, attempts to translate subjects into reproductions of British society meant disrespecting local laws and customs that seemed completely incomprehensible to the foreigner and in opposition to liberal ideas, especially 'the rule of law' (Furnivall 1948). In the interactions between colonisers and colonised, both invariably changed, so these changes can be written as translational histories that broke solidified patterns of identification and created new ways in which communities negotiated their collective identities (Saha 2012).

It is within these contours that contemporary rule of law promoters intervene with technologies that derive from an international law, modelled in the colonial project (Benton 2018; McBride 2016; Parfitt

2019). Even when practitioners try to build the rule of law entirely from the bottom up, they draw on a set of similar technologies that contribute to their rule of law ideal and that they embody by means of background and education (Simion and Taylor 2015) rather than some local adaptation of the concept. Next, I provide an overview of some of the 'technologies' that dictate rule of law and what these can achieve in developing or fragile settings across the globe.

## 2.2   RULE OF LAW TECHNOLOGIES

How are concepts made into authoritative models? Supported by their 'technologies', models are animated by ideas of what they can achieve in development settings (Behrends et al. 2014). Most often, these are created and promoted by global actors that facilitate actions from a distance (Rottenburg 2009), and they encapsulate politics (Riles 2005). This section unpacks the understanding of rule of law as something that development actors seek to propagate and transfer by claiming universality through the model's technologies (Carruthers and Halliday 2006). For example, facilitated action is seen in the creation of legal instruments that are intended to regulate behaviour in settings far removed from where they were created. Other persistent technologies include fact-construction by global actors found in the authoritative rule of law discourse they create; evaluative technologies, such as rankings and performance metrics; processes of monitoring and evaluating legal institutions; and the production of rule of law research.

### 2.2.1   Macro Actors and Argument from Authority

While there is no universal organisation that officially controls or enforces fragments of the ideas, principles, knowledge, and technologies that the rule of law field accepts as universally true, it is not far-fetched to nominate the WB and the UN as typical 'macro actors' (Callon and Latour 1981) that produce some of the field's most stable and repeated 'truths' through copying practices (Meyer 1996). These actors produce discourse and texts (Rajah 2014) that unlock 'argument from authority' of the kind that other actors constantly refer back to as persuasive descriptions of what rule of law is and what it can achieve in development contexts. Consequently, they are powerful enough to represent a collective 'global voice' of which they become the spokesperson (Callon 1986; Callon and Latour 1981).

In the early 1980s the WB did not explicitly mention 'rule of law'; rather, 'legal reform' was referenced as a component of the property rights, fiscal reforms, trade liberalisation, and so on that formed part of structural adjustment loans (Santos 2006). Law was seen as a central component of economic progress, and it was in the late 1980s that rule of law entered the organisational discourse more clearly as the organisation developed its focus on 'good governance' (Decker 2010: 228). In the late 1990s, the WB was criticised for failing to show enough consideration for the local context in settings where development programmes were implemented (Blake 2000; Faundez 2010). Inspired by a version of the rule of law that drew on the ideas articulated by Amartya Sen, a Nobel Prize winner and Harvard economics professor, the WB president at the time, James Wolfensohn, proposed a new 'Comprehensive Development Framework' to consider economic development in tandem with human, social, and structural aspects to better address long-term issues of development (Wolfensohn 1999). Sen was singled out as the main architect of new ideas that related to legal aspects of development (see, e.g., Perry-Kessaris 2014) and he was invited by the WB to give his view on the interconnectedness of legal and judicial reform with broader development processes. He emphasised the need to view economic, social, political, and legal development as connected means and ends, and stressed that legal and judicial reform was to be considered as contributing to, and crucial for, the general process of development (thus important on its own) and not as a separate fragment of legal or economic development (Sen 2000). As a result, the WB gradually replaced its old paradigms with new ideas that incorporated 'the social' in the rule of law reform agenda (Rittich 2006). The result of the new connection between governance and law was an expansion of legal reform projects that left few areas of the law out (Decker 2010; Faundez 2010).

Sen's ideas return in later WB discourse on rule of law (e.g., World Bank Legal Vice Presidency 2009:2). In 2012, a paper that introduced a new approach to justice system strengthening drew on Sen's ideas, suggesting that meaningful WB work on the reform of justice systems necessitated a 'vision of justice at the forefront' and thus 'an ongoing engagement with the substantive question of how justice is advanced' (World Bank 2012:1), through 'a justice reform agenda conceived in terms of "actual realizations and accomplishments" that matter to users (and potential users) of the justice system, more so than "the

establishment of what are identified as the right institutions and rules'"
(World Bank 2012:1, citing Sen 2009:9).

While WB discourse on rule of law has shifted into more substantive understandings, earlier ideas about the linkages between rule of law and economic development continue to be stated as some of the most fundamental 'truths' of the rule of law field. Also, although no coherent rule of law definition has been agreed for and within the WB (Santos 2006), guidance on confirmed views of the concept is found in the Worldwide Governance Indicators, where the rule of law is defined as 'the extent to which agents have confidence in and abide by the rules of society, and in particular the quality of contract enforcement, the police, and the courts, as well as the likelihood of crime and violence' (World Bank 2007:3). The rule of law is here linked to the justice chain and contract enforcement, which are important components of causalities between rule of law and economic development.

Consequential statements that link rule of law and economic prosperity are interesting because the story and the reality align imperfectly. The available evidence that an increase in rule of law will lead to economic development is ambiguous (see, e.g., Ginsburg 2000). In particular, several studies find that illiberal states have managed to develop their economies without a substantive rule of law system (Rajah 2012), which leads scholars to suggest that there might exist alternative and acceptable variations of rule of law (Jayasuriya 1999; McAlinn and Pejovic 2012). WB discourse that stresses the concept's linkages to economic development remains more palatable in authoritarian settings, where a less political approach that focuses on the economic gains of rule of law is welcomed more readily than approaches that focus on the model's substantive aspects, such as human rights (Wang 2015). In some ways, WB discourse thus differs from the dominant focus of the UN, which I outline next, on rule of law in connection with human rights and conflict prevention, differences that are in line with different organisational interests. However, the organisations' different stances are seldom seen as contrasting. Instead, the rule of law is a concept that is everywhere and seldom questioned. Here, Chesterman's (2008:2–3) suggestion that the 'high degree of consensus on the virtues of the rule of law is possible only because of dissensus as to its meaning[, a]t times ... [seen] as ... synonymous with "law" or legality[ and] on other occasions ... appear[ing] to import broader notions of justice' presents a reminder as to why organisations with different fundamental objectives can share common ground when it comes to questions of rule of law.

According to the UN, rule of law is both a fundamental aim of the organisation and a means to achieve its ends, including peace, security, and sustainable development (United Nations Report of the UN Secretary-General 2008). The UN policy that has evolved is comprehensive, and rule of law is included as a key element in everything from establishing law and order in conflict-affected settings to economic development and democratic governance (Farrall and Charlesworth 2016). The UN Security Council (SC) holds regular thematic debates on rule of law and often stresses its importance. Especially, a 2003 thematic debate on 'Justice and the Rule of Law: The United Nations Role' resulted in a statement from the president of the SC that mandated the Secretary General to report on rule of law in conflict and post-conflict societies (United Nations Security Council 2003). As a result, in 2004, the report 'Rule of Law and Transitional Justice in Conflict and Post-Conflict Societies' launched a rule of law definition common for the whole organisation (S/2004/616 23 August 2004). The UN Secretary General's 2004 statement has become influential in defining the rule of law as:

> a principle of governance in which all persons, institutions and entities, public and private, including the State itself, are accountable to laws that are publicly promulgated, equally enforced and independently adjudicated, and which are consistent with international human rights norms and standards. It requires, as well, measures to ensure adherence to the principles of supremacy of law, equality before the law, accountability to the law, fairness in the application of the law, separation of powers, participation in decision-making, legal certainty, avoidance of arbitrariness and procedural and legal transparency
>
> (S/2004/616 23 August 2004).

The institutional scope of the UN definition is broad and sets out to encompass not only legal and judicial institutions but also law enforcement, corrections institutions, and administrative agencies. It can be interpreted as a 'substantive' or 'thick' version of the rule of law (contrastingly 'formal' or 'thin') because it stipulates that the content and meaning of laws and regulations should also adhere to (international) standards of law and human rights or some other substantive criteria of justice (Tamanaha 2004). Nevertheless, the definition to some extent remains formalist as it fails to acknowledge or take into account the wide plurality of legal actors found in many of the world's hybrid systems (Tamanaha 2008; von Benda-Beckmann 2002). Divisions of 'thick' or 'thin' rule of law understandings permeate discourse in the field in Myanmar. For example, a foreign rule of law programme manager in Yangon (Interviewee #29, 23 October 2014) expressed irritation about the United Nations Development Programme (UNDP), which he said was providing rule of law trainings that were 'formal' and lacked a clear 'substantive' human rights component. The programme manager suggested that donors were giving in to the will of an authoritarian regime when they provided trainings that only presented a 'thin' version of the rule of law. Strategies of promoting rule of law had, in this case, been adapted to fit the local setting by intermediaries working on the project. Still, such an approach resulted in criticism from foreign practitioners because the model's substantive features had been stripped of meaning in light of the political context.

At the UN World Summit in 2005, the rule of law was repeatedly mentioned in connection to international law, acknowledged as key 'for sustained economic growth, sustainable development and the eradication of poverty and hunger', and as interlinked with human rights and democracy (United Nations General Assembly 2005). Focus on the connection between rule of law at the national and international levels was further emphasised during the Sixth (Legal) Committee of the General Assembly in 2006 (United Nations n.d.) and thereafter the General Assembly debated and adopted annual resolutions on rule of law at the national and international levels.

Several attempts have also been made by the Secretary-General and different UN entities to provide concrete guidance by describing specific justice components, tasks, and functions of rule of law assistance. For example, a 2008 Guidance Note on the 'UN Approach to Rule of Law Assistance' introduces, for the first time, a framework for strengthening rule of law by identifying a number of substantive and procedural elements in relation to aspects like constitutions and legal frameworks, and their implementation (United Nations 2008). To this end, some topical areas have gained specific attention. One example is 'legal aid', which has been the focus of global studies (see, e.g., the joint UNDP and UNODC global study on legal aid that was launched during 2015, United Nations Development Programme and United Nations Office on Drugs and Crime 2016), a major conference in Johannesburg in 2014 (United Nations Development Programme and others 2014), policy guidance (United Nations Office on Drugs and Crime and United Nations

Development Programme 2014), the adoption of guidelines and declarations (Johannesburg Declaration 2014). This particular topical focus is of interest for Myanmar where legal aid, inspired by experiences from South Africa, became a key focus of rule of law reform efforts after the political transition in 2011 (Thomson Reuters Foundation 2013).

In 2012, the UN held its first high-level meeting on rule of law in order to stress the central place that the rule of law had assumed in UN operations and to discuss and agree on a forward-looking agenda to strengthen it at national and international levels (United Nations Secretary General 2012). At the meeting, the General Assembly again adopted a Declaration 'on the Rule of Law at the National and International Levels' (United Nations General Assembly 2012). The scope and size of the 2012 meeting suggests that the UN views rule of law as a central aspect covering most of its activities.

The UN has produced a comprehensive rule of law discourse that links the concept to sustainable peace and security, development, human rights, and democratic governance. The 2004 definition has gained widespread usage as both an operational and an ad hoc definition by UN as well as non-UN rule of law actors active in Myanmar (see, e.g., Friedrich Naumann Stiftung für die Freiheit n.d.). The 2004 definition is often cited as a universally agreed-upon definition by rule of law promoters from the Global North (see, e.g., United Nations 2011:v–vi). For example, in a 2013 United States Institute of Peace (USIP) report that outlines the potential for rule of law activities in Myanmar, it is suggested: 'While explaining that there is a multiplicity of definitions and understandings of the Concept, USIP introduced participants to the term from the perspective of the international assistance community, specifically, the definition agreed to by UN member states in 2004' (United States Institute of Peace 2013:17). The UN definition is presented as representing the 'perspective of the international assistance community' in its entirety (ibid.).

In Myanmar, the UN definition is used in rule of law assessments; for example, a section entitled 'any law reform process must begin with a common understanding of the rule of law' states the definition as authoritative of explaining rule of law (New Perimeter et al. 2013). In addition, foreign practitioners in Myanmar often referred to the UN rule of law definition as being an authoritative expression of the concept, as do practitioners elsewhere (Evers 2010).

The rule of law discourse created by global actors is applied and adopted in creative ways by intermediaries in Myanmar who often find it too encompassing and politically difficult to discuss or implement. For that reason, intermediaries engage in processes of adapting global technologies to local circumstances to permeate reform initiatives. At the same time, intermediaries repeat and use global discourse for 'staging' purposes (James 2011) to showcase an understanding of concepts during workshops and trainings and in their discussions with foreign actors (Interviewee #3, 8 May 2014). For example, a rule of law programme manager suggested that her staff had no idea of what rule of law means, while the staff themselves referred to the 2004 UN definition as 'the rule of law' in my discussions with them (Interviewees #6, 19 May 2014; #35, 19 November 2014). Even though local actors may lack an understanding of the concept as expressed through UN discourse, they view it as necessary to express their understanding of the concept for career purposes. Macro actors create an environment in which global institutions formulate normative and institutional understandings of rule of law which are translated into development assistance on the ground in Myanmar (see, e.g., Friedrich Naumann Stiftung für die Freiheit n.d.) and beyond. They have thus classified and ordered a world of definitions and practices of things that are good and desirable (Latour 1987). The complexity of such normative suggestions, regardless of their authenticity, is that local-level adaptations remain ignored and are seldom allowed room to recursively influence macro actors' authoritative statements against which local-level reforms are measured. Understandings remain static and steered towards 'global' rather than 'local' (Bergling, Ederlöf, and Taylor 2009) which leaves little room for alternative (non-Western) conceptions of the rule of law (Peerenboom 2004) that emerge when intermediaries translate the concept to the local context. Feedback loops instead stop at the country level, where the individuals working to implement donor agencies may well understand the difficulties in using the organisational discourse and therefore adjust their communication with local counterparts in accordance with suggestions made by local intermediaries (discussed in Chapter 8).

### 2.2.2 International Legal Instruments
International legal instruments can also be viewed as a technology that helps animate rule of law, through claims of universality via instruments such as conventions, declarations, model laws, and best practices

(Carruthers and Halliday 2006). International legal instruments are used by both local and global actors in attempts to set normative examples (Meetings Coverage: United Nations General Assembly 2012). For rule of law assistance purposes, workshops are delivered to lecture on the meaning and practical application of international legal instruments, in attempts to advocate for amendment of national legislation (Fortify Rights 2015); they are used as benchmarks for rule of law monitoring and evaluation and applied as frameworks in the design of rule of law interventions. An example of the latter is the United Nations Basic Principles on the Independence of the Judiciary (1985), the United Nations Basic Principles on the Role of Lawyers (1990a) and the United Nations Guidelines on the Role of Prosecutors (1990b) that help guide judicial reform as a component of rule of law assistance (see, e.g., United Nations Office on Drugs and Crime 2017).

In Myanmar, where the government historically has paid little regard to international law (Milbrandt 2012) and has ratified relatively few international treaties (United Nations Human Rights Office of the High Commissioner 2017), INGOs as well as local NGOs use international law to advocate for change and to promote awareness of human rights. Already in the early 1990s, the International Labour Organization engaged in Myanmar in an attempt to end forced labour (Horsey 2011). One of the strategies employed was to draw on the regulatory power of international legal instruments to put pressure on the military leadership (Horsey 2011) who, despite their oppressive behaviour, also sought some political legitimacy (Cheesman 2013). In 2004, local NGO Equality Myanmar created a Universal Declaration of Human Rights cartoon (Equality Myanmar 2004) that has since been used to advocate for human rights in the country. Through visual aids, the cartoon illustrates, for example, article seven and article ten of the Universal Declaration in ways that communicate the articles' main messages of legal equality and the right to a fair trial.

International legal instruments are also applied in attempts to amend national legislation, for example by the International Commission of Jurists (2013) as an assessment framework for the analysis of problematic areas of the law in Myanmar in order to advocate for a change of legislation. Also, Fortify Rights draws on international standards to advocate for the abolition of repressive legislation, in this case a piece that requires individuals residing in Myanmar to report (and obtain permission to host) overnight guests to government officials (Fortify Rights 2015). Such regulation is based on the colonial 'Village Act'

that stipulated a system of collective penalties for resistance or reluctance to report criminals, the deportation of friends and family of
suspected criminals, and the requirement of villages to keep fences
and report any activities of strangers (Furnivall 1948). Originally passed
during the pacification campaign (1886–90) 'as an instrument of mar-
tial law', '[t]he Act', as Callahan suggests, 'broke up traditional local-
level administrative organizations' seen as 'giving rise to banditry and
organized resistance to British rule' but counterproductively 'paved the
way for a longer-term trend of lawlessness and disorder' (Callahan
2004:23–4). Compliance with the relevant sections that regulated the
obligation to report overnight guests in the 'Ward or Village Tract
Administration Law' was ensured through household inspections often
carried out at night. Fortify Rights suggests that the legislation is
repressive as it 'impinge[s] on various human rights, including the
right to privacy and rights to freedom of movement, residency and
association' (Fortify Rights 2015:7). The Act was amended in 2016
(Pyae Thet Phyo 2016) to come to terms with some of its most draconic
practices, but it remains problematic in many of its central features
(Action Committee for Democracy Development and Progressive
Voice 2018).

International courts may explicitly seek to bind parties before them
(including states) through the use of international legal instruments.
As an example, Myanmar has yet to sign (and become a party to) the
Rome Statute of the International Criminal Court (ICC) in order for
the Court to be able to investigate and prosecute alleged war crimes
committed by members of the Myanmar Army (Guilfoyle 2019; Hale
and Rankin 2019; Pedersen 2019). Still, many respondents who were
foreign rule of law practitioners referred to such investigations as the
ultimate expression of rule of law being applicable in Myanmar, most
certainly because the core idea of the rule of law is to limit the powers of
the sovereign so that law is applicable to all (Fuller 1964). Respondents
who were Myanmar nationals expressed neither a desire nor an expectation that 'the Generals' would ever be subjects of the rule of law and
such investigation. One foreign lawyer expressed the problem as she
perceived it:

> People get very offensive if you mention the ICC, people are less inter-
> ested in it, they think it would provoke the military. It is better to stay
> away from it. Some think it could happen in 5–10 years. This differs from
> other countries where there is some government interest in transitional

justice. This also raises the question if we should do things here when the government is not interested? Or is what we are doing here actually the way we should do transitional justice in other places? I am starting to raise the issue.

(Interviewee #15, 22 September 2014)

To this foreign practitioner, transitional justice was clearly connected to criminal prosecution. David and Holliday (2018) present a more nuanced picture of possible strategies for transitional justice in Myanmar to include reparation, retribution, revelation, and reconciliation. In Myanmar, they find, retributive justice that includes prosecution of former crimes is less supported by popular opinion than are reparatory or revelatory measures, but, in any case, the possibility for even more general debates on transitional justice is likely to remain underprioritised in light of the fragile political transition.

Tensions between universals and particulars are uncovered in the application of international legal instruments. After the transition in Myanmar, international law is advocated for more systematically by foreign development actors. Local activists seek to create awareness of international norms in a society that has been isolated from the international community for decades (Ahsan Ullah 2016). Clashes arise between international norms and local understandings (David and Holliday 2012; Holliday 2011, 2014). With regard to the lack of belief in transitional justice and the adherence to local beliefs, in this sense, the dismissive attitude towards international criminal law demonstrates international law's weakness.

### 2.2.3 Rule of Law Indicators

Macro actors have also developed means of evaluating the uptake of rule of law by target states through indicators that measure and rank professed discourse and concepts. The use of indicators as a technology for global governance by international development actors has been extensively analysed (Davis, Kingsbury, and Merry 2012). Such indicators have been referred to as 'technologies of truth' (Merry and Coutin 2014) referring to their power in defining the truths of social realities and knowledge (see also Rottenburg et al. 2015).

Several indicators have emerged to specifically measure, monitor, and evaluate rule of law (see, e.g., Merry, Davis, and Kingsbury 2015; Taylor 2016). Parsons et al. in 2010 identified a total of fifty-three justice indicators (Parsons et al. 2010). Some of the most well-known examples include the World Justice Project (WJP) *Rule of Law Index* (World Justice Project 2014); the WB's *Worldwide Governance Indicators* (World Bank 2017); and the UN *Rule of Law Indicators* (United Nations 2011). The UN indicators focus primarily on the criminal justice sector, contradictory to the organisation's attempts to advocate for a broad understanding of the rule of law (see United Nations 2011). Also, the UNDP recently developed a comprehensive user's guide to measuring rule of law, justice, and security programmes in development settings (Kutateladze and Parsons 2014).

Indicators are commonly used to benchmark and evaluate national justice systems. For example, in a 2016 'Briefing on the Rule of Law in Myanmar', Booth writes:

> Myanmar continues to earn dramatically low marks in global rule of law and governance indicators. In 2015, The World Justice Project placed Myanmar at 92 out of 102 countries ranked due to poor ratings in open government, absence of judicial corruption, and fundamental rights. The same year, the World Bank gave Myanmar one of the lowest scores possible in rule of law, along with meagre rankings in other public sector governance issues.
>
> (Booth 2016:1)

Through such a statement, the author presents indicators as authoritative and, in Rajah's (2014:356) words, 'impenetrable', meaning that they are presented in a format that few care to question.

Indicators are frequently built into project designs as part of the required outcomes for an intervention (Taylor 2016). They are applied as quantifiable benchmarks intended to 'prove' whether or not rule of law development aid 'works' and to 'measure host legal system compliance with selected forms of the rule of law' in attempts to standardise rule of law assistance (Taylor 2016:39). This line of thought can also be seen in the development of impact evaluations and other ways of measuring rule of law assistance (Cohen et al. 2011).

In their design, rule of law indicators tends to be top-down, ahistorical snapshots of how select respondents perceive the functioning of formal legal institutions (Ginsburg 2011; Taylor 2007). They are also intended to broadly generalise and influence perceptions of rule of law within individual states, measured against an idealised yardstick of what desired 'rule of law' attributes or institutions would look like. Taylor (2007), for example, argues that rule of law indicators support simplified representations (overly complex realities) that inform commercialised global templates of branding that help rule of law organisations build their profile (Taylor 2016).

Recently the importance of rule of law indicators was highlighted in relation to the 2015 Agenda on Sustainable Development Goals (SDGs) (Arajärvi 2017; Bergling and Jin 2015). In the planning stages, it was suggested that '[d]efining and measuring goals, targets and indicators on justice and rule of law is both technically feasible and a key component in ensuring that the post-2015 agenda is equitable and inclusive' (Permanent Mission of Pakistan and the United Nations System through the Rule of Law Coordination and Resource Group 2014:2). However, the optimism, especially in relation to Goal 16's (Peace, Justice and Strong Institutions) 'measurability', was increasingly recognised as presenting challenges. An example of the increased complexity of these indicators would be the challenge of measuring the twelve targets that accompany Goal 16: for example, 'Promote the rule of law at the national and international levels and ensure equal access to justice for all' (Global Goals for Sustainable Development n.d.). Countries are expected to provide annual reports on their progress in achieving the targets, which feed into a report by the UN Secretary-General (United Nations Economic and Social Council 2017). Generating statistical data will be difficult for national governments, and there are likely to exist profound political disagreements over concepts that are the target of measurement, for example war, peace, institutional autonomy, and justice (Tommasoli 2017). To engage with some of the complexities of applying official indicators, a specific Goal 16 Data Initiative has been created that supplements the officially agreed indicators with indicators that try to capture citizens' perceptions, based on surveys or expert assessments (SDG 16 Data Initiative n.d.).

Rule of law ranking and measuring tools are becoming more complex. Further explorations into their structure would reveal multiple layers that prompt questions about the nature of their construction (Davis et al. 2012; Merry et al. 2015; Parsons et al. 2010; Restrepo Amariles 2015; Rottenburg et al. 2015). An analysis of their 'commensuration' – the process of translating diverse social conditions and phenomena into comparable units (Merry 2015) – is important when increasing weight is being attached to indicators, because they decontextualise people, events, actions, and objects to create points of comparison and similarity. Indicators contribute to the construction of a rule of law model that is more often formal and limited to certain areas of rule of law programming, rather than considerate of local complexities and power dynamics.

### 2.2.4 Rule of Law Research and Theory

Science as a technology has authority and influence in the field of rule of law assistance, yet little attention has been devoted to the way it influences and informs the way that rule of law is considered when applied as an intervention. For example, what ideas and perspectives become accepted as the 'truths' of the rule of law model? How do global rule of law actors make use of rule of law research and theory to support their claims and authoritative discourse?

Organisational theorist Meyer (1996:247) suggests that, through research, organisations 'search externally for consensual and scientifically "valid" standards'. Involved consultants and scientists often serve what is considered a higher set of truths and not simply a market of consumers (ibid.). Callon's (1986) foundational science and technology study exemplifies how a couple of scientists became the central translators of the 'will' of several groups while establishing themselves as spokespersons. Recently, the role of experts as spokespersons is stressed in relation to the SDG's. For example, the UN Secretary-General has appointed 'scientists' to work on a quadrennial Global Sustainable Development Report that is intended to 'strengthen the science–policy interface', incorporate 'evidence in a multidisciplinary manner', and 'provide guidance on the state of global sustainable development from a scientific perspective' (Risse 2017). Such stressed importance on scientists' knowledge empowers certain actors as they obtain 'power' to represent 'the rest' while they manoeuvre the 'authority to speak or act on behalf of another actor or force' (Callon and Latour 1981:279).

Since the initiation of the law and development movement, academics have been involved in the field's establishment and characterisation (Newton 2006; Trubek 2006). Academics' work has been used to justify activities and illustrate that they have 'impact' (see, e.g., Legal Vice Presidency 2003). In particular, rule of law research has come to focus on defining what the rule of law *is*. In attempts to provide conceptual clarity and define the rule of law, subsequent scholars will usually start from an account of a historical truth originating with theorists such as Weber, Dicey, and Hayek (see, e.g., Santos 2006). These writers commonly list components needed for a state to be regarded as one where the rule of law prevails (Dicey 1999; Hayek

1944); for example, laws need to possess certain qualities such as being publicly known and available, not retroactive or contradictory, being comprehensible and fairly stable, and being reflective of both societal rules in action and officials' behaviour (Fuller 1964).

An important question that springs from these fundamentally liberal definitions (Tamanaha 2004:32; see also Humphreys 2010) is whether or not the rule of law can exist in a setting without formal institutions or written laws. Hayek (1955) recognised that it matters relatively little if the core of the rule of law exists in the bill of rights, or in the constitutional code, or if it is just a strong, established tradition, because the essential basis of the rule of law lies in confidence in the concrete rules which set up the relations among individuals. Even though it was recognised that law takes the form of both written and unwritten rules about behaviour, legal scholarship has often neglected the input side of law, that is, the forces in society that contribute to the shaping of law (Friedman 1975). For development purposes, neglecting the social 'inputs' that constitute law often contributes to a misunderstanding of law as a formal ideal that reflects a 'modern' system. The consequence of such a conception is that legal development initiatives are often expressed in terms of their form rather than as a reflection of the political and socio-economic functions that law plays in society (Decker, Sage, and Stefanova 2005; Peerenboom 2009; Trubek and Santos 2006). Krygier (2006:1) reacts against universalist and formal conceptions of the rule of law and proposes that, in order to understand what rule of law is, it is necessary to look

> beyond legal institutions to the societies in which they function there, and what else happens there which interacts with and affects the sway of law. For the rule of law to exist, still more to flourish and be secure, many things besides the law matter, and since societies differ in many ways, so will those things. So a universal, institution-based, answer to what the rule of law is, is implausible. And it will often mislead. Indeed it might well lead us away from the rule of law.

Krygier's argument resonates with a travelling model's framework because it recognises that universal approaches are far-fetched. Such recognition also resonates with the law and society and anthropological scholarship that explore less formal aspects of rule of law and see the concept as being as much about culture and perceptions as about formal institutions (Calavita 2010; Merry 1988).

It appears as if liberal theorists have had more influence on rule of law theory than sociologists. Still, we cannot be certain that they play a significant role for development practitioners today, who, by contrast, often cite the UN as the 'inventor' of rule of law (see, e.g., Evers 2010) or focus their development work on the post-colonial enterprise of mapping and detecting justice systems they deem 'customary' (see, e.g., Kyed 2017). Nevertheless, scholars reinstate the work of this select group of legal and political theorists and often express surprise that development practice looks different from what these theorists once described (see, e.g., Humphreys 2010; Santos 2006). Rule of law theorists also support a tradition of analysing countries through these technologies and benchmarks as a way of determining whether or not they 'have the rule of law' (see, e.g., Cheesman 2009).

By reinforcing the importance and supremacy of this theory, researchers are feeding a set of technologies into rule of law, leaving out alternative explanations of the concept (Hurst 2018) and theoretical work by scholars from non-Western countries, thus concentrating knowledge in an elite part of the world (Said 2003). Interestingly, in Myanmar, in addition to the influence of newly arrived foreign organisations and researchers, local practitioners often refer to this form of Western theory when asked how they inform themselves about rule of law. This contrasts with the responses of foreign practitioners, who more often refer to international legal instruments and discourses. So, for example, when I asked one of Aung San Suu Kyi's advisers about her knowledge of rule of law, the reply I got was that 'She read Tom Bingham's book on rule of law' (Bingham 2011; Interviewee #41, 11 December 2014). A former political prisoner and now local rule of law activist said that for purposes of his own knowledge and curricula development for trainings: 'I read many books by western scholars, for example[] Hart, I slightly use parts of these' (e.g., Hart 2012; Interviewee #30, 24 October 2014). A rule of law programme staff member suggested that he read many political works and translated texts by Thomas Jefferson to learn about the rule of law: 'I translated the text, it means absolute objectivity in the application of law, people representing people' (Interviewee #55, 27 September 2015). This is interesting because it indicates that global discourses that contribute to perceptions of rule of law for purposes of development assistance may be too encompassing and confusing to adapt at local and national levels. Instead, local actors resort to older theoretical work void of development trends and buzz-words.

On a more practical level, some researchers are engaged in justifying involvement in rule of law assistance and in creating a feeling of assurance through validated science and research. For example, the WB has made efforts to justify its involvement in legal reform through the 'voluminous literature' it has produced (Faundez 2010). The WB has continuously attempted to prove empirical relationships between rule of law and economic growth through quantitative research (Thomas 2005). To that end, the organisation established and managed a trust fund with support from donor countries such as Australia to support research and operational innovation through the 'Justice for the Poor Programme' (Justice Reform Practice Group of the World Bank's Legal Vice Presidency 2012). Until its phased conclusion in 2018–19, the programme offered a 'Justice and Development Working Paper Series', briefing notes, research reports, policy notes and literature reviews on rule of law and justice-related topics (World Bank 2011). The WB has also on several occasions sought statistical validation and quality assurance of its influential WJP *Rule of Law Index* through an opinion piece from a group of European scientists (Saisana and Saltelli 2012). A web portal on 'Justice and Rule of Law' (World Bank 2015) informs us that the WB also carries out extensive research through case studies and working papers. For example, for purposes of judicial reform, a 2013 paper from the Justice and Development Working Paper Series on 'Caseflow Management: Key Principles and the Systems to Support Them', by Gramckow and Nussenblatt, provides a comprehensive introduction to 'caseflow management' as a tool for 'courts across the globe … to better organize and manage their caseload' (Heike Gramckow and Nussenblatt 2013:1). The call for caseflow management through a research piece is interesting because 26 per cent of the WB's total spending on technical assistance for justice reform was at the time devoted to court and case management (Justice Reform Practice Group of the World Bank's Legal Vice Presidency 2012:4). Other development actors also focus on case management systems as components of judicial reform; for example, in Myanmar, Tetra Tech was introducing such systems in local courts at the outskirts of Yangon (Interviewee #59, 15 December 2014).

## 2.3 CONCLUSION

In this chapter, I applied a 'travelling models' framework to illustrate the authoritative features that rule of law takes on as a model for development intervention. The framework emphasises rule of law's mediated necessities rather than universalities. It does not claim that models are coherent and static; rather, they are fluid, but they always present a contrast to domestic worldviews and understandings, and thus they are an intervention of some sort. Even when adapted and adjusted by skilled development workers, models need mediation and translation because they will never be fully promoted from the bottom up. I suggested that this way of thinking about rule of law as a model that travels allows us to draw on theories and insights from sociology and anthropology with less focus on trying to define what rule of law *actually is* and more focus on the agents that broker the field's disparate but authoritative technologies and ideologies to better understand how such normative concepts intervene in illiberal or semi-illiberal regimes.

I did not attempt to claim that there was a coherence as to what rule of law is, but I argued that, while competing definitions exist, we find features of a model among these shattered elements that inform the work of rule of law practitioners active in the development field who seldom question 'simple arguments' of the casual connection between rule of law, democracy, and peace (Merry 2016).

I suggested that technologies are created and promoted by global actors that facilitate actions intended to promote the model from a distance. First, I argued that macro organisations are formulating a global rule of law agenda through their discourse and authoritative arguments and that local-level adaptation seldom recursively influences the discourse of macro actors; instead, the latter remains the benchmark against which local-level reforms are measured. Such practice leaves little room for alternative conceptions of rule of law to emerge or be publicly articulated. The discourse used by macro actors thus remains static and steered towards explanations and understandings that are described as global rather than local. Even when practitioners proclaim bottom-up approaches (van Rooij 2009) that explore aspects such as customary justice (Kyed 2017), they arrive in the field with their own legal training and understanding of what the rule of law ideal should look like (Simion and Taylor 2015); hence, they promote a model, even if incoherent or unconscious, that is part of their baggage, if not the stated aim of the donor.

Thereafter, I suggested that international legal instruments constitute one technology through which translation happens as they are used to advocate for change and promote awareness of human rights and are applied in attempts to amend national legislation. Moreover, indicators measure and rank rule of law to entrenched discourse and concepts and thus contribute to the construction of a model that is more often formal and limited to certain areas of programming rather than considering local complexities and power dynamics.

I suggested that 'research' is used to justify involvement in rule of law assistance and to create a feeling of assurance through validated science. In particular, research has come to focus on defining and conceptualising what rule of law *is*, and Western scholars are often deemed the inventors of such theory. Science as a technology has authority and influence in the field, yet little attention has been devoted to the way rule of law research and theory influences and informs how rule of law is considered when applied as a model for intervention. For example, little work has been done to track the practices that 'create giants' (Calkins and Rottenburg 2014) through citation practices in the rule of law field while ignoring other authors. By reinforcing the importance and supremacy of certain theorists, researchers are feeding a set of technologies into the rule of law, leaving out both alternative explanations of the concept as well as the theoretical work by scholars from non-Western countries.

Local adaptation and translation, which intermediaries engage in, is key for success in rule of law development attempts. My take on rule of law as a model emphasised the mediated processes needed for the model to gain traction in places of development intervention where universals intercept with particulars. In settings where political, cultural, and social norms are fluid, the implementation of rule of law implies unintended consequences if local context, authority, and power relations are overlooked. The result of intervention and intermediaries' work goes to both ends: while donors would have preferred a more 'on the book' version of the authoritative model and intermediaries would have been better off promoting a version more apt for the societies where they operate, both sides are pushed to find a middle ground, with results that include semi-illiberal versions of the concept, even when promoted with the best intentions (Liljeblad 2019; Pompe 2005).

CHAPTER THREE

# INTERMEDIARIES: WHO, WHAT, WHEN?

How does the contemporary intermediary in the rule of law assistance field differ from the colonial village 'headman' who helped administer the powers of imperial rule or from the individuals that mediated new regulations and values imposed by central powers on the peripheries? When we examine the typical profile of intermediaries in Myanmar's transition period, we see that, in fact, these characters bear much resemblance. Then, and as I show is also the case now, intervening actors who lack linguistic knowledge and socio-legal understandings of law and custom have to rely on local intermediaries (Merry 2010) because their actions result in an intervention that involves differences in values and new forms of regulation that claim universality of some sort, even if well-meaning. This revelation, however, might be an uncanny one since it suggests that the field of rule of law promotion today remains connected to the historical legacy of the legal colonial project (McBride 2016) and that it involves aspects of *intervention* rather than *co-operation* (Rottenburg 2009).

Scholars of political anthropology emphasise the intermediary role as central throughout this history and propagate for a 'return of the broker' in more contemporary political anthropology scholarship (e.g., James 2011). They focus especially on the emergence of intermediaries as a result of an intervention in the realms of law and regulation during colonial administration or from a central power on local communities. For example, Benton and Ford (2018) show how the administrators and those at the core of the law of the British Empire kept trying to bring legal order to the colonies with intermittent but numerous interventions, but with results that amounted to a tolerance of countless legal pluralisms. The 'local' repeatedly got in the way of the effort to bring order through British law and legal practices, and thus the British had to employ and empower locals and expatriates as intermediaries who in turn detoured and transformed the policies in all kinds of ways in different places and at different times (see also Benton 2002).

There has also been a renewed interest in intermediation and translation among anthropologists and social scientists studying international development aid (Koster and van Leynseele 2018). Seminal work in this field includes Bierschenk, Chauveau, and de Sardan's (2002) ethnography of development intermediaries in Africa, which outlines how such actors rose to exceptional significance, especially in relation to the redistribution and circulation of development revenue, in the aftermath of colonial independence when colonial rule was replaced by aid dependency from the same sources. More recently, Koster and Leynseele (2018) explore a variety of brokers, their role as agents, and dimensions of their work in transitional settings to highlight development processes and dynamic societal settings, where multiple forms of power and influence overlap. Examples are youth workers that bring together and negotiate different worldviews captured in the development policies propagated by the state in their aim to 'socialise' the youth, often in opposition to the needs and aspirations of the other side (Chalhi, Koster, and Vermeulen 2018), and brokers that mediate the struggles that follow the introduction of international models for land regulation (Leynseele 2018).

Early anthropological scholarship on intermediaries has been criticised for depicting societies as 'locked in' in a relationship of 'encapsulated' and 'encapsulating', an influential 'top' and a peasant 'bottom', where the colonial administration influences a rigorous hierarchy and dichotomy, limiting mediation of these linear relationships (Kuper 1970). More recently, scholars emphasise the importance of viewing the intermediary as an analytical starting point for understanding broader processes of global to local interaction (Lindquist 2015b) among multiple sites (Marcus 1995). Within the field of international law and human rights, Merry (2006a, 2006b), for example, examines women's rights as they are defined at 'global' levels and traces their translation to the 'local' level and back through people in 'the middle': those who vernacularise global norms to the specific national or local context, as 'translators' or 'intermediaries'. Merry's ideas are taken up by sociologists Carruthers and Halliday (2006) in their analysis of the translation of global insolvency scripts that shows how ideas, norms and ideologies, developed in global settings, are conveyed to local settings through intermediaries.

Also, international relations scholars who draw on a tradition of 'norm translation' (Acharya 2004; Finnemore and Sikkink 1998) analyse the implementation of global norms in local arenas, which they find is often made possible through support by non-state actors and transnational networks. Rule of law can diffuse locally through the implementation of foreign-assisted development projects through national and local contestation, which in turn affect foreign actors recursively – back and forward (Zimmermann 2017). Non-state justice institutions play a crucial role in translating global norms to local courts where change (e.g. the empowerment of the poor and the marginalised) happens when grassroots-level fieldworkers translate transnational norms in ways that resonate with the social and political worldview that poor and marginalised people hold (Berger 2017).

These classical studies of intermediation and brokerage assist the analysis of current phenomena of global rule of law assistance (cf. de Jong 2018) as this chapter introduces an in-depth account of who rule of law intermediaries are in Myanmar, based on empirical research conducted in the country's transition period. I initiated my search for the who and what of rule of law intermediation in a setting of unprecedented opportunity to forge connections with foreign actors and ideas amid political flux and upheaval. Scholars have identified intermediaries in the transnational rule of law field to include NGOs (Merry 2006a, 2006b), local activists (Chua 2019), government officials and international consultants (Halliday and Carruthers 2009), lawyers (Dezalay and Garth 2012), and amorphous judicial networks (Dallara and Piana 2017). In general terms, they are persons who occupy ground from where they broker ideas, models, and templates for change. They oscillate between different roles, depending upon what the circumstances call for. More particularly, rule of law intermediaries work as interlocutors between foreign donors and domestic institutions (see Nicholson and Low 2013).

This book argues for an emphasised focus on the role of intermediaries, as an embodiment of broader contexts and processes of transnationalism (Lindquist 2015a), in settings where rule of law assistance is rolled out under the auspices of development: where institutional failure and success have been heavily analysed, but the intermediaries responsible for fine-tuned relationship building between configurations of actors and conceptual adaptations remain under-investigated. This chapter confronts the expanding scope of rule of law assistance by focusing on the concept of the intermediary, which offers an analytical means of identifying the social nodes in a network of relative positions and influence. The discussion about various conceptualisations of intermediation sheds light on the role that intermediaries play, and the challenges they face, at the interfaces of the different knowledge and value systems that accompany the development industry.

Rule of law intermediaries in Myanmar come from various backgrounds and draw on different forms of capital (foreign, political, social) while they move within central and peripheral domains of informal and formal processes concerning complex interventions into law and legal institutions in dynamic yet problematic struggles of allegiance and distrust. They are local lawyers, busy consultants who try to establish a connection to Myanmar actors and learn about local culture and custom, eager development agency staff, ambitious NGO leaders, as well as less satisfied government officials. After I have presented who intermediaries are in Myanmar, I turn to a reflection of their characteristics and what they do to emphasise that they are not neutral go-betweens but people who stand to gain or lose from different transactions and capital (see Long 1975; Silverman 1965).

## 3.1 WHO IS A RULE OF LAW INTERMEDIARY, IN MYANMAR?

While it might be tempting to pre-define who intermediaries are, such an approach limits our socio-legally informed understanding of active agents around and in between the law (see also Moore 1973) in the same way as a formal, rather than a pluralistic, approach limits our understandings of what law *is* (see, e.g., Calavita 2010). Therefore, I entered the research setting with a set of open-ended questions through which I sought the individuals who 'played a role' as intermediaries in the rule of law assistance field in Myanmar.

Intermediaries were located through interview data that described them (i.e., other people talking about them), their own biographical presentations and answers to interview questions, as well as my own personal observations. My research took as a starting point a 'bottom-up' approach where I used exploratory, rather than explanatory, strategies in order to help locate rule of law intermediaries. For that reason, I decided to leave out words linked to what I was after (e.g., intermediary) beforehand and instead described my project as being about rule of law development in more general terms. The approach allowed more variation and insights into personal perceptions than a 'deductive' one with predetermined categories of who should be defined as an intermediary. For example, I asked a foreign rule of law programme manager who he relied on to reach out to counterparts, who his 'key player' was, and what that person did. I was told:

> He [the intermediary] is the nexus, or one point, between us and the world. He is the link between this international body and engagement with real people with real problems. Few internationals in all these organizations know how to get to them and how. I would not know who to call the way he does. It would be hard to find someone who could do it as good as him, he has it in his DNA. He has one foot in and one foot out at the same time. A bit schizophrenic and difficult . . . he is at the interface.
>
> (Interviewee #20, 30 September 2014)

The understanding conveyed here is that the intermediary, while being the central connection to the counterparts, is also in a difficult and ambivalent position. This portrayal of the intermediary from Myanmar in 2014 bears resemblance to Szasz's (1994) historical depiction of such individuals that emerged following the white settlement of North America, because there was an evident need for intermediaries who possessed 'extraordinary skill' to mediate between the 'clashing worlds' of native communities and initial contacts by foreigners (see also Richter 1988). She writes about intermediaries who

> became repositories of two or more cultures; they changed roles at will, in accordance with circumstances . . . They knew how the 'other side' thought and behaved, and they responded accordingly. Their grasp of different perspectives led all sides to value them, although not all may have trusted them. Often they walked through a network of interconnections where they alone brought some understanding among disparate peoples.
>
> (1994, 6)

Then as now, intermediaries were described as being absolutely essential for co-operation (illustrated by Table 3.1), but they were also perceived as Janus-faced and never fully trusted (reviewed in Chapter 7).

After several similar interviews that described individuals or organisations as typical intermediaries, I sought contact with the identified persons. I asked them simply 'Tell me about your work' or 'Tell me what

TABLE 3.1 Rule of law intermediaries described

| Terms and phrases intermediaries used in their narratives | Terms and phrases foreign practitioners used in their narratives |
| --- | --- |
| Fixer | Link |
| In-between | Nexus |
| Co-ordinator behind the scenes | Peace-maker |
| Bridge | Point of contact |
| Translator | The one with all the connections |
| Facilitator | One foot in and one foot out |
| Mediator | At the interface |
| Diplomatic interferer | Open doors |
| Aligner of social and political capital | |

you do' and felt as if I had hit the mark when they answered in ways that indicated that the individuals viewed themselves as playing an inter-mediary role. For example:

> I try to just be the bridge, not favouring my side – the one who likes to help the one who needs help. I don't think for myself. I am not standing just for my employer. I am representing both sides – the local people and the ones who want to help us develop. I coordinate the two sides. They both need to understand that they should adjust.
>
> (Interviewee #27, 7 October 2014)

At first glance, this intermediary's explanation illustrates a position of neutrality, of not wanting to favour any side or think for herself. This self-perception is quickly transformed into an expression of how the intermediary may try to wield influence as she voices her opinion that 'both need to understand that they should adjust'. As this book shows in the chapters that follow, intermediaries were not shy about exerting their influence on both sides of the development configuration with results that illustrate intermediaries' effect on the understanding and development of rule of law in an illiberal setting.

I identified rule of law intermediaries across several institutional positions. The most common, broadly classified, included the local lawyer, the local NGO, the locally employed staff who work for an international organisation, the government employee, and the international consultant. This is not to suggest that everyone who is employed in these roles is an intermediary, but that it is usually across these professional groups that we find individuals who perform an intermediary function. Thus, while positioned in different roles and assignments in the rule of law development field, what they all have in common is that they perform the delicate and intricate task of relating larger, globally oriented ideas to the Myanmar locale, in a key middle position among foreign, national, and local actors.

The exercise of creating labelled categories to some extent benefited from the use of a conceptual lens that I applied after intermediaries had been initially identified. Bierschenk et al.'s (2002) approach to the study of intermediaries helped in this regard. The group of anthropology scholars suggest that 'intermediary' is a 'role' that 'does not refer to a concrete status or to any official, or informal position in an institution, or to an emic notion calling on conceptions which exist at a conscious level, in the awareness of the persons involved'; rather, they suggest, 'intermediary' is a conceptual lens that 'allows us to distance ourselves from the self-representation of actors and thus to produce analytical insights of the way actors, who are not able to perceive themselves from this angle, behave' (Bierschenk et al. 2002:19). Through inductive methods, I attempted to avoid the application of a top-down lens. Also, contradicting the authors' suggestion, in Myanmar, many of the individuals interviewed were very aware of the intermediary role they played (as indicated by their self-descriptions). However, Bierschenk et al.'s (2002) approach helped in distinguishing official work titles from the intermediary role and provided guidance when I experienced challenges because research participants self-identified in ways that contradicted interview data from other practitioners or from personal observations. Some individuals seemed quite eager to refer to themselves as 'brokers' or 'fixers' while it was fairly evident that they had no such influence in the rule of law community. I also detected a difference between foreigners' willingness to self-identify as playing an intermediary function compared to nationals'. For example, when describing my project to a foreign rule of law programme manager with the intent of getting her to tell me about the intermediary I knew was working with them, she instead confidently retorted, 'Oh, someone like me!' Another one commented: 'We want to play that intermediary function', while a third constantly told me that he was one of those 'fixers' who broker deals and that he knew people within the government.

I got the impression that for many foreigners, acquiring the level of trust needed to play a bridging role was something desirable and respectable. For nationals, the situation was slightly different, as they would not necessarily describe the role as something they aspired to; rather, it was a position they were at times 'stuck' with.

In the overview that follows, I present rule of law intermediaries as they were characterised and identified across several institutional roles. They are presented as composite sketches of actual individuals in each category, with the known facts about them. I use pseudonyms to protect the identities of my participants. Nonetheless, the characteristics of each intermediary type will be familiar to the rule of law development actor, and for the outsider, they should offer some explanatory power.

### 3.1.1 The Myanmar Lawyer

Local lawyers who are young, good English speakers, and charismatic took on a role as intermediaries in Myanmar's transition period as they brokered ideas of rule of law that they had picked up from various sources of international law.

Scholarship with inspiration in Dezalay and Garth's (e.g., 2011, 2012) socio-legal studies explores elite lawyers as active brokers in a quest for rule of law change (Hammerslev 2006; Kisilowski 2015; Tungnirun 2017). These lawyer brokers are depicted as more than 'neutral translators' because '[t]hey use the various forms of capital (social, legal, political, economic) that they have already accumulated to build their credibility (and power) as brokers' and may provide 'the full menu of multiple services as go-betweens but also as translators and mediators' (Dezalay and Garth 2011:5, 260; see also Halliday, Karpik, and Feeley 2007). A contrast to the focus on elite lawyers as legal intermediaries is Munger's (2012a) response that champions the other 'end', which he defines as locally embedded 'cause lawyers' (see also Sarat and Scheingold 2008) who use the language and norms of rule of law to instigate and influence social change in the confined setting of Thailand's authoritarian rule (see also Cheesman and Kyaw Min San 2014). Munger (2012b) argues that the study of elite legal professionals influences the understanding of globalisation as a top-down enterprise while these processes are also facilitated from the bottom up. The studies in question all start from their respective 'ends' – the 'global' or the 'local' – which become problematic dichotomies because they easily isolate those spaces. In a sense they recognise processes in the 'middle' but still glue together (and 'black-box') relationships, however these are characterised. For example, 'local' views and understandings, in the case of development assistance, are often a distorted understanding of the intermediary or 'middle' view (cf. Manji 2006). Likewise, this book focuses on fluid processes in the 'middle' rather than those more commonly defined as 'local' (Bosch 2016; Nicholson and Low 2013) or 'international' (Magen and Morlino 2009).

Lawyers who brokered influence in the field of rule of law assistance in Myanmar were not quite the elite lawyers depicted in Dezalay and Garth's (2010) explorations nor active cause lawyers. There, the legal profession had already become nationalised in the 1970s when the freelancing members of the Bar were transformed into People's Attorneys with the state as their headman under direct control by the legislature (Huxley 1998). When they were severely reprimanded for any political involvement and marginalised to the point of extinction during military rule in the 1990s (see also Cheesman 2015; International Commission of Jurists 2013), they often remained vested in underground politics and local political activism. Consequently, Myanmar lawyers who brokered influence in the rule of law assistance field often had a background in local politics (reviewed in Chapter 6), as expressed with a smile by one respondent: 'We are all chance politicians' (Interviewee #49, 11 December 2014). Rule of law intermediaries are more commonly found among marginal positions than within community elites (cf. de Jong 2018) and their political engagements are often more prominent than their work as lawyers active in everyday court practice (cf. Batesmith and Stevens 2019).

In terms of identifying local lawyers, foreign donors were cautious about whom to engage with. Similar to what Hammerslev (2006) observed in the case of Bulgaria, where foreign donors found both 'Westernised' lawyers and those who were more reluctant to pursue the reforms, in Myanmar foreign interveners deliberately worked with people 'who agreed on the priorities of the development of law' (2006:75). In Myanmar, these lawyers were not necessarily the most influential ones; rather, they knew what donors wanted to hear in terms of global rule of law discourse. In contrast, scholars have found that when the local legal community takes ownership of brokering its preferred version of the rule of law (even if not the preferred liberal system as desired by international development actors) in lieu of excessive foreign aid models and incitements, the result can be institutions that, in the longer run, are more open to democratic transition (Kisilowski 2015). In transition settings, foreign development actors become an established but delicate feature of social, political, and economic life that people encounter on a daily basis. In such a new landscape, intermediaries become responsible for navigating local and national institutions, values, and people. These new conditions of living with foreign development actors and models are a complex undertaking because intermediaries are torn between counterparts' conflicting worldviews (see also Tungnirun 2018).

These Myanmar lawyers had the leverage to broker influence in the rule of law assistance field because they knew how to act as informal brokers of law: manipulators and strategists adept at working with the law, but not always working within it (see Batesmith and Stevens 2019; Prasse-Freeman 2015).

### 3.1.2 The Local NGO

Individuals (who are often intermediaries in their own right) assemble to carry out collective intermediary activities in the rule of law field (see also Massoud 2015; Munger 2014). Already in the primes of the law and development movement, Gonzalez (1972) provided one of the earliest analyses of a group of individuals constituting the 'Development Association' that channelled international sources from the United States to the Dominican Republic. She outlines how these development intermediaries gained their influences within US–Dominican relations due to their financial powers, access to information, and prominent networks. These development intermediaries used their capital – language skills (English and development lingua), foreign manners, and networks – to attract investment in the form of grants from the US Agency for International Development (USAID), the Ford Foundation, and the World Bank (WB). Seeley (1985), in her study of social welfare development in a Kenyan town, similarly shows how intermediary organisations built up and used their relational capital in order to negotiate with both 'sides' of the development configuration, cautious about granting outside access to the personal networks they had invested in.

In Myanmar, individuals gather through coalitions or NGOs with head offices in Yangon that, according to foreign practitioners, are 'run by charismatic leaders' (e.g., Interviewee #1, 6 May 2014) who are 'instrumental for driving the agendas' (Interviewee #28, 22 October 2014). NGO leaders reveal similar backgrounds and include both lawyers and non-lawyers, with some degree of previous political engagement at the village level or as student activists (see Chapter 6).

The rationale behind gathering in NGOs and coalitions can be manifold. The traditional role of civil society associations – as an intermediary function between the state and the people (Shigetomi 2002; South 2008) – may morph with the introduction of outside development aid. Bierschenk et al. (2002) suggest that individuals assemble as a response to increased donor presence (because donors prefer to channel funding through groups over individuals) or successively transform existing coalitions to meet donor needs (see also AbouAssi 2013). The influx of foreign donors may thus result in organisations that are more likely to 'respond to the dynamics of project availability' than to promote initiatives representing 'true' local needs (Bierschenk et al. 2002:24). On the other hand, in illiberal settings, there is also the tendency by donors to rule out local NGOs that express different needs from those deemed legitimate by foreign donors (Décobert and Wells 2020). In relation to lawyers who started their own NGOs, Dezalay and Garth's (2011) observation that lawyers who are intermediaries promote their own NGOs in order to build credibility at local levels was also observed in Myanmar.

Three distinct types of local rule of law NGO's were detectable in Myanmar. There were the ones that 'came out of Nargis and then expanded into rule of law' (Interviewee #9, 23 May 2014); this common expression that indicates that the NGO was set up in the aftermath of the devastating Cyclone Nargis in 2008, which provided some room for local NGOs to mobilise without as much government control as previously (Seekins 2009). These NGOs had initially worked on issues of humanitarian character (Décobert and Wells 2020) and then progressively moved into work on justice and rule of law-related issues. Also, there was an upswing in NGOs that were presented as local initiatives but were either fully set up by foreign donors or established with significant support from such: often they continued to operate under significant donor involvement, of which some were later dissolved as a result of internal contestation and lack of legitimacy with key local counterparts. There were also newly established local NGOs run by eager lawyers from various sectors of society. Many of these managed to gain significant funding through major donor projects; for example, the European Union funded the 'MyJustice' Programme.

NGOs broker influence because they channel aid money to local counterparts, and they can easily adapt foreign ideas and package them as their own initiatives. For that reason, they can easily become powerful actors in a setting that is new to foreign practitioners when they struggle to make sense of the local setting. As later chapters show, NGO influence is often mitigated by foreign donors who try to steer the direction and focus of activities and who position foreign technical experts to control lines of communication.

### 3.1.3 The Local Staff

Individuals from Myanmar who work for foreign development actors, commonly referred to as 'local staff' in development lingua, included a mix of lawyers and non-lawyers (see also Massoud 2015). Local staff constitute an 'interface' between foreign donors and 'recipients' in developing countries (Roth 2015) and act as 'interlocutors' between foreign donors and state actors, thus providing 'insights into what does and does not work' (Nicholson and Low 2013:6).

Many of the local staff in Myanmar had previous development experience from working during the decades of military rule, where they learned core aspects of the aid industry. Several of the 'local staff' whom I categorise as rule of law intermediaries identified as belonging to one of Myanmar's ethnic minorities (for an overview see, e.g., Ganesan and Hlaing 2007). This is perhaps a result of a deliberate policy by international organisations to hire only ethnic minorities as a way to try to mitigate direct links to a government primarily made up of the majority Bamar ethnic group (see Walton 2013). One respondent believed that it had taken him more time to build up a relationship with government actors because he belongs to a minority ethnic group: '[T]he government trust the majority – Bamar' (see also Holliday 2010). However, he was confident that 'it depends on the individuals, when they know who I am, it's OK. It all depends on individuals' (Interviewee #6, 19 May 2014).

Crewe and Fernando (2006) discuss the racial connotations and unequal relationships that the dichotomies between 'local' and 'international' staff create. I observed that the 'internationals' would often bundle together everyone who was from Myanmar as 'local' staff, while the employees themselves would variously define their role in more detail; for example, when I asked them to tell me what they do, I received various replies including 'strategic adviser', 'programme officer', 'focal person', and 'programme assistant'. One interviewee related that he was not sure what his title meant and felt as if his work was to be an 'in-between person' who carried out 'translating and liaison work' (Interviewee #6, 19 May 2014) rather than a subject expert of some sort (see also Roth 2012).

Local staff broker influence in the rule of law assistance field, for example, by providing parallel lines of communication before and after official meetings between foreign and Myanmar development partners. As native or second-language speakers of Burmese, even though employed by foreigners, they can help clarify language aspects that have been lost in translation during meetings and that are unclear to the counterparts and also gain the trust of the Myanmar side quicker than that of the foreign organisation.

### 3.1.4 The International Rule of Law Consultant

Foreign individuals have managed to acquire a role as rule of law intermediaries. Previous ethnographies of aid have established how consultants mediate and interpret different meanings between donor policy and project operation on both sides (Mosse 2004). They 'provide policymakers and aid managers with valuable reflective insights into the operations and effectiveness of international development as a complex set of local, national, and cross-cultural social interactions . . .' (Lewis and Mosse 2006:1). As representatives of donor agencies on the ground, they 'must juggle at times competing motives, as they make difficult decisions within complex political contexts' (Roth 2012:296).

The foreign consultants active in Myanmar often had some previous connection to the country through their family history and background. When self-reflecting, they saw this background as important; for example, one respondent wanted me to identify her ethnicity because she 'think[s] it matters' (Interviewee #3, 8 May 2014). Another respondent (Interviewee #1, 6 May 2014) believed that his background (Burmese mother and English father) mattered for his work: 'I had a desire to do something more socially worthwhile, it was meant to happen . . . In some way, I see my place here in a romantic way – a circle of life. This place matters to me a lot, and I think my background matters to the people I work with. I tell them about my background.'

Not all development consultants repatriated to Myanmar because of family connections (see Williams 2012 for a discussion on Burmese diaspora activities) but instead had a long-term engagement with the country often because they had worked out of Thailand, on the Thai–Burma border (Ware 2012a), or in nearby places in South-East Asia. For example, a locally employed staff member told me that one foreign consultant became synonymous for the otherwise unknown foreign organisation he represented because 'national actors don't really know about the foreign organization, but they know about the consultant from his time with another big organization – that influences the work' (Interviewee #6, 19 May 2014). Similarly, a local lawyer told me that he happily supported one foreign consultant because she had spent a long time – and showed an interest – in the country and because he liked her (Interviewee #17, 23 September 2014). The work that she was assigned to do and for what international organisation seemed to matter less. The quotes reflect that personal relationships between 'internationals' and 'locals' (Roth 2015) may be a key determinant of successful development work.

Some international consultants were placed within a local or national institution to provide 'technical expertise' (see also Roth 2015, and for a critique Easterly 2014). Such placement meant that they were able to access spaces that would otherwise be hard to gain entry to for foreigners. By being foreigners and positioned at a national or local institution, they thus provided a link that carried different values and understandings from the 'international' to the 'inside'. John was one such example. As a consultant for a multilateral organisation, he worked hard to gain the trust of his local colleagues but often felt as if they saw him 'as a spy of some sort'. The suspicions about him were not improved by the fact that his international employees often communicated with him directly, instead of going through the Myanmar director (who, in theory, was supposed to be John's boss). The international donor also tried to gain influence through their direct communication with John. He was not comfortable with their approaches because he wanted to keep his independence and show loyalty to the 'Myanmar side', because he felt as if it mattered which side he was on.

This category of intermediaries can broker influence when they start to understand that they must adapt their actions and language to local reality. While they get criticised by the organisations they represent for failing to adhere to idealised conceptions of rule of law, and have to use one kind of language to their superiors to secure funding and jobs, foreign practitioners apply mediated approaches in the interactions with their local counterparts.

### 3.1.5 The Government Employee

In Myanmar's transition period, government employees who had studied abroad and spoke English were positioned as intermediaries to communicate with foreign visitors and buffer their demands. Gillespie (2004), in his study of Vietnamese legal reform, shows how 'elite level legal and economic technocrats in central ministries are responsible for importing borrowed law and adapting it to Vietnamese conditions'. As active 'change agents', these government employees navigated the interface that emerges when foreign actors coax staff in central ministries (and who are equally pressured by their minister) with their belief in 'legal ideas as technical fragments unconstrained by cultural borders [with] an unwavering conviction in the instrumental power of law to engineer social change' (2004:163).

In Myanmar circa 2014, the small group of government employees that spoke English better than their colleagues and therefore got 'bombarded' (Interviewee #3, 8 May 2014) with meetings with foreigners perceived their situation as undesirable because it involved complex translation and mediation activities rather than opportunities to actively broker influence as in more established aid settings (e.g., Halliday and Carruthers 2009). For example, Hla Aung Shwe, who works for a justice institution in the newly constructed capital Nay Pyi Taw, had since his sudden and unexpected move to the city in 2005, like many other government employees, found his personal and professional life increasingly scrutinised. He lives in an apartment block with his colleagues from the justice institution from where there is a shared commuting service to and from work every day. The opportunity to meet and talk openly with foreigners is limited, and, before Hla Aung Shwe agreed to meet with me, I had to contact him several times to assure him that I would come by myself and that our conversation would be fully on his terms.

When we met, Hla Aung Shwe was more relaxed and seemed to enjoy sharing stories about work and personal life. After our meeting, he said that it felt good to 'talk'. I offered to buy a bottle of wine – Hla Aung Shwe told me that he preferred a foreign wine over the 'crappy' Myanmar wine; he had learned to appreciate good wines when he studied abroad. Mid-career, he got a chance to complete a Master's degree abroad through the government's co-operation with a foreign university – often the offer comes with a signed bond to serve in the ministry for up to ten years after coming back. Hla Aung Shwe was one of few fluent English speakers at his government department. He told me shyly that he did not 'want to brag or anything' but that yes, his English was 'better than his colleagues'. Because of those language skills, Hla Aung Shwe needed to attend 'all meetings with foreign delegations'. He was not satisfied with his situation because he had little time to manage his usual work when having to 'deal with foreigners all the time'. Hla Aung Shwe's position as 'that person' who always had to deal with foreigners and do translation work, he told me, tormented him as he did not feel well prepared for the task and it did little good for his chances of being promoted.

Government intermediaries are able to exert influence over high-level development co-operation in the rule of law assistance field, not so much because they are power brokers in themselves but more so because they provide the communication channel to the Myanmar side. Because government counterparts do not trust ordinary translators, they want their employees with them at meetings to do the translation. In this role, they are able to both facilitate and gatekeep potential development co-operation.

## 3.2  WHAT DO INTERMEDIARIES DO?

Intermediaries are put in situations where they operate as brokers, mediators, or translators in roles that more often coalesce than demarcate differences (Meehan and Plonsky 2017; Stovel and Shaw 2012). They have been found to variously operate as gatekeepers, representatives, liaisons, itinerant guides, or co-ordinators, and often as combinations of these (Stovel and Shaw 2012).

In Myanmar, intermediaries act as development brokers when they acquire funding allocations to their local areas and to causes they support – for example, a court reform project or rule of law workshop – thus actively shaping the way rule of law is promoted and implemented with various results (see also James 2011, 2018). The term 'broker' (*pweza-r*) has derogatory connotations for the actors involved because it suggests that the individual is interested in economic gains and it is also the common term used for people that facilitate the exchange of bribes in the courts (Cheesman 2012). Even though, in some cases, the economic benefit of the development brokerage was observable over time, a preferred description of such activities, according to intermediaries, was 'a person who act effort for someone' (personal communication, Yangon, November 2014).

Intermediaries in Myanmar are caught in different situations where they are needed to mediate between development counterparts that view rule of law differently or because local partners distrust foreign-funded initiatives (see also James 2011). This theme appears in the history of legal intervention. For example, with the arrival of foreign legal ideas in Japan and the transformation of domestic law, there was an identified mismatch (Hasegawa 2009). In effect, the 'mediator' was an individual who faced different cultures, identified foreign values, and interpreted them domestically so that they became compatible with local beliefs and understandings. The mediator is facing two different directions, burdened in a middle space, feeling as a Janus-like figure while championing modern ideas (ibid.).

Intermediaries 'filter' and 'carry' values and ideas from national spaces to local communities (Silverman 1965). Gluckman, Mitchell, and Barnes's (1949) seminal study of the village headman in British Central Africa shows how he acted as a go-between and local intermediary, torn between principles in a delicate position. The headman inhabited the space where two worlds met: the 'modern' political system pressured her to impose values and rules that were not accepted at the local level. The headman found himself in ambivalent and problematic situations, trying to balance the collision of the 'modern' and the 'traditional'. Intermediaries in Myanmar face similar ambivalence as the newly emergent and active development field creates pressure for the imposition of law and values that are being branded as more modern, universal, and especially superior to what is in place (see also Massoud 2011), which is disregarded as an outdated authoritarian 'rule by law' opposite.

As 'translators', intermediaries alter meanings of models that can never be fully controlled by their senders (Berger and Esguerra 2017). Translation empowers a few actors, like intermediaries, to represent the 'rest' because they manoeuvre the 'authority to speak or act on behalf of another actor or force' (Callon and Latour 1981:279) in a manipulative act of power (Berger and Esguerra 2017) for a particular purpose which becomes reflected in the meaning that is constructed in the process (Callon 1986).

Intermediaries' success in what they do springs from a combination of personal 'charisma' (see Lidholm 2018), the possession of large networks, and the control of knowledge. Intermediaries have 'development skills, English skills, confidence, [and] know[] how to interact with foreigners' (Interviewee #48, 10 October 2014). This is a theme that runs through the history of intermediation. Bierschenk et al.'s (2002:22–3) depiction of development brokers resembles rule of law intermediaries in Myanmar in the communality of their knowledge and backgrounds: rhetorical skills, organisational competence, scenographic competence, and relational capital, needed because intermediaries must be able to 'master the linguistic and cultural codes' and be able to adapt the latest trends in development lingua (de Sardan 2005), manage co-ordination activities within an office or association, showcase for the outside world the positive aspects of the aid received, and build relationships and networks. Even though each epoch and each context generate specific types of intermediary, the role remains similar.

Intermediation exhibits a dual quality (Stovel and Shaw 2012). Intermediaries can facilitate social interactions and relationships where these are absent and with positive benefits for all involved. But intermediation also has a 'dark side', potentially fostering exploitation and personal gains. The moral ambiguity of the intermediary – as an actor who carries out fine-tuned navigation in between, potentially in order to maximise individual gain – has remained constant (James 2011). The colonial brokers were not neutral transmitters of information. They brokered influence over colonial policy and practice by drawing on their political and social capital and interests, in order to enhance status, wealth, and power (Lawrance, Osborn, and Roberts 2015). Similar patterns of influence are found in contemporary aid settings. Seidel (2017), for example, from her contemporary study of rule of law implementation in South Sudan, finds that what local actors accept, adopt, and appropriate from international tools depends in large part on the question of whether the offers strengthen their own position. Or in the words of James (2011:319): 'Brokers are not only products but also producers, of the kind of society in which they re-emerge.'

As an effect of developmentalist frameworks and planned interventions by state and non-state actors, coercion and resistance spur experiments aimed at reconciling old and new subjectivities and modes of organisation (Koster and van Leynseele 2018). In contexts of transitional fluidity, foreign donors establish their presence by merging several aspects of social, political, and economic life that people encounter on a daily basis. In such a new aid landscape, intermediaries become responsible for navigating local and national institutions, values, and people. The changed conditions in Myanmar after the acceleration of foreign-assisted rule of law promotion and the new conditions of living with foreign development actors and models are a complex undertaking for intermediaries that are torn between development counterparts' conflicting worldviews. Here they are in an exposed position because they have to 'face in two directions at once' while serving both the community and the actors at the national level, and thus know how to handle potential conflicts when interests collide (Wolf 1956).

## 3.3 CONCLUSION

This chapter charted what we know about intermediaries across settings and times in history in order to provide a comparative perspective for transnational rule of law assistance. In line with this book's central argument, the chapter illustrated the continued role of intermediaries in illiberal settings where rule of law assistance is rolled out under the auspices of development support: where institutional failure and success have been heavily analysed, but the intermediaries responsible for fine-tuned relationship building among configurations of actors remain under-investigated.

The chapter focused on the concept of the intermediary as an analytical means of identifying the social nodes in transnational networks of relative positions and power. It highlighted the role that intermediaries play, and the challenges they face, at the interfaces of different knowledge and value systems that appear as the development industry intervenes across the globe.

Moreover, I showed how my use of an inductive approach was key for locating individuals who played an intermediary role in Myanmar's rule of law assistance field. A central aim of the chapter was thus to answer two questions: who is an intermediary, and what do they do? Intermediaries would often self-identify with labels that indicated such a role in response to a set of open-ended questions. The exploratory nature of the method provided a first clue in opening the 'black-box' of rule of law intermediation because it revealed who they were and how they self-identified.

Rule of law intermediaries were found across several institutional positions: the local lawyer, the local NGO, the locally employed staff that work for an international organisation, the government employee, and the international consultant. Myanmar lawyers who acted as intermediaries often had a background in politics. Collective intermediary activities in the rule of law field included NGOs and coalitions, often assembled as a response to increased donor presence. 'Local staff' included a mix of lawyers and non-lawyers with previous development experience. They related that a significant part of their work involved intermediary activities as they became 'in-between' persons, a role they were not always satisfied with. The case was similar for government employees who often felt as if they struggled in an undesirable position that involved complex translation and mediation activities and that did not further their career. Some international consultants were placed within a local or national institution to provide technical expertise. Such placement meant that they were able to access spaces that would otherwise be hard to gain entry to for foreigners. By being foreigners and positioned at a national or local institution, they provided a channel and linking function that carried different values and understandings from the 'international' to the 'inside.' Such foreign individuals who managed to acquire a role as a rule of law intermediary in Myanmar often had some previous connection to the country through their family history and background.

Not everyone who was employed in the roles presented was an intermediary, but it was usually across those professional groups that individuals who performed an intermediary function were found. Thus, while positioned in different roles and assignments, what they all had in common was that they performed the delicate and intricate task of relating larger, globally oriented ideas to the Myanmar locale, in a key middle position among foreign, national, and local actors.

This book shows that intermediaries use their language skills, personality, knowledge, capital, and network to broker influence in the rule of law assistance field. While they are mistrusted by some, they are essential to many for establishing links to counterparts. This ambivalent role that intermediaries play has been constant throughout the history of intervention. Such a revelation can have us questioning the nature of development intervention itself and the structure of an industry that, just like colonial intervention, between its universals and its particulars is dependent on these actors.

# CHAPTER FOUR

# RULE OF LAW ASSISTANCE: ACTORS AND TECHNOLOGIES

After the political transition in 2011, Myanmar saw an increase in development assistance, especially to sectors that worked with democratisation, governance, rule of law, and justice. Even though aid links had already been established before the transition, especially in the aftermath of Cyclone Nargis in 2008 (Décobert and Wells 2020), the historic event of the political opening of one of the 'last frontiers' in terms of authoritarian pariah states of the world meant that civil society, the Myanmar government, and foreign development agencies were able to meet in-country and work to accommodate increased project supply and funding (Ware 2013). Accompanying the acceleration of development assistance was the introduction of a rule of law development model that matched national rule of law rhetoric but that differed significantly from the meaning the term had come to have in Myanmar, where it was more easily read as 'law and order' or 'rule by law' (Cheesman 2009).

The foreign organisations that sought to introduce rule of law in Myanmar were thus met by local and national counterparts who held different values and understandings of how best to approach development processes that involved the thing they all called 'rule of law'. In the confusions that accompanied new relationships being established, intermediaries emerged to navigate the spaces where development counterparts got together. Development anthropologist Long (2001) describes these spaces as the 'interfaces' that emerge when development actors contest, accommodate, or bridge their different values and understandings. The interface is a space that intermediaries navigate and where change happens in their hands as they 'appropriate a model and relate it to their own understanding of both the model's origin and intention and situation to which it is supposed to be immersed' (Behrends et al. 2014:14). In an authoritarian setting like Myanmar, the interface may have been especially contested because the country had for a long time been isolated from the outside world as a result of decades of military-enforced isolation. The interface highlights the dynamic of interactions among rule of law counterparts and uncovers a space of contestation that has been overlooked by many studies of the rule of law assistance field. This chapter reveals some of those points of contestation: the actors' differing motivations for engaging in rule of law development work; donors' lack of knowledge of the local setting; and the dynamics of power relations among donors, local counterparts, and intermediaries. To learn more about the outcomes and the potential unintended consequences of aid in illiberal states, these are aspects that need to be unpacked.

In this chapter, I present the field of rule of law assistance as it was established in Myanmar after 2011. Having the chance to observe the initial moment of rule of law assistance and the relationships that were created among new development counterparts was significant for my being able to build the main analysis and argument of this book. I outline accounts of rule of law assistance from exemplar rule of law actors and projects, rather than providing an exhaustive inventory of the field, and show how the various ways of translating the rule of law model resulted in contestations among development counterparts. This overview should raise questions about *what* rule of law could realistically be introduced on the reform agenda in a place like Myanmar.

This chapter concludes that because international, national, and local understandings and approaches to rule of law development differed and were challenging to align, intermediaries emerged to mediate friction about issues such as monetary compensation; applications for funding; the best approach to achieve rule of law development; donor involvement in local affairs; and institutional constraints that, according to intermediaries, foreign actors were not able to fully grasp.

## 4.1 RULE OF LAW ON THE REFORM AGENDA IN MYANMAR

Development actors from abroad intervened to promote rule of law in a well-established military-led authoritarian regime that had now decided to roll out its controlled plan for engagement with the outside world. While donor engagement had been established before the point of the 2011 transition (Décobert and Wells 2020), the introduction of a 'civilianised' government under (then) president Thein Sein (Skidmore and Wilson 2010) signalled an increased space for foreign promoters in terms of working on rule of law-related issues. The previously isolated regime re-engaged with the international community in various forms to attract foreign investment or to seek assistance with processes of political or social change (Rieffel and Fox 2013). Political transition opened up a reform space with a unique range of opportunities for both political and civil society actors and for relationships to be established with actors outside Myanmar's borders (Macdonald 2013). A changed political climate was followed by the relaxation of foreign sanctions (the country had for decades been subject to one of the toughest sanctions regimes globally, Pedersen 2008) and in 2012 a new foreign investment law was passed that eased legal restrictions on foreign investors (Hookway 2012). Several other laws were repealed or drafted to create a legal infrastructure to support an internationalised market economy (Turnell 2014). Other notable reforms the Myanmar government embarked on included eased censorship (Government of Myanmar 2012), the release of political prisoners (Burke 2012), new laws that allow trade unions and strikes (BBC News 2011), and establishment of a Human Rights Commission (Liljeblad 2016a; Taylor 2012). Paradoxically, while the government illustrated an engagement to 'reform' through this range of activities, the carefully crafted 2008 Constitution remains even in 2020 an instrument with which the military controls Myanmar at its will (Crouch 2019).

In the transition period, there was an increase in discussions of rule of law as part of the political reform agenda. Local and foreign practitioners felt more confident to engage in rule of law activities after having heard (then) president Thein Sein mention the term in his speeches, because (then) opposition leader Aung San Suu Kyi had been appointed chair of the newly formed 'Rule of Law and Tranquillity Committee' and thus spoke more often about it, and because of the increased openness of national media that published rule of law-related news of a character that had not been allowed in the past, when they had been under government control and strict censorship (Nirmal 2012). After the political transition in 2011, such past regulatory practices were eased and issues that previously had been deemed too sensitive to write about, including the rule of law, were increasingly reported and debated (Pedersen 2014). A local rule of law programme manager explained how being at the start of transition felt: 'Media allowed articles that were not allowed in the past. Then anything they wrote was linked to the rule of law … The word "rule of law" became more and more prominent' (Interviewee #43, 1 October 2014). The paradox of this is the limited space journalists were allowed again after elections in 2015 when, as in one example, Reuters journalists Wa Lone and Kyaw Swa Oo were sentenced under colonial legislation for reporting on the crisis in Rakhine state (Prasse-Freeman 2019; Samet 2018). The conviction was defended by Aung San Suu Kyi as rightfully upholding the 'rule of law' (Amnesty International 2018).

### 4.1.1 Aung San Suu Kyi as Rule of Law Advocate

In 2011, democracy icon and Nobel Peace laureate Aung San Suu Kyi was released from house arrest and subsequently appointed to head the Rule of Law and Tranquillity Committee in 2012 (Nyein Nyein 2012b). Her appointment caused some confusion about the regime's intentions in this transitional moment because Aung San Suu Kyi had long been considered a political force that the regime sought to eliminate (see, e.g., Pedersen 2008). For example, a somewhat sceptical government employee suggested that the Committee possessed little influence and that the appointment of Aung San Suu Kyi as its head was intended to expose her inability to achieve reform (field notes, 5 September 2014). Nevertheless, her new status as a global rule of law advocate had observers wondering if Myanmar was finally ready to receive international assistance for capacity building of the justice system and rule of law (e.g., Skidmore and Wilson 2010:12–14). Soon after Aung San Suu Kyi's appointment, she was invited to several influential institutions around the world – her first ventures out of the country in twenty-four years (Spillius 2012). In Thailand, she appeared at the World Economic Forum (WEF) meetings to discuss the need for the rule of law in Myanmar and particularly emphasised rule of law's importance for investment opportunities and the need for a 'clean' and independent judiciary (World Economic Forum 2012). At around this time, Aung San Suu Kyi also sought advice on the proposed new foreign investment law and enrolled Hong Kong-based Anglo-Myanmar commercial dispute resolution lawyer Robert S. Pe as her senior adviser on legal affairs. Robert S. Pe initiated his professional engagement in Myanmar when he chaired a seminar on international arbitration – 'A Practical Introduction for Myanmese Businesses' – for the

Federation of Chambers of Commerce & Industry in Yangon in May 2012. He was an active spokesperson on topics including 'Law Reform in Myanmar', 'Reforming Myanmar's Legal System', and 'Myanmar: Time to Invest?' and organised seminars for the Myanmar Parliament on 'International Arbitration and the New York Convention' (Orrick Lawyers n.d.). At the London School of Economics, Aung San Suu Kyi said that only under the rule of law could fairness and freedom be restored to Myanmar (London School of Economics and Political Science 2012). She stressed the importance of rule of law and judicial reform for a 'democratic Burma' when she visited Yale University (Gonzalez 2012). When speaking at Harvard University's Institute of Politics, she expressed a need for assistance from other countries, including lawyers and judges, to establish the rule of law in Myanmar (Harvard Kennedy School 2012).

Aung San Suu Kyi's international tour was not, however, the debut of her ideas about rule of law and its importance for Myanmar. She and the National League for Democracy (NLD) had talked about rule of law after the elections in 1990 (local programme officer, Interviewee #24, September 2015). We also find references to rule of law in her early writings, where she links the concept to the prevention of corruption and highlights its importance for a society where people can live with 'human dignity' and with 'freedom from fear' (Aung San Suu Kyi 1991). In 2002, she described the government's practices of incarcerating political dissidents as the 'misrule of law' (Aung San Suu Kyi 2002).

Still, it was after the more open political environment in 2011 that Aung San Suu Kyi began to speak more frequently and broadly about rule of law and especially, as shown just now, in relation to democratisation and foreign investment opportunities (see also local rule of law practitioner, Interviewee #46, 9 December 2014). On the one hand, her expansiveness in speaking of the 'rule of law' should perhaps not be too surprising. In a setting where the military for decades used rule of law to signify 'law and order' (Cheesman 2015) and after transition tried to hijack the term to signal positive reforms, it might be that she had to claim the concept any way she could in opposition to the uses by the military and its affiliated politicians. However, Aung San Suu Kyi's broad and inconsistent use of the term did attract some mockery (Burma Tha Din Network 2013) but also some well-calibrated critique, particularly in relation to her statements on citizenship rights, which often contradicted her other uses of it (Cheesman 2014b). The easy slip into the language of 'obedience' and 'security' has Cheesman (2014:-230–1) conclude that Aung San Suu Kyi and her party

> have failed to articulate a conception of the rule of law that might travel with them during the ups and downs of democratization, towards whatever goals that they think matter for people in Myanmar. By going along with the seeming consensus about the rule of law, rather than by making plain what they want from it, Aung San Suu Kyi and her party have done a disservice to the concept, and to themselves. They have failed to discharge a duty of care that I think they owe to the rule-of-law ideal on behalf of their constituents. By playing fast and loose with the rule of law, they have jeopardized it rather than defended it. And when confronted with an idiom for the rule of law hostile to democratization, an idiom that resonates more with the language of dictatorship than with the language of democratization, they have had no rejoinder.

As NLD won a landslide victory in elections on 8 November 2015 (BBC News Asia 2015) the conceptual confusion of what the 'rule of law' means for Aung San Suu Kyi became even more obscure as she suggested that tensions in Myanmar's Rakhine state were being handled according to 'principles of the rule of law' (Funakoshi 2016), while foreign observers variously suggested that the military treatment of Rakhine's Muslim minority, the Rohingya, constituted genocide or crimes against humanity (Aljazeera 2016). In 2020, with the benefit of hindsight, we know that the symbolism of Aung San Suu Kyi's appointment, her electoral victory, and the resulting optimism about rule of law change in Myanmar were to disappoint her supporters domestically and internationally and that she was little able to protect rights indiscriminately in the country (David and Holliday 2018).

### 4.1.2 The Government's Transitional Discourse on Rule of Law

In March 2011, then-president Thein Sein gave his inaugural address to the Parliament (*Pyidaungsu Hluttaw*). The address demarcated an important turning point for possibilities to work on rule of law in the country. A foreign development practitioner who had spent several years in Myanmar before the transition explained:

> Thein Sein's inaugural speech mentioned rule of law and good governance. It was a surprise to all. However, nobody knew where to start, how far can we go, what can we do? We had to test the water. We were very careful when designing a project so that it would not be too political. 'rule of law' is a good kind of frame for it, what does it mean? I mean it

can mean anything. It gave us a nice wide frame to use. Because it had been used in an official speech, it was a good opportunity to bring actors together and show that 'hey he said it' so we can do something here. We keep it more amorphous without being wishy-washy.

(Interviewee #20, 30 September 2014)

The importance the foreign practitioner put on the term's repackaged use in official speech is interesting because it demarcates the perceived belief that the Myanmar government was ready for a different rule of law, one that was outward-looking and connected to substantive rights. Décobert and Wells (2020) have unpacked this period of aid relationships and, through their empirical work, illustrate a sort of 'Thein Sein effect' as the then president was 'really good at making donors believe they can push the space' (Interview with INGO manager, cited in Décobert and Wells 2020:306) and because 'the right language was coming out of Nay Pyi Taw' (Interview with INGO director, ibid.). In fact, Thein Sein's inaugural address tells a rather confusing, but still progressive, story that is both historical and forward-looking and mixes messages of law and order, substantive rights, and military control:

> We guarantee that all citizens will enjoy equal rights in terms of law, and we will reinforce the judicial pillar ... So, we will amend and revoke the existing laws and adopt new laws as necessary to implement the provisions on fundamental rights of citizens or human rights ... we need to convince some nations with a negative attitude towards our democratization process that Myanmar has been committed to see the interests of the nation and the people to serve those interests only in the constitutional framework and not to try to disrupt democratization process outside the constitutional framework and harm peace, stability and the rule of law ... we sincerely thank all the people, all the Tatmadaw members and all service personnel for achieving peace, stability and the rule of law and building development infrastructures instrumental to a democratic nation.
>
> (New Light of Myanmar 31 March 2011)

The rule of law announced here clearly connects to democratisation, which might have followed from the overall goals of the transition and may be functioning as a way to engage with the international community (Pedersen 2014) because it matches broader democratisation discourse at the time (Cheesman 2014b). Nevertheless, many aspects of the speech remained linked to elements of law and order, expressed, for example, in the continued regard for the military as an achiever of 'peace, stability and the rule of law' (ibid.) which shows that the concept was still prone to hijacking for illiberal ends (Rajah 2012).

A more procedural use of the rule of law was expressed in Thein Sein's speech delivered to the Parliament in August the same year:

> [T]he judicial body … has assumed its charge of duties in accordance with the principles of the State Constitution such as to administer justice independently according to law; to dispense justice in open court unless otherwise prohibited by law and to guarantee in all cases the right of defence and the right of appeal under law … We are also implementing the proceedings we have pledged to this Hluttaw such as ensuring good governance, clean government and democratic practices, fundamental rights of citizens, the rule of law ….
>
> (New Light of Myanmar 22 August 2011)

The major pitfall with such a pledge is that the principles of the 2008 Constitution fall short in several ways with regard to procedural guarantees of justice (Myint Zan 2017; Williams 2014) and continue to this day to present the main obstacle to democratic transition (see, e.g., Crouch 2019). The 2008 Constitution, recognised through a sham referendum held nationwide only two days after one of the country's most devastating natural disasters of modern times, Cyclone Nargis (Taylor, R. H. 2009, 2012), is the product of a National Convention that was announced in 1992 to draft its principal guidelines, including the military's permanent control over a civilian government, its right to 25 per cent of the seats in the Parliament (Diller 1997), and its continued influence over the police force (Fuller 2015b).

Thein Sein's speeches in 2011 were not dramatically different from some of the public statements on 'rule of law' or 'law and order' that had been made by the previous military regime (Cheesman 2009). However, the changed political climate and the fact that Thein Sein represented a civilian government might have given his words a different resonance. The context he was operating in suggests a desire to signal that change was underway and that Thein Sein could be seen as a reform-minded leader, brave enough to challenge hardliners (Nyein Nyein 2012a; Pedersen 2014). Because of the increased attention given to 'transition' in Myanmar by outside observers, the government took an interest in showcasing its 'reforms' to the world (see Risse-Kappen, Ropp, and Sikkink 1999:10, 12 for a discussion of how national governments change their human rights rhetoric and practices in order to 'access the material benefits of foreign aid').

Rule of law was also discussed in official planning documents such as the 2013 Nay Pyi Taw Accord for Effective Development Cooperation, which affirmed new guidelines on donor-government co-operation. The Accord, described as the localisation of global accords, drafted in co-operation with 'development partners in a spirit of mutual benefits and accountability' (Government of the Republic of the Union of Myanmar 2013:1), '[m]arked a key milestone in the normalisation of aid relations between the state and international bilateral and multi-lateral donors, and in transition towards Western donors supporting the state's development priorities – whereas in earlier phases Western aid had been mainly humanitarian and had largely bypassed the state' (Décobert and Wells 2019:305).

As part of these new directions in aid funding with the state considered a competent partner, the Accord commits to the strength-ening of rule of law and improved access to justice as a national priority (Government of the Republic of the Union of Myanmar 2013). Moreover, the 2012 Framework for Economic and Social Reform, which affirms the Policy Priorities for 2012–15 towards the long-term goals of the National Comprehensive Development Plan, discusses rule of law in relation to 'improv[ing] citizens' access to law, and to increase[ing] public confidence in [laws]' while also mention-ing a need to increase the public's abiding by existing laws, which hints at the usual formalist understanding of the concept that laws disregarding their quality should indeed rule (see Krygier 2017a; Munger 2017). The latter understanding is further established as rule of law is discussed as a social control mechanism in relation to immigration, in the suggestion that the government will establish 'an effective monitoring system in the border areas in order ensure [sic] that the rule of law will prevail' as a solution to 'inward migration ... that is causing friction with local populations' (Government of Myanmar 2012:37). The escalation of the crisis in Rakhine shows a bifurcated trajectory: where governance and access to justice may have improved for citizens in general, the treatment of the stateless minority, the Rohingya, is repeatedly being referred to as dealing with 'illegal migration' (Ahsan Ullah 2016).

While foreign practitioners picked up on rhetorical showcasing in public speeches, local actors remained more sceptical. For example, a local rule of law programme manager was convinced that, for the president and the military, rule of law continued to mean 'following their law and according to their law, they want a lot of law to rule the people and also see security as an important part' (Interviewee #24, 14 October 2014). In lieu of detailed proof of substantive reforms in order to improve the conditions of those who suffered under malfunctioning 'rule of law', the programme manager's scepticism is not surprising. The term (adopted as part of a new reform language) might have added more confusion to what the concept actually had the potential to mean for Myanmar's transition (Cheesman 2014b).

Such notions of scepticism are shared by other practitioners. For example, when I met with a former Myanmar judge who was now working for a foreign donor, she lowered her voice and whispered: '[P]eople think that you can speak freely now, but it is still only within a certain frame' (Interviewee #27, 7 October 2014). This comment reflects the common belief that the military could at any time resort to its old behaviour (Callahan 2009). It is a notion that has been examined in more depth by Skidmore (2003); she analyses how conceptions of time centred on the wait for violence pervaded people's minds during military rule, and thus people wait on 'events' and things that 'will happen'.

In 2014 some interviewees told me that they were uncertain about the government's intentions while they used newly risen opportunity to engage more openly in reform work that they had already been involved in previously. For example, one intermediary showed me that his work had been featured in a local newspaper (Interviewee #17, 23 September 2014). However, even three years after the initiation of reforms, he confessed that he was concerned over that exposure. That concern is something that I perceived in conversations with other interviewees who were also reluctant to reveal too much about their work, especially when it involved working with foreign organisations – not always because they felt that there was a risk involved, but simply because they did not know what the government 'was up to' this time. Such concerns are not surprising as Myanmar has gone through similar flirtations with the international community throughout its history, only to resort to old practices. For example, in the late 1990s, when in need of foreign investment, the regime tried to carefully open up to a foreign private sector (Steinberg 2001). In early 2000 the government improved its co-operation with international human rights and humanitarian organisations, including the International Committee of the Red Cross, the International Labour Organization, and the United Nations Children's Fund, as these were allowed to increase their activities in the country. The government also ratified a number of international human rights conventions, and the release of Aung San Suu Kyi from house arrest in 2002 contributed to improved foreign relations (Pedersen 2008). However, 'the growing willingness of the regime to discuss human rights … was not matched by a commitment – or ability – to redress the general climate of impunity' that was prevalent in Myanmar (Pedersen 2008:8). Instead, relationships with the outside world deteriorated again, especially after the 2003 attack on NLD members and Aung San Suu Kyi (and her subsequent detention for endangering the security of the state under section 10(a) of the 1975 State Protection Act). Moreover, the special rapporteur on human rights was not allowed to visit Myanmar from 2003; discussions about releasing Aung San Suu Kyi ceased that year; and in 2004 several INGOs had their activities constrained again (Pedersen 2008:221), a behaviour that had Pedersen (2008:8) conclude: 'The army and other security forces show few signs of changing their heavy-handed behaviour.' In hindsight, it is ever so obvious that any attempts at 'democratisation' in Myanmar have always been part of calculated transition crafted by the military to guarantee its continued grip on power (Huang 2020).

In the initial frenzy, post-2010 elections, donors experienced a state that finally seemed willing to step up as a competent and able development partner; rule of law was a topic worthy of discussion with national counterparts in Naw Pyi Taw's new government buildings, with local lawyers who labelled themselves democracy activists, and with ordinary citizens who were trying to make sense of how the concept could help them improve their rights (see, e.g., Cheesman and Kyaw Min San 2014). While old donor relationships with major powers such as Japan, the United Kingdom, and the United States were slowly transgressing, newcomers to the country were quick to offer their 'expertise' and solution to the rule of law situation. Next I introduce such influx of actors, their stated rationales for intervention, the issues they sought to engage with, and the activities they focused on.

## 4.2 ESTABLISHING ROOM FOR FOREIGN INTERVENTION

When foreign development actors arrived to work with rule of law assistance in Myanmar, they were faced with the country's malfunctioning law and justice institutions (see, e.g., Cheesman 2012), with the legal plurality (Merry 1988) of Anglo–Burmese statutory law, Burmese and non-Burmese customary law, colonial legal codes and military decrees, and diverse social and cultural norms about law and justice (Crouch and Lindsey 2014a; Denney et al. 2016; Kyed 2017). In this setting, finding legal sources was a process cloaked in mystery (Beyer 2015). Coercive military decrees and colonial codes continued to rule, the latter especially a remnant from the rule of former dictator Ne Win's proclaimed socialist and anti-imperialist rule, which saw the bulk of colonial criminal instruments remain in force without any significant amendment (Cheesman 2011) because it came in handy (and so continues) to suppress dissent of various kinds (Steinberg 2001). On this theme, Callahan shows how the colonial legal definitions of 'crime' and 'internal security' brought murderers, cattle thieves, robbers, rebels, Buddhist monks, labour organisers, and starving, scavenging peasants into a legal system that treated them all similarly and for the first time ever as enemies of the state (Callahan 2004). For authoritarian leaders, keeping the colonial codes meant that blame for inefficiencies in the new system could be referred to the colonial legacy (Cheesman 2015).

Back to the transition period, development promoters realised that access to justice was scarce and informal justice resolutions common in the regions (Denney et al. 2016; Kyed 2017). The lack of legal aid was recognised as a significant obstacle for people seeking legal remedies. Also, lawmaking processes were non-transparent and only open to public knowledge through the general news (Booth 2016). Legal system infrastructure was in a dire condition: individuals waiting for trial were locked up in minuscule cages; courtrooms were littered with case files; technical equipment was lacking; and buildings were in a poor state (personal observation, Yangon, October 2014).

Foreign rule of law promoters were especially perplexed by Myanmar courts and their peculiar practices. For example, a foreign lawyer explained the disturbance she felt while observing a court hearing:

> During one case, the prosecutor was cross-examining someone, and the judge was not there. This made me perplexed and frustrated. But for them [the lawyers] they did not want to adjourn and upset the judge. What is the meaning of these actions? The judge wanted it to go on. It is an administrative process; the end goal was to go through the entire process to get someone guilty, and then pay off the judge.
>
> (Interviewee #3, 8 May 2014)

The comment above reflects the fact that the court hearing took on a form similar to an administrative process, with little regard for procedural justice. Instead, the process sought 'to move the defendant from one part of their administrative processing to the next' while showing adherence to 'principles for law and order' as Cheesman (2015) has shown is common practice. Courts in Myanmar are known as endemically corrupt, characterised by the prevalence of 'court brokers' (e.g., court clerks, prosecutors, or a judge's relative) that facilitate the selling of case outcomes (Cheesman 2012). As previously mentioned, the term for a broker in Myanmar – *pweza-r* – had negative connotations for the often reform-minded individuals that participated in this study, the corrupt court broker perhaps being a typical embodiment of such negative views. Continuing on the theme of corruption, a foreign human rights lawyer was puzzled by the conversation he had had with a local lawyer: 'I asked a lawyer if the judge was fair and he told me that the judge was very fair as he only accepted "little money"' (Interviewee #2, 7 May 2014). The foreign lawyer concluded that the understanding of what rule of law means in Myanmar is 'so different' from what 'we know'. When foreign development actors arrived in Myanmar, lawyers thus possessed little institutional autonomy because corrupt practices influenced 'every aspect' of their career (International Commission of Jurists 2013:3). A local lawyer proudly stated that he 'never pays' because 'when you know the law you don't need to pay' (Interviewee #17, 23 September 2014). However, this seemed to be the exception rather than the rule (Cheesman 2015). As a system characterised by endemic corruption is the reality of most local lawyers, it is not too surprising then, as Batesmith and Stevens (2019:585) suggest, that 'Myanmar lawyers do not consider themselves as agents of the rule of law'. Batesmith and Stevens's (2019) focus on local lawyers active in court contrasts the focus of this book on lawyers also vested as active norm entrepreneurs for rule of law in the development field.

### 4.2.1 Simplified Narratives

The rule of law deficiencies that foreign development actors found upon their arrival in Myanmar contributed to assessment conclusions with simplified narratives, bundled together in the mantra 'There is no rule of law' in the country. This form of narrative presents a simple storyline that becomes easier to communicate in settings where foreign promoters possess only superficial understandings and lack detailed and nuanced information of a setting deemed 'complex' (Autesserre 2012).

To establish room for intervention in response to the narrative of the 'lack of rule of law in Myanmar', the International Bar Association's Human Rights Institute (2012:6) conducted a 'fact-finding mission' for seven days in August 2012 'to understand Myanmar's prospects and needs at this important juncture and, more specifically, to find out how far it has begun to adhere to globally prevalent understandings of the rule of law'. Country visits and fact-finding missions are part of a 'rapid response mechanism' allowing the organisation to 'react quickly to sudden events in countries, which may threaten human rights, the rule of law or independence of the judiciary' (2012:9). New Perimeter, Perseus Strategies, and Jacob Blaustein Institute for the Advancement of Human Right's 2013 joint 'Myanmar Rule of Law Assessment' claims to offer an 'in-depth assessment of rule of law reform needs in Burma' that will 'provid[e] guidance and recommendations to all those who will engage with local actors in Burma' and 'allow international actors to help move the law reform process from the current state where promises are made by Burma to the international community to one where reforms are implemented . . . both on paper and in practice' (JBI Human Rights 2013). Also, the US Institute of Peace published a 'Rule of Law Trip Report' (2013) from a visit to the country together with a US government inter-agency rule of law mission – from 9 February to 3 March 2013. The stated purpose of the visit was to collect information from actors in the country on suggested strategies, priorities, and challenges in strengthening the rule of law reform process as well as to explore how external actors could take part in supporting such process.

For the assessment authors, the rule of law is not national or local business as all references to the concept's origin are made to regional and international documents such as the Venice Commission Rule of Law Checklist (2006); the Charter of the Association of Southeast Asian Nations (2008); and the 2004 former UN Secretary General's definition (S/2004/616 23 August 2004). The assessments generally seek to demarcate gaps in Myanmar's national law and justice system and stress substantive aspects of global justice. More specifically, New Perimeter et al.'s (2013:8) assessment includes a section titled 'Lack of Understanding of Rule of Law' in which they assert: 'While there is substantial talk about the need for rule of law and law reform, most people believe it means rule by law, and fail to appreciate the range of elements necessary for the rule of law to exist in a society.' Similarly, USIP's report describes key discoveries as including the fact that the law is seen as irrelevant for people's lives:

> [T]here is no common understanding of the meaning of the term 'rule of law.' Communities lack knowledge of basic laws, legal procedures and mechanisms for accessing their rights. Many perceive the rule of law

simply as a set of laws and institutions that, as currently constituted, are designed to reinforce existing power dynamics including the dominance of the security services and the wealthy over the society.

(United States Institute of Peace 2013:5)

Simplified narratives explain that 'there is not a broad understanding of what the rule of law actually is', but that nevertheless 'government officials and the people of Myanmar repeatedly assert its fundamental importance to sustain any reform process' (New Perimeter et al. 2013:7). Such narratives are perplexing in light of conclusions that '[a]ny law reform process must begin with a common understanding of the rule of law' (International Bar Association's Human Rights Institute 2012:69).

Another recurrent mantra is the national lack of capacity to accept offers of assistance: the government is trying to undertake too much too quickly, without the 'ability to implement programmes' (New Perimeter et al. 2013:8), while, at the same time, it is this type of assistance that the assessment authors seek to offer. One example is in the field of legal education: '[T]here is a strong international desire . . . to assist in improving legal education in Myanmar' which is made difficult by the 'Ministry' who 'needs to enable law programmes to accept this assistance easily' (ibid.:36). Fast forward a couple of years, and there is fatigue among urban law schools, especially Yangon law faculty, from handling the many offers – often poorly co-ordinated and ill-suited to local realities – to support legal education (Liljeblad 2016b).

The assessments provide narratives of how the rule of law is used as a template through which development actors try to comprehend and diagnose local complexities. In this way, rule of law assistance actors separately, but at the same time collectively, contribute to the discourse of 'intervention needs' in Myanmar – needs that they eventually will, or have already, become involved in. These templates are powerful; the basic assumptions made in these documents tend to be continuously repeated until they gain the status of authoritative 'truths' that will guide development programming for years onwards (Roe 1989, 1991). While the assessments can help translate impressions into an understandable format that is in turn modelled after the international actors' own understandings of a model (Behrends et al. 2014), they leave little room for local or national legal variations and hybridity as well as non-superficial understandings by foreign promoters of local realities. Next, I present the rule of law assistance activities that foreign actors introduced to engage with the issues they identified as needs in the reports just presented.

### 4.2.2 Rule of Law Development Actors from Abroad

Foreign rule of law development actors became more visible in Yangon after 2012 as they arrived to set up offices, negotiate possible interventions, and initiate projects and programmes. Yet while the transition was ongoing, their engagement remained cautious and mindful of the previous operational context (Ware 2012b) – Myanmar remained, and remains to this day, under the influence of a militarised leadership.

One expression of this concern was seen in the informal and ad hoc nature of rule of law reform-focused INGO engagement. For example, a foreign lawyer described how, when trying to start activities in Myanmar, his organisation 'just showed up and started networking, going to courts and visiting offices of lawyers and then initiated [its] own trainings, which was good for meeting local people' (Interviewee #3, 8 May 2014; for similar suggestions see also Interviewee #4, 15 May 2014 and Interviewee #15, 22 September 2014). In addition, several of the INGOs that I interviewed had begun, and today continue to operate, without formal registration under the 1988 Associations Law. A foreign practitioner explained: 'We now have unofficial status, but the government knows we are here. We are not registered and are not pursuing registration' (Interviewee #2, 7 May 2014). Some suggested that they would continue to work without registration after the passing of new legislation on associations in 2014 because the new regulation would entail reporting duties heavy enough to constrain them from conducting any substantial activities (e.g., Interviewee #3, 8 May 2014). These comments suggest that these INGOs continue to operate in a space that is overshadowed by similar legal constraints on civil society as those that were in force during previous military rule (see Liddell 1997).

The lack of registration has also had implications for how INGOs have been able to engage the government as counterparts. One foreign practitioner suggested that the INGO had 'no formal relationship with the government counterparts' but used 'advocacy as a strategy to keep in contact with them' (Interviewee #8, 22 May 2014). When INGOs attempted to operate under the government's radar, they also tried to limit the amount of public information available about their activities (Interviewee #4, 15 May 2014). These strategies again indicate the character of foreign actors' engagements in a country with history of authoritarian rule, violence, and cautious international involvement (Ware 2012b).

Multilateral and bilateral engagements of other kinds also remained to some extent problematic even though the state had become an acceptable counterpart after elections in 2010 (Décobert and Wells 2020). Historical donor policies and sanctions towards Myanmar that sought to prevent funding from reaching the hands of individuals connected to the military regime on the one hand, and government officials' suspicion regarding foreign actors' motives and interests on the other (Ware 2012b; see also Interviewee #14, 13 December 2014), meant that co-operation within some fields was particularly challenging to set up even after official agreement. For example, while the United Nations Development Programme (UNDP) had been present in Myanmar for more than three decades working on livelihoods (i.e., food, water, shelter, clothing) and related fields, due to the sanctions regime, it was hindered from working on subjects considered too political (Pedersen 2008). Thus, it took the UNDP almost a year of negotiations after the new order was established before it was able to expand its country programme to include topics like 'justice'. The change was significant with regard to UN policy for Myanmar, especially since it meant working more closely with the government, which required approval from the highest UN director level (Interviewee #9, 23 May 2014; Interviewee #35, 19 November 2014).

The slow process of initiating UN co-operation was a result of the decades of sanctions where policies towards Myanmar led it to become the 'only country in the world where the first priority of the UN [was] to promote democracy' and, in addition, it 'receive[d] less international assistance than any other least developed country' (Pedersen 2008:22). After pressure from Western governments, the UNDP Governing Council imposed an 'extraordinary mandate' that restricted UNDP Myanmar's activities to areas where government interaction could be limited. In addition, Myanmar was added to the US Congress list of 'outlaw states', 'which under the provisions of the Foreign Assistance Act of 1961 mandates that voluntary U.S. funding for any UN agency be automatically reduced if the agency conducts programs in Burma' (Pedersen 2008:45). Such a move put a great deal of pressure on the UNDP because its programmes were 'carefully scrutinized by Washington, thus forcing UNDP officials to balance their responsibility to the people of Burma against the risk of upsetting the U.S. government' (ibid.). Working on anything related to Myanmar was problematic, not only because of the authoritarian rule exercised by the country's domestic leaders but also because of the authority exercised by the sanction's regime (see Chapter 7).

Foreign rule of law donors were situated differently in relation to Myanmar. One element shaping their connections after 2011 was their historical links to the country. Thus, while countries such as Finland and Australia made rule of law development a stated priority of their aid programmes (Foreign Economic Relations Department and the Development Partners Working Committee), it was the United Kingdom (DFID), Japan (JICA), the United States (USAID), and the European Union (EU) that emerged as the most visible bilateral rule of law donors. Three of these had intrusive historical engagements with the country, the United Kingdom as colonial ruler, Japan as an occupying force, and the United States as the main enforcer of the rigid sanctions regime just mentioned.

The UK's post-Anglo–Burma war appropriation of the territories of Ava, Tennasserim, and Arakan came to form 'Burma' and initiated rule under British power, justified by describing the conquered territory as a political state with totalitarian royal rule and little social organisation (Thant Myint-U 2004). In the early years, Burma was governed under the rules and regulations of India as the government had no legislative powers (Taylor, R. H. 2009) until 1872 when a Judicial Commissioner was appointed (Furnivall 1948) and in 1897 a Legislative Council was established in the capital (Taylor, R. H. 2009). Thus, as Callahan points out, '[t]he British never built a colonial state in Burma; they merely packed up some components of administration in India and shipped them to the new territory' (Callahan 2004:23). As an append-age to India, Burma was never a priority for British imperial policy and state building; rather, it was used as a means to achieve economic benefits (ibid.).

British rule was brought to an end during World War II as the country turned into a battlefield between Allied and Japanese forces that ultim-ately led to invasion of the latter (Silverstein 1977) and a subsequent 'collapse of the colonial state' (Callahan 2004). British-Indian armed forces were removed, and civil servants were replaced with Japanese army officials and civilians or loyal Burmese politicians and officials (Taylor, R. H. 2009). While, for some, these were initially seen as liberators, the accelerated takeover by the Japanese soon crushed dreams of independ-ence (Callahan 2004). Through harsh rule and regulatory and adminis-trative reforms, the Japanese took over economic enterprises, transports, and communications while the Burmese authorities retained control over revenue collection and law, order, and justice institutions (Taylor, R. H. 2009), a slight shift from Japan's usual strategies of setting up public and legal administrations in its colonies, in which it had become experienced (Kublin 1959; Myers and Peattie 1984). The aftermath of the Japanese invasion, however, resulted in a collapse of the Burmese police force and social control became difficult to maintain (Taylor, R. H. 2009). In regional areas, the exodus of indigenous bureaucrats 'stripped the countryside of police [and] jail attendants' and 'the physical evidence of the colonial state (jails, offices, courts, etc.) was torn down by either retreating imperial troops or angry mobs led by BIA [Burma Independence Army] units' (Callahan 2004:47). Ultimately, the Japanese army and military police (the *Kempetai*, one of the most feared organisations of the time) became the most effective and brutal force to establish control as common in other settings of Japanese dominion (Lamont-Brown 1998).

With various previous linkages and relations to Myanmar, ranging from colonisation and occupation to long-term diaspora activism or no previous experience whatsoever, in 2015 multiple multilateral organisations, bilateral donors, private actors, and INGOs worked on rule of law assistance in Myanmar. As an example, the UNDP's monthly rule of law co-ordination meetings with local and international organisations working on rule of law (as defined by the organisations themselves) is illustrative (see Table 4.1). Except for general updates on what the members were doing, meeting topics could include discussions about the 'need to coordinate better on how to communicate "core" rule of law concepts and terminology' (monthly RoL co-ordination meeting protocol, 16 December 2014, on file with the author). International members were in a significant majority, a few local NGOs participated, while no national (i.e., Myanmar government) actors were present at the meetings. While national and local actors, although invited, were often absent from the co-ordination meetings, they were sought as counterparts to rule of law assistance. They included government actors such as the Union Attorney General's Office, the Supreme Court, the Myanmar police force, the Rule of Law and Tranquillity Committee, the Parliament, and Myanmar Courts. Local NGOs included, for example, Loka Ahlinn, Myanmar Legal Aid Network, Myanmar Legal Clinic, and Justice for All.

Table 4.1 shows who was included in the rule of law co-ordination meetings in 2014 and 2015, which is interesting because it shows the plethora of foreign actors who self-identified as working on rule of law

TABLE 4.1 UNDP rule of law co-ordination meeting members
(2014–15)

| | |
|---|---|
| Multilateral organisations | United Nations Office for Drugs and Crime (UNODC) |
| | United Nations High Commissioner for Refugees (UNHCR) |
| | United Nations Children's Fund (UNICEF) |
| | International Labour Organization (ILO) |
| | International Development Law Organization (IDLO) (Intergovernmental) |
| Bilateral donors | British Council (BC) |
| | European Union (EU) |
| | United States Agency for International Development (USAID) |
| | United States Institute of Peace (USIP) |
| International non-governmental organisations (INGOs) | Namati |
| | International Bar Association's Human Rights Institute (IBAHRI) |
| | Action Aid |
| | Justice Base |
| | International Senior Lawyers Project (ISLP) |
| | Bridges Across Borders Southeast Asia Community Legal Education Initiative (BABSEA CLE) |
| | Central and East European Law Initiative Institute (CEELI) |
| | International Centre for Transitional Justice (ICTJ) |
| | International Commission of Jurists (ICJ) |
| | Justice Trust |
| | Mercy Corps |
| | Public International Law and Policy Group (PILPG) |
| | Friedrich Naumann Foundation (FNF) |
| | Centre for Humanitarian Dialogue (HD Centre) |
| Local NGOs | Justice for All |
| | Loka Ahlinn |

in Myanmar. During the course of my fieldwork, new international development actors would frequently arrive in Myanmar, for example, to initiate training activities (e.g., Avocats Sans Frontières, personal observation), set up an office (e.g., Justice Trust and USIP, personal observation) or to assess what they could do within the rule of law assistance field (e.g., East-West Center, personal observation). Also, while the list of foreign actors is rather extensive, during my fieldwork, it did not appear as if all of them actually worked on rule of law assistance in Myanmar.

The overview of the participants in the UNDP co-ordination meetings and the data presented in this section (interview responses, project documents, and publicly available information about Myanmar local actors) indicate that a multiplicity of parties constituted the rule of law assistance field. They included the usual proponents of international development assistance, such as bilateral donors and INGOs; their counterparts such as national government agencies; and their implementing partners such as private contractors and local organisations. Rule of law assistance projects brought actors together not only vertically but also horizontally, as foreign donors competed for government collaborations and local access. While they worked alongside each other and asserted that they co-ordinated their efforts, actors often sought to translate their own particular organisational view of what was needed (or feasible) for rule of law development and in the process became competitors for local counterparts and competent intermediaries. Intermediaries were often the actors who facilitated such interactions between counterparts, which added another layer of complexity to projects when these were steered in directions that were based on the interests of the individual intermediary. Next, I review such projects in more detail.

## 4.3 RULE OF LAW ACTIVITIES

How was rule of law operationalised on the ground in Myanmar amid political transition? An overview of foreign development actors and their activities shows the several ways in which rule of law was translated into activities based on ideas of legal aid as necessary for access to justice (British Council 2015), of lawyers needing good education and an independent bar association (United Nations 1990a), and of the judiciary needing to be independent and efficient (United Nations 1985).

The branding of the activities carried out by foreign development actors resembled that of those found in other developing and post-conflict settings (see, e.g., Sannerholm et al. 2012). For example, almost fifteen years ago, Bergling (2006:196) observed that even if settings vary in ideas and identity, the trending activities and modes of implementing rule of law assistance remain largely the same. At first glance, the same holds true for Myanmar, where, as in many other developing settings, rule of law assistance actors focus on 'needs assessments, expert advice to lawmakers, topical training, book tours, conferences, resident advisors, acquisition of information technology, production of information materials, etc.'

### 4.3.1 Access to Justice, Legal Aid, and Legal Awareness

Enhancement of 'access to justice' is a central component of rule of law development strategies (see, e.g., United Nations 2008). Its rationalities are based on the presumption that if people cannot access ways of solving their conflicts (e.g. because spaces that provide such services are too distant or unknown to the individual), a rule of law system is not in place (see, e.g., van de Meene and van Rooij 2008).

In 2012 the UNDP initiated activities on access to justice in Myanmar. The 2013–15 Myanmar Country Programme included a rule of law and access to justice component that sought to build 'the capacities of justice sector institutions and their staff to effectively implement justice sector reform', enhance 'the legal awareness of vulnerable groups', and improve 'governance by strengthening the rule of law and access to justice for poor men, women and children' (United Nations Development Programme n.d.). However, one UNDP representative was not sure how to match the global ideals of rule of law with the locality: '[W]e aim to bring in a lot of international stuff, but it is hard to describe how to bring that in here ... how it will fit?' (Interviewee #9, 23 May 2014). In 2013, an access to justice mapping was carried out to better assess needs and priorities for the justice sector and individuals in strengthening the rule of law 'to ensure that future UNDP rule of law and access to justice programming is not only relevant but also sensitive to diverse local contexts' (United Nations Development Programme 2014:1). The 'Summary Report of Rule of Law and Access to Justice Mapping' asked state officials and ward/village and township levels about the priority of local justice concerns, how people felt that they could address concerns and what their perceived obstacles to accessing justice were. The report found 'that there is a lack of trust that negatively affects the relationship between State and citizens; and, second, that there is a need for greater legal awareness by the public'. It also found that such 'issues are seen as requiring efforts by the government to encourage the public to obey the law' and that 'rule of law tends to be viewed synonymously with law and order'. Regardless of that translational confusion over what the 'rule of law' means for the actors involved, the report is confident that officials were open to collaboration with 'the UNDP in strengthening the rule of law' (2014:1–2).

To assess questions of rule of law and access to justice, the UNDP thus applied 'research' as a technology. One of the practitioners involved stated that the research was carried out in areas where the UNDP managed to gain access through known networks and through researchers who were 'chosen carefully' to make sure they had knowledge of 'legal terms and concepts' and with the support of 'interpreters [who] knew exactly what [the UNDP team] wanted' (Interviewee #7, 21 May 2014). Such a statement supports one of this book's main arguments, namely that intermediaries help enable access, which in turn results in development activities being steered in certain directions.

Also working on access to justice-related issues, in 2014 the Myanmar government and the United Nations Office on Drugs and Crime (UNODC) signed a 'landmark' collaboration agreement after a year of negotiations that sought to enhance Myanmar citizens' confidence in the justice system 'to provide stability and access to justice' (Mizzima News 2014, citing Jeremy Douglas from UNODC). The UNODC had been working on drug control in the Golden Triangle for more than thirty years (United Nations Office for Drugs and Crime n.d.; for an overview of crime and drug control in the Golden Triangle, see Broadhurst and Ferrelly 2014). After the political transition, UNODC Executive Director Yury Fedotov visited Myanmar in 2012 and met with Aung San Suu Kyi to express his organisation's willingness to support rule of law reforms linking its importance to the establishment of economic and social development (United Nations Office on Drugs and Crime 2012). After further negotiations with government counterparts, it was decided that the UNODC would support efforts to transform the Myanmar police force in line with international standards and principles (Mizzima News 2013). When I met the UNODC Police Adviser at that time, he was excited over his move to police HQ in the capital Nay Pyi Taw where he was the only foreigner and would be given a driver and police car to 'work with the police to write a road map for the future, to reflect their move to a democratic system of governance' (Interviewee #1, 6 May 2014).

Promoting 'legal awareness' is another rationale that donors believe will enhance access to justice. The DFID (UK Department for International Development) was active in promoting legal awareness via its support to the British Council (BC), which implements much of the UK's aid to rule of law assistance projects in Myanmar (Interviewees #20 and #21, 30 September 2014). The BC has been present in Myanmar for decades and has had engagements across the country since 2000 through initiatives like the library network 'Millennium Centres' where English and 'much more than English' was being taught (Interviewee #20, 30 September 2014). The BC started its capacity building projects in 2005–6, some of them in support of rule of law, including the set-up and support of local rule of law organisations (ibid.). One of these organisations was the 'Pyoe Pin' programme which was established to serve as 'a credible facilitator and broker that responds to the needs of the people' (British Council n.d.a). In 2014, Pyoe Pin operated as a translator of the BC's objectives of enhancing legal awareness in Myanmar. One such initiative included the creation of a rule of law-themed television drama (*The Sun, The Moon and The Truth*) to raise awareness of rule of law and legal rights (see, e.g., Cassrels 2015). The soap-opera-style drama portrays a young female lawyer who works for a 'legal clinic' in rural Myanmar where she helps people who have been treated unjustly. In early 2020, I learned that Pyoe Pin, long critiqued for being controlled by foreign interests, had been dissolved and a new organisation created.

Another long-term donor was the European Union, present in Myanmar since the early 1990s (with a bilateral aid programme active since 2004). In 2008, the European instrument for human rights and democracy was introduced; however, for the Myanmar context the name was changed to the 'good governance country-based support scheme' because '[o]therwise – if keeping human rights, etc. in the name – the government would know about it too easily and people would get jailed' (Interviewee #32, 30 November 2014; see Ware 2012a:329 for an overview of similar INGO strategies to not put local actors at risk). Engagement with the government did not start until 2010, and still, in 2014, much support was channelled through international organisations in support of civil society and human rights (Interviewee #32, 30 November 2014). A foreign EU representative suggested that '[m]any international and local organizations applied for funding in partnership – still local people did not understand what this big EU thing was' (Interviewee #32, 30 November 2014). Other donors provided similar opportunities for local organisations to apply for funding. However, the intermediaries who worked for those donors suggested that local organisations lacked an understanding of the application and reporting process, and therefore refrained from seeking funds. Some who had gone through the process said that they would never do so again (Interviewee #27, 7 October 2014). Intermediaries mentioned that the main issue that arose in relation to funding applications was donors' focus on 'money matters' and reported that they had to 'mediate' issues pertaining to 'money' because 'the Burmese mentality' was different from foreigners', and thus:

> They [the 'Burmese'] don't care much about money so if they don't like something they won't work even if it pays well and vice versa if they like the work and work with friends they could work without money. Some people are getting a bit tired of donors, especially the ones pushing their own agenda. It is mainly the donor's focus on money and monetary compensation that bothers people, as Myanmar people generally care very little about money.
>
> (Interviewee #17, 23 September 2014)

This is one of the issues raised by local participants in relation to what they perceived as the conflicting motivations of themselves and their foreign counterparts with regard to engaging in rule of law development work. It is a matter of debate, of course, whether there is such a thing as a single 'Burmese mentality' which encourages people to stay away from 'money matters' in a setting known for its ethnic diversity and endemic corruption. Factors that complicate such speculation include the decades of 'socialist' influenced politics as introduced by Ne Win and the common contemporary references to intermediaries being in the rule of law assistance field 'for the money' (e.g., Interviewee #3, 8 May 2014). It may also be that these local interviewees wanted to demarcate a normative 'Burmese' order as an expression of 'strategic essentialism' (Spivak 2007) to signal a shared culture, belief, or representation that differed from what was brought in by foreigners (see also interviewee #27, 7 October 2014). Nevertheless, this is just one example of where the introduction of foreign funding for rule of law projects in Myanmar meant that values, perspectives, and worldviews (Interviewee #17, 23 September 2014) came into contact and created interfaces of competitive and contested ideas and approaches. Such aspects needed careful balancing by rule of law intermediaries who had to mediate (Interviewees #14, 5 October 2014; #17, 23 September 2014; #39, 22 November 2014; #42, 5 November 2014; #55, 26 September 2015) and co-ordinate the 'two sides' that 'need[ed] to understand that they should adjust' (Interviewee #27, 7 October 2014).

Some local organisations did not shy away from acquiring EU funds. For example, the EU funded a €20 million 'MyJustice' programme, which was implemented by the BC and a local organisation called 'Loka Ahlinn'. The local organisation did not seem an obvious choice for such a major justice project, being described as an 'atypical' rule of law organisation for the EU to support because the organisation's members consisted mainly of artists and 'wishy-washy' people (Interviewee #20, 30 September 2014). The organisation's history also sheds doubt on its ability to handle large sums of donor money for justice activities. Loka Ahlinn was founded in 2006 to prepare community groups for future national development through capacity building and networking, then in 2008 the organisation assisted with emergency and relief activities in the aftermath of Cyclone Nargis and partnered with the UNDP and other international organisations in 2009 to work on agriculture and livelihood recovery activities and community development trainings. After 2012, Loka Ahlinn worked variously with 'Community Development', 'Civic and Political Engagement', and 'Governance and Accountability Promotion'. It implemented 'Farmer Field School', 'Rule of Law Promotion', 'Youth Empowerment', and civil society organisations strengthening projects. It raised awareness of legislation and provided training on rule of law and judicial system reform (Loka Ahlinn n.d.). Loka Ahlinn also ran an earlier BC-funded 'Capacity Building for Rule of Law Promotion' project in Myanmar (Namati: Innovations in Legal Empowerment n.d.). One foreign lawyer complained that Loka Ahlinn 'do any project they get money for, they are not a well-known rule of law organization, they don't know rule of law' (field notes, 5 December 2014). But it might also have been the case that the organisation had well-established networks and influence that mattered more for its ability to achieve local change as compared to those organisations that more obviously branded themselves to match donors' rule of law idioms. Loka Ahlinn itself describes its work as a 'right-based [sic] social development organization which [is] strengthening the actors of both individuals and institutional [sic] for civil society movement through rule of law and human right-based [sic] democracy' (Namati: Innovations in Legal Empowerment n.d.).

The MyJustice Programme that Loka Ahlinn helped implement aimed to improve access to justice, through legal aid, community mediation and paralegal services, especially for the poor, vulnerable, and marginalised (British Council 2015). Through the programme, legal aid centres were established across the country (British Council 2015). It was a legal aid model that had been elevated from South Africa's experiences to a global level, promoted by the UN, and introduced by foreign actors in Myanmar (Thomson Reuters Foundation 2013). The rationale that legal aid is a necessary component for access to justice had thus travelled to Myanmar, where it was identified that a legal aid system was lacking. On that theme, in addition to setting up legal aid centres, a legal aid bill was passed in Parliament, and foreign legal aid advisers were embedded with local organisations to provide technical assistance (Interviewee #40, 9 December 2014). Also, a Myanmar Legal Aid Network (MLAW) that consisted of law firms and civil society organisations was established (Interviewee #46, 9 December 2014). Like Loka Ahlinn, MLAW faced significant demand from foreign development actors and came to occupy a central position (see also de Sardan 2005) as an intermediary to foreign organisations.

The translation of a legal aid system in Myanmar did not, however, come without friction, as foreign, national, and local actors tried to align their different understandings and knowledge. This was exemplified by one of my participants (an American lawyer) who recounted some of the issues that had appeared in her work. The foreign lawyer had been discussing legal aid with the local lawyers with whom she was working and came to the conclusion that sometimes she thought they were 'on the same page and then I hear something so very surprising'. She recalled:

> [T]hey told me about the challenges for local lawyers working with legal aid: they have been insulted and under attack for providing free services. Then someone raised the question of whether it is possible that we are supporting higher levels of crime because we provide free legal advice. Could this really be a legit concern people have?
>
> (Interviewee #53, 5 October 2015)

The example illustrates how the imported rationales for an accessible legal aid system did not translate smoothly to the Myanmar setting, neither semantically nor ideologically, as reflected in the concern by the local lawyer (see also Interviewee #58, 30 September 2014).

### 4.3.2 National Rule of Law Institutions

Multilateral and bilateral donors approached the Myanmar government as counterparts to rule of law assistance. The Supreme Court of the Union (SC) and the Union Attorney General's Office (UAGO) in Nay Pyi Taw were especially targeted as central law and justice institutions. Institutional constraints of these government actors were mentioned, for example, in New Perimeter, et als. rule of law assessment (2013:18) which portrayed the UAGO as having strong leadership that appreciated international co-operation and support, but that was overburdened and had few lawyers with knowledge of legislative drafting, international law and 'basic skills, tools to do their jobs, and capacity to absorb outside help'. The judiciary was described as in need of a 'shift' of 'culture' because judges 'are expected to adhere to the rule of law and explain in written rulings the reasoning for their decisions' (New Perimeter et al. 2013:31). Training programmes run by international agencies were suggested as 'highly valuable' for effecting such a 'culture' shift (ibid.).

While it seemed as if the Myanmar government was active in its rule of law reform attempts, foreign practitioners mentioned the low capacity among government counterparts and the tiresome processes and negotiations they had to go through to reach agreements on reform (e.g., Interviewee #9, 23 May 2014). In practice, intermediaries variously suggested that they had to mediate or 'be the go-between' because foreigners did not understand the limitations that such constraints put on proposed and implemented rule of law activities (e.g., Interviewee #17, 23 September 2014). One intermediary complained about 'the ones from DC' (referring to her US donor representatives) who, in their attempted collaborations with the government,

> want to skip the local completely and do their own thing, I try to convince them of how they cannot do that as the problems they will encounter are not what they can predict from the outset, they will come to a point where there is a stop. When they don't want to listen to me, I tell them 'good luck.'
>
> (Interviewee #10, 12 May 2014)

Another intermediary suggested that 'international staff' did not understand that 'a lot of flexibility' was needed 'to work with the government in a place like this' and that therefore 'you might have to bend the rules a little bit' (Interviewee #6, 19 May 2014). In effect, on their side, government intermediaries were central for managing the different expectations held by foreign actors and government counterparts (Interviewee #6, 19 May 2014; Interviewee #7, 21 May 2014).

While foreign practitioners did not experience rule of law as a priority reform area for the Myanmar government (e.g., Interviewee #7, 21 May 2014), collaborations with international actors were established. To get closer to government counterparts, in 2013, a UNDP position of chief technical adviser on rule of law and access to justice to be located within the UAGO in Nay Pyi Taw was advertised (UNDP Jobs 2013, on file with the author). The chief technical adviser was to provide assistance with 'institutional capacities for participatory coordinated planning and policymaking' for the Office of the SC, the Ministry of Home Affairs, police services and justice sector parliamentary committees. The UNDP's initial initiatives on rule of law reform were thus mainly framed as developing national counterparts' planning capacity (see also Interviewee #35, 19 November 2014). Such focus is interesting in light of the suggestion by a UNDP programme officer that 'it is still very sensitive what we are doing here on the rule of law' (Interviewee #31, 10 November 2014). Emphasis on enhancing planning capacities seemed like a relatively safe approach adapted in lieu of digging deeper into aspects of law and justice that may have been deemed more sensitive or rather the only approach that government counterparts were willing to accept at this stage.

Like the UNDP, JICA positioned rule of law advisers within the offices of UAGO and the SC (Interviewee #39, 22 November 2014). JICA worked with a similar capacity, building focus as the UNDP, but there was little co-operation between the two organisations on a daily basis (Interviewee #35, 19 November 2014). According to one interviewee, JICA's involvement in rule of law assistance had a strong focus on law and economic development which was 'quite different from other places' because it was 'much more focused on business interests and in quick solutions for the business community' (Interviewee #39, 22 November 2014). This was an approach that the practitioner questioned, and again the focus of activities indicates the narrow space for foreign assistance. Regardless of the impact and room for manoeuvre that the placement of foreign advisers within key justice institutions could possibly have, the fact that the Myanmar government agreed to such placements indicates a noteworthy change in a country that to a large extent remained off-limits to foreigners for decades.

The UNDP's strategy to focus on 'planning' did result in the first ever Judiciary Strategic Plan ('Advancing Justice Together' for the years 2015–17) to improve the Myanmar justice system and the services of the courts (Supreme Court of the Union of Myanmar 2014). The plan was drafted with support from USAID and JICA and its focus areas, including public access and awareness, enhancing independence, accountability, equality and integrity, and the strengthening of swift case processing, translated some donors' priorities: enhanced case processing (USAID), and access to justice and legal awareness (UNDP). A review of the plan's first year suggested that reforms that had been implemented included the identification of pilot courts where public information centres had been set up, modern equipment provided, the judiciary trained, and case management procedures implemented. At the SC, electronic case information systems had been developed, and several new departments had been established. Progress had also been made to enhance the public's and the media's access to information about the court and its services (Supreme Court of the Union of Myanmar 2016). The SC also published the Code of Judicial Ethics for Myanmar Judges in 2017 as 'a standard to be able to assess the judicial activities by the Executive and Legislative branches of the State, and by the lawyers and the public' (Supreme Court of the Republic of the Union of Myanmar 2017).

Reforms within UAGO were said to be slow (Interviewee #35, 19 November 2014). However, they also launched a first strategic plan as a result of the collaboration with the UNDP (Union Attorney General's Office 2015) and subsequently a Code of Ethics for Law Officers following Myanmar's ratification of the United Nations Convention Against Corruption in 2012.

It might be that in 2016 the effects of practitioners' work during previous years bore some fruit as two main government counterparts finally produced well-designed and genuine plans for the future directions of their work. Or, do we see here an example of how a government can make public commitments to the rule of law and present reform plans and commitments that look stellar on paper while continuing to abuse central principles of the concept in practice (Ginsburg and Moustafa 2008)? In 2020, we know that Myanmar remains an illiberal regime that disregards core aspects of rule of law, for example equal rights under the law for all, regardless of ethnicity, and equal application of the law, and while government reforms might look good 'on paper', their significance for rule of law 'in practice' and especially people's increased confidence in the justice system as an effect of the reforms remains to be seen. An important question, then, is whether or not foreign actors' support to 'planning capacity' and intermediaries' work in promoting and supporting the drafting of these plans, in fact, contribute to illiberal versions of rule of law that remain focused on discourse and texts rather than actual implementation (see especially Rajah 2012). When I visit Yangon in 2020, a discussion with a local lawyer is telling as he disappointedly tells me that 'much change has happened on paper, but little in practice' (informal interview, February 2020). Rights exist in documents, though, for ordinary people, they remain absent.

Back to the immediate transition period when USAID re-established its mission and for rule of law promotion purposes approached national courts to support the set-up of electronic court filing systems (United States Agency for International Development 2016b). While more recent humanitarian assistance had been provided by the agency since 2000, the last time the USAID had any presence in the country was in 1988. One of the expressed aims of the development assistance delivered by the USA to the country is to lend support to the initiated economic and democratic reforms undertaken in favour of rule of law, human rights, and good governance that take into account the diversity of Burma and its civil society (Bureau of East Asian and Pacific Affairs 2013; Cartwright and Truong 2012). While USAID is presented as a main rule of law donor, the Inaugural Rule of Law Project in Myanmar (United States Agency for International Development 2016a) is implemented through consultancy firm Tetra Tech. In August 2013, Tetra Tech sought candidates for 'Justice Sector Positions in Myanmar' with significant experience in one of the listed areas of expertise (nothing less than judicial governance and training, access to justice, legal aid and education, implementing legal frameworks, legislative drafting, grant management, campaigning, gender mainstreaming, strengthening civil society, monitoring and evaluation, finance, admin, and human resources) for various long-term positions for the USAID-funded 'Promoting the Rule of Law Project in Burma' (on file with the author). In November 2013 a 'Myanmar Legal Specialist' was sought to carry out several tasks including travelling to various regions, carrying out activities in co-operation with the government and advising on legal themes (on file with the author). The fact that a search was done for someone who could travel 'to various regions' shows how intermediaries are needed to travel with the rule of law across Myanmar to promote the aims and objectives of the donor (see also Cheesman and Simion 2022; Desai 2014).

The Myanmar government also accepted foreign support through the various trainings and workshops organised for government staff in Nay Pyi Taw. For example, in 2014, the International Commission of Jurists (ICJ) convened a seminar on 'The Role of Judicial Independence and Integrity in Improving the Effectiveness of the Rule of Law' for the SC (International Commission of Jurists 2014). The UNDP arranged trainings on constitutionalism, lawmaking, and substantive skills for UAGO and the SC (United Nations Development Programme n.d.). Trainings that involve international legal concepts are common for promoting the rule of law and often seen as one of the most straightforward ways of delivering development promotion, but what results can be expected from excessive training? Scholars have pointed out that training as a method for rule of law development has many shortcomings and limitations and leaves much to ask for genuine and long-term change unless the training is followed up by evaluations and reviews in combination with longer-term relationship building with training participants (e.g., Andrews, Woolcock, and Pritchett 2017).

Was foreign donors' enhanced co-operation with the government seen as something positive by involved actors and counterparts? Important to remember is that foreign actors arrived in a situation where, for decades, co-operation with the government had been banned (due to the sanctions regime), or it had been excessively opposed via an active activist diaspora and human rights groups. Showing up and mingling with government actors was a necessity for some donors, and perhaps in some cases the only way to achieve reform on higher levels, but it was not necessarily going to make these foreign organisations popular with either the international or the local NGO community. Switching strategy from keeping aid money away from the previous military government to suddenly engaging with the government had local intermediaries and counterparts suggesting that foreign organisations lacked sufficient knowledge of the local setting and power relations as they pushed their own agenda (see also Décobert and Wells 2019). A representative from an intermediary NGO suggested that foreign donors' increased engagement with the government constituted 'a moral crisis' for him that he perceived as 'a big damage for civil society and the democracy movement':

> [T]hey want us to engage directly with the government … but morally … we want to base our work on our moral ground. When

working with the [foreign donor] I have to report my meetings to them, this gives some sort of score, high-level people matter more and gives a higher score, so I always have to mention the very important people we meet, and I have to invite them to trainings. Before 2010 we should not talk to them [the government] but then yes. Historically we are a country of social movement, but after 2010 foreign donors engaged directly with the government, social movements became marginalized, many organizations changed their strategy now, and there are very few social movements now.

(Interviewee #30, 24 October 2014)

Perceptions of partners thus shifted, while NGOs had emerged as suitable collaborators in humanitarian aid that bypassed the military government (especially after Cyclone Nargis in 2008). However, their influence began to be marginalised as Western donors sought to normalise their relations with the Myanmar state (Décobert and Wells 2020). There were additional complaints that donors' push for engagement with government counterparts was inappropriate or potentially harmful. A foreign practitioner explained a typical situation of 'international supervisors [that] don't understand sensitivities in the country':

Local staff still feel unsafe; they refuse to go to certain areas and work on certain issues. The special branch is still here. If you met with officials, they will follow you. They will take Myanmar citizens aside and question them and ask why they were with a foreigner, what the mission is about, etc. National staff don't even want to call ministers. Perhaps it's paranoia.

(Interviewee #02, 7 May 2014)

Both of the suggestions raise important questions in relation to donor engagement which should be sensitive to the context and strive for ensuring ownership without risk for local participants (Ware 2012a). As an effect of the 2015 elections and the accelerated belief in the NLD government as a suitable donor partner, NGO marginalisation increased, only for them to again be requested as counterparts in light of 'donor interpretations of the NLD government' (Décobert and Wells 2019:311).

### 4.3.3 The Legal Profession and Legal Education
When rule of law organisations from abroad arrived in Myanmar, they identified several issues of concern with the legal profession and legal education (International Commission of Jurists 2013). With the understanding that they were facing a Common law system, domestic realities and historical contours were little regarded (Crouch 2014).

Lawyer-to-lawyer collaborations were introduced with the aim of strengthening the capacity of the legal profession. For example, in January 2014 the ICJ announced the opening of a new Yangon office (via the Myanmar Law Google Group) with an International Legal Adviser for Myanmar. The ICJ voiced criticism of the current state of legal and judicial affairs, especially in relation to the legal profession (Aguirre and Sathisan 2016; International Commission of Jurists 2013).

Another configuration of lawyers, the International Bar Association's Human Rights Institute (IBAHRI), which 'works to promote and protect human rights under a just rule of law' in transitional settings (International Bar Association's Human Rights Institute), established presence in Myanmar after undertaking a fact-finding mission in August 2012 'to understand Myanmar's prospects and needs at this important juncture and, more specifically, to find out how far it has begun to adhere to globally prevalent understandings of the rule of law' (2012:6). Following the initial assessment, in November 2013 an International Legal Specialist was recruited 'with the necessary skills to function effectively as the national representative body for lawyers, to promote the rule of law and law reform and to act as a counter-balance to the state' to work on a development project to 'establish a professional, independent and active bar association in Myanmar (Burma)' (on file with the author). The selection fell on a younger Australian lawyer who managed to build up strong relationships with key intermediaries, in combination with the understanding of the importance of good admin and travel assistance via a local travel agency that helped her establish contacts and some levels of trust across the country. The IBAHRI representative took any chance at travelling across Myanmar with the intermediaries that pushed the project forward (personal observation during 2014).

The legal specialist's approach to her work and her ability to foster key connections with intermediaries were central to IBAHRI's work in supporting the establishment of an independent Lawyers' Association in Myanmar. For IBAHRI, the rule of law was thus translated into a need for a Lawyers' Association and, to that end, in 2014 seminars were arranged on topics that included international and regional best practices on bar associations (Workshop Report, on file with the author) and comparative views on laws regulating the legal profession (International Bar Association's Human Rights Institute 2014). To raise awareness of the initiative and mobilise support for the establishment of a national bar association, representatives from IBAHRI travelled across Myanmar to meet with local lawyers during 2014 and 2015 (personal observation). As a result of that work, in January 2016, after state elections, the Independent Lawyers' Association of Myanmar (ILAM), supported by the Rule of Law and Tranquillity Committee, was launched as it held its inaugural meeting in Nay Pyi Taw.

Was this work a success story of an 'international expert' adapting to the local setting in combination with excellent support on the ground? Reports by the IBAHRI would likely tell you that was the case; as one foreign lawyer who was associated mainly with national actors expressed: 'I see how they brag about it on their web page and in their newsletters.' In fact, the work in establishing a Lawyers' Association was filled with conflicting worldviews and misunderstandings that needed careful navigation and mediation by key intermediaries. For example, one local lawyer noted that, for people in Myanmar, aspects other than 'democracy' (e.g. seniority) were considered more suitable for deciding who should become a member of the national bar (Interviewee #14, 5 October 2014). These differences in the views of the most suitable selection criteria for the Bar led to conflicts with lawyers across the country that needed to be mediated and resolved by local intermediaries (ibid.). Attempts at establishing a national bar association were also criticised for sidelining existing local initiatives: '[T]hey often use their name and then take over ... [T]hey call it the IBA initiative to start a national bar association', an intermediary critiqued when speaking about IBAHRI. Instead, he suggested:

> I played a key role. It is not their initiative ... they want it to be their initiative. They flew in a lot of people who knew nothing about the country or about MLA [the already existing Myanmar Lawyer's Association], which is a local initiative that was just starting. I asked local lawyers if they knew about MLA and if they think it is a good start, some said yes, when I told the IBA, they replied that it is a biased government initiative. None of the internationals knew about it, IBA said it is no good. I think the IBA wanted to be the 'steerer' of that, and they want to brag about it.
>
> (Interviewee #41, 11 December 2014)

This quotation captures the major issues of the development field, including those of respecting local ownership (Bosch 2016) and engaging in settings without sufficient knowledge of local power relations.

An example of the latter was observed by Dunlap (2014) in Cambodia where, she argues, because of the lack of well-grounded insights, IBA's rule of law assistance efforts helped support corrupt and elite government interests instead of contributing to rule of law development. In the Myanmar case, foreign actors mentioned the 'un-democratic' aspects of the existing Myanmar Lawyer's Association (MLA) as an explanation for sidelining an existing local initiative. An often-retold story among foreign rule of law practitioners in 2014 concerned an impromptu break-out meeting that was convened by several senior local lawyers during an IBA conference. According to the story, members of MLA felt that there was no need to establish a new association when they had already achieved temporary registration and were working towards being a representative, national bar association. However, other lawyers expressed the view that MLA was unfairly focused on lawyers who were mainly from Yangon. There were also questions raised about the group's political affiliations (e.g., Interviewee #8, 22 May 2014; Interviewee #14, 5 October 2014). A foreign lawyer captured his experience of attending the meeting that had become the talk of the town:

> It was a horrible meeting for me. Some say that MLA is too Yangon-focused, but they had advertised the meeting in the newspaper, maybe it was not broad enough, but they tried. On the second day at lunchtime, I sat down with some guys and told them: 'You should speak with the MLA, they probably didn't want to exclude you.' I got them all talking with each other; they were shouting at each other, [local intermediary] was helping me to turn it to a more positive discussion. MLA is founded by local lawyers. IBA wants to do it. This is not consistent with international best practice; you need to let the locals do it.
>
> (Interviewee #41, 11 December 2014)

The essence of the foreign lawyer's experience is captured in Liljeblad's (2019) analysis of the local challenges of IBAHRI's attempt to establish a Bar Association in Myanmar. Liljeblad conceptualises IBAHRI's model for a national Bar Association as a 'Legal Transplant' with the aim to 'introduce IBA conceptions about an independent national bar association' (2019:211). Contrasting IBAHRI's goals of building support for and setting up a legally registered national and independent bar as well as backing the legal reforms necessary for this to realise, Liljeblad suggests that the 'transplant' that resulted in ILAM was unsuccessful because it has not been able to gain the status of a national or independent body. As suggested by the foreign lawyer cited already, Liljeblad also finds that IBAHRI's transplant intruded 'a domestic space of pre-existing actors' (2019:220). IBAHRI's attempts to gain national exclusivity resulted only in addition to the many already existing alternatives of lawyers' configurations across the country and thus created 'uncertainty as to the position of ILAM vis-à-vis other lawyer organizations with similar purposes' (ibid.).

To work towards the development of the legal profession, major donors also supported legal education as opportunities emerged when in 2013, for the first time in almost two decades, undergraduate degrees (including law) began anew at the University of Yangon and Mandalay University (Crouch 2013; Ei Thae Thae Naing 2013). Since Ne Win's rule from the 1960s onwards, universities were shut down for long periods of time, mainly as a response to student protests, which were common. During the periods when legal education was ongoing, legal scholar Myint Zan's ethnographic experience from the time tells of an education full of inaccuracies and socialist ideology reflecting 'the propagandistic nature in which the subject [of law] was presented and display[ing] either total ignorance or willful distortion' (Myint Zan 2008:71, 74). Another factor that affected legal education was the changing of the language of instruction from English to Burmese, a phenomenon that materialised in 1976 as universities were reopened (they had been shut down in 1974 and 1975 when student protests came to an end with the use of military force (Taylor, R. H. 2009)). Correspondence courses in law were introduced, and a huge increase in students was enabled. Myint Zan (2008) observes that the government under Ne Win intentionally lowered the standards of legal education, and tried to keep students away from campuses (thus serving political and security purposes of stability and control) through the introduction of such distance education. The system of distance education, including aspects such as the use of extremely generalised questions, requiring no more than copying the course material, and the high amount of students (50,000 enrolled in 2005), with, consequently, little time for serious marking, created a mass production of law graduates who easily obtained high marks from overburdened staff.

The rationale for providing legal education as development (for its common uses, see Taylor 2010a) easily translated to the Myanmar setting where legal education for decades deteriorated in the face of hostile political strategies, thus leaving it in a poor state, incapable of producing well-prepared lawyers (Liljeblad 2016b; Myint Zan 2000a). The education sector was also a relatively smooth counterpart for development assistance because it is easy to articulate why a good education system is important for development (Tun Lin Moe 2008). Two local programme assistants explained that their work on legal education was successful because they refrained from 'touch[ing] sensitive parts' which would make their work less successful; however, they admitted, 'the larger goal is of course justice for all' (Interviewees #60 and #61, 3 December 2014). However, because the education sector – and Yangon and Mandalay University in particular – became a counterpart in demand (Esson and Wang 2016), it became overburdened with development initiatives which led to several issues of efficiency and recipient concerns 'about the manner in which aid was being provided' (Liljeblad 2016b:143).

The UNDP also prioritised work in support of universities as a key dimension of strengthening rule of law and access to justice in Myanmar. It thus supported organisations such as Bridges Across Borders Southeast Asia Clinical Legal Education (BABSEA CLE) which worked with universities to introduce the US concept of 'clinical legal education' to aid the poor in lack of legal services (Owen 2011). The organisation explains that clinical legal education is 'a progressive educational ideology and pedagogy that is most often implemented through university programmes. Clinics are interactive, hands-on classrooms that promote learning by doing' (Bridges Across Borders Southeast Asia Clinical Legal Education n.d.). In essence, clinical legal education seeks to educate lawyers so that they can promote and work towards social justice (Ashford and Mckeown 2018; Bloch 2011).

Pro bono lawyers from the USA, Australia, Vietnam, and other countries contributed to the clinical legal education programme (personal observation; Interviewees #60 and #61, 3 December 2014), some of whom were associated with the global, mainly corporate, law firm DLA Piper (DLA Piper 2013). In March 2013, DLA Piper's pro bono legal assistance organisation for developing and post-conflict settings, New Perimeter et al. had stated in its 'Myanmar Rule of Law Assessment' that the organisation would support law reform in Myanmar by contributing 'thousands of pro bono hours from the law firm' (2013:2). This type of pro bono service of law firms often translates into goodwill and an opportunity to network with government officials or potential employees. Some firms run seminars for government officials and law students and some help government officials with law and regulatory reform. For example, DLA Piper provided funding to NGOs to conduct the rule of law assessment in Myanmar seemingly as part of its global pro bono account the main purpose of which is to increase the share of pro bono account relative to profits (this has an impact on the ranking of law firms in the USA) and to show that they are an international firm (see further Tungnirun 2017).

In 2013 JICA and Nagoya University funded a Myanmar–Japan Legal Research Centre at the University of Yangon to enhance research capacities and to provide teaching. The centre 'aims to carry out legal assistance in Myanmar, which is facing an urgent need for human resource development of judicial officers in its rapid progress toward democracy and a market economy' and 'disseminates research and legal information of both countries' (Nagoya University 2013). Japanese academics lectured on topics including 'the legal essence of Myanmar law and common aspects of Myanmar and Japanese law' and carried out research on Myanmar's legal system to 'help facilitate processes in a historical moment when many laws are amended' (Interviewees #51 and #52, 12 December 2014). Involvement in legal education illustrates Japan's role as an emerging 'soft power' donor also within the realms of democracy, human rights, and rule of law (Ichihara 2017).

In addition to its support to university education, the UNDP worked to enhance education for already graduated legal professionals (and others) through collaboration with the Rule of Law and Tranquillity Committee. Based on an idea prepared by the Committee in 2013 (San Pe 2014) and a UNDP feasibility study that included comparative examples and consultations with stakeholders in Myanmar (United Nations Development Programme 2014) the constellation set up 'Rule of Law Centres' across the country including Mandalay, Lashio, and Yangon. The set-up of the centres meant that the UNDP moved from its less sensitive planning activities to the actual implementation of rule of law reform. For the Rule of Law and Tranquillity Committee (and especially Aung San Suu Kyi), the establishment of the centres helped illustrate some tangible results of rule of law development (conversation with foreign diplomats, field notes, 30 September 2014).

The rapid implementation of Rule of Law Centres was, however, debated. A foreign rule of law practitioner expressed her surprise over Aung San Suu Kyi's push for the implementation of the centres, because, as the practitioner explained, she was used to the opposite happening, that is, to foreigners being the ones driving hasty reforms (Interviewee #9, 23 May 2014). A local programme officer who was involved in the project was concerned about the sustainability of the centres because they had been implemented quickly, with little research conducted on local needs and their feasibility (Interviewee #6, 19 May 2014). Also, the set-up of the Rule of Law Centres had been the subject of various political and donor struggles. For example, it is noteworthy that the International Development Law Organization (IDLO), also involved in the project, in 2014 announced that a consortium of partners had been established in light of then-president Then Sein's repeated calls for the strengthening of rule of law, and in 2015 announced that the consortium of partners was linked to the proposal by the Parliamentary Committee (on file with the author), which indicates various moves in trying to please different factions of the former government. In addition, at its initial launch, the centre's project was presented as a UNDP and another foreign donor initiative – with no recognition of the Rule of Law and Tranquillity Committee (Interviewee #41, 11 December 2014). The foreign donors' initially cautious approach to being visibly affiliated with the Committee may have reflected the uncertain political environment that many of them felt that they were operating within during that time.

## 4.4 CONCLUSION

After the political transition Myanmar saw an increase in development assistance, especially to sectors that worked with democratisation, governance, rule of law, and justice. The historic event of the political opening of one of the 'last frontiers' in terms of authoritarian pariah states of the world meant that civil society, the Myanmar government, and foreign development agencies were able to meet in-country and work to accommodate increased project supply and funding.

This chapter presented the field of rule of law assistance as it was established in Myanmar after 2011. The chance to observe the initial moment of rule of law assistance and the relationships that were created among new development counterparts were significant for my being able to build the main analysis and argument of this book. I outlined accounts of rule of law assistance, exemplar rule of law actors and projects, rather than an exhaustive inventory of the field, and showed how the various ways of translating rule of law resulted in contestations among development counterparts. I suggested that the foreign organisations that sought to introduce rule of law in Myanmar were met by local and national counterparts who held different values and understandings of how best to approach development processes that involved the thing they all called 'rule of law'. In the confusions that accompanied new relationships being established, intermediaries emerged to navigate the spaces where counterparts needed to negotiate their different values and understandings. Development anthropologist Long's (2001) concept of an 'interface' – the spaces that emerge when development actors get together to contest, accommodate, or bridge their different values and understandings – uncovered the dynamic of interactions among counterparts. I suggested that the interface is a space that intermediaries navigate and where change happens in their hands. By analysing the interface, a space of contestation that has been overlooked by many studies of the rule of law assistance field was uncovered: the actors' differing motivations for engaging in rule of law development work; donors' lack of knowledge of the local setting; and the dynamics of power relations among donors, local counterparts, and intermediaries. To learn more about the outcomes and the potential unintended consequences of aid in illiberal states, these are aspects that need to be unpacked.

I argued that because international, national, and local understandings and approaches to rule of law development differed and were challenging to align, intermediaries emerged to mediate friction about issues such as monetary compensation; applications for funding; the best approach for achieving rule of law development; donor involvement in local affairs; and institutional constraints that, according to intermediaries, foreign actors were not able to fully grasp. I showed that issues were raised by local participants in relation to what they perceived as a divergence between their motivations and those of their foreign counterparts for engaging in rule of law development work. Issues were also raised that pertained to the knowledge of the local setting and power relations as donors were pushing their agenda. Competitive and contested ideas and approaches needed careful balancing by rule of law intermediaries who had to mediate between, and co-ordinate, counterparts. Reforms in Myanmar thus reopened or created fields of action for a great number of intermediaries.

# CHAPTER FIVE

# THE EMERGENCE OF INTERMEDIARIES

The reforms in Myanmar and the resulting development assistance reopened or created fields of action for intermediaries. In response to these new features, certain actors transformed themselves into intermediaries, either by drawing on their own capital to establish themselves as such or through their enrolment as part of foreign actors' desperate search for them.

Myanmar conforms to political anthropological theories about the emergence of intermediaries: a process of political change and/or intervention (Koster and Leynseele 2018). That political change can include, for example, authoritarian regimes transitioning to more democratic systems (Bierschenk et al. 2002). As a result, foreign development aid may increase and lead to new relationships between foreign and local actors that in turn give rise to intermediaries who negotiate between the two parties (de Sardan 2005). As one of the 'mechanisms' that separate groups can use to interact (Stovel and Shaw 2012:140), intermediaries become 'both product and producers of a new kind of society' (James 2011:335).

This chapter takes as its starting point the way intermediaries emerge in periods of societal transformation and governance transition. This emergence was possible to observe in real time, due to Myanmar's recent and unique transition, where international, national, and local structures gradually connected as development intervention escalated after 2010 (Décobert and Wells 2020). Civil society, the government, and foreign development agencies worked to accommodate increased project supply and funding (Ware 2013).

In response to the transition, young lawyers, seasoned NGO activists, consultants, and government officials became established in positions as intermediaries, either by drawing on their own capital to gain such position or through their enrolment as part of foreign actors' frantic search for individuals that could help them navigate unfamiliar systems and connect them to counterparts.

Observing intermediaries' emergence provides deeper understandings of the structure of development assistance. In this chapter, I argue that foreign development actors do not anoint intermediaries in an indiscriminate way: they are particularly cautious about engaging actors too closely connected to the military or who do not share their ideas of what human rights constitute. They look for intermediaries who understand their aims and objectives and who can function as representative 'vehicles of control' (Latour 1987) who believe in the facts that foreign donors wish to promote and who are willing to invest in such truths because they speak to their own interests. As a result of high demand but a limited supply of suitable intermediaries, foreign development actors compete for individuals who possess valued characteristics; to bolster the lack of supply, they support the creation of coalitions and invest in NGOs that can serve as competent intermediaries.

The chapter shows why foreign rule of law development actors seek intermediaries and why they view them as essential. It also examines the intermediaries' perspective to show how they compete for this development space and acquire their positions. Such revelations are fundamental for understanding aspects of structure and agency in the development sphere: for example, who gets to be included, who gets to exert influence, and why. What social processes transform certain actors into intermediaries, and why do foreign rule of law assistance actors seek them out?

The chapter concludes that the tendency of foreign actors to seek individuals with likeable personalities who are easy to work with has implications for rule of law assistance because it indicates that foreign actors chose people to work with out of convenience rather than influence. In addition, the inclination of foreign donors to work with the same group of intermediaries who move between donors and assignments resulted in the perception that many people supported foreign-funded initiatives while in fact, at the time, only a handful of people channelled much of the rule of law assistance to Myanmar.

This chapter proceeds next with an overview of how foreign practitioners expressed their need for intermediaries to build relationships with their intended counterparts. I show how intermediaries become imperative for foreign development actors attempting to gain traction because they can help them to understand a new cultural and linguistic setting. I argue that development actors enter into a competitive struggle to find competent intermediaries because of the difficulties of engaging in rule of law development work in a new setting.

Also, the strategies employed to create intermediaries was easily observed in Myanmar's young development setting. I show how foreign development actors affirmatively gathered individuals to form local NGOs. Some did this in order to fill their need for intermediaries while others based their development model on creating institutions deemed necessary for the rule of law. I then proceed to an illustration of how new opportunities in the rule of law assistance field resulted in local actors that drew on their established capital and new connections to set up organisations, or shifted their organisations' prevailing focus, to work on rule of law-related issues: they reinvented themselves as development consultants, local staff, and NGO leaders parallel to the processes of enrolment that donors engaged in.

## 5.1 A NEW MARKET: THE NEED FOR INTERMEDIARIES

In order to understand the demand for intermediaries in Myanmar and thus their emergence, it is necessary to review the challenges that foreign practitioners experienced when they arrived to promote rule of law in the country after the political transition in 2011.

As a reply to my questions about what it is that intermediaries do, foreign practitioners variously suggested that they required the assistance of intermediaries to gain access to, and build relationships with, their intended counterparts (Interviewees #7, 21 May 2014; #8, 22 May 2014; #9, 23 May 2014; #10, 12 May 2014; #20, 30 September 2014; #29, 23 October 2014; #40, 9 December 2014; #54, 25 September 2015; #56, 26 September 2015). For example, a foreign practitioner exclaimed: 'Burma is a new market, so how do we do it? It is incredibly difficult to get in' (Interviewee #20, 30 September 2014). What the practitioner was referring to was the general lack of understanding of how, or who, to best support when seeking to develop rule of law in Myanmar. The comment also touched on technical aspects of doing development and gaining access; intermediaries' abilities to exploit difficulties of access is a common theme in studies of intermediation globally (James 2011).

His comment was followed by a detailed explanation of the role played by his local staff (and intermediary), and other foreign develop-ment practitioners described similar sentiments – a perceived need for the assistance of intermediaries and the impossibility of performing development work without them:

> It would not be possible to do what I do without these players. It's important for me to go and talk to these people in their context. To understand what happens in states and regions, I don't know how I could have organized it without them. I would be less successful. It would have a direct impact on peoples' motivations.
>
> (Interviewee #8, 22 May 2014)

The quote suggests that there was a view that the foreign organisation would not have been able to implement rule of law assistance activities without the assistance of the local intermediary, who was responsible for enabling both access and ideas for how to support rule of law development.

There was a tendency by foreign development actors to look for intermediaries who could help them access the counterparts they sought. For example, one organisation that worked with local courts enrolled a former judge and had been 'thinking about hiring someone to "get to" the Attorney General, for example, a former employee' (Interviewee #25, 3 October 2014), although it had realised the prob-lems that might arise if hiring someone 'just because of their connec-tions' (ibid.). The differences in how development actors translated the rule of law and whom they sought as counterparts thus influenced the background characteristics of the intermediaries they enrolled.

This overview mirrors a common theme in development studies, that 'outsiders' need the help of 'insiders' who act as 'gatekeepers' to access new settings (Anderson and Olson 2003; Autesserre 2014; Roth 2015). The tendency for outsiders to become dependent on the insiders who act as gatekeepers results in their significant 'influence over the direc-tion and conduct of programs' (Anderson and Olson 2003:41). Such influence can result in foreign actors being out of touch 'with important sectors of society' (Mosse 1994). D'Exelle (2009) shows how intermedi-aries exert influence because they control information flows to aid providers that they are able to manipulate since they can deliver distorted messages of 'local needs' upwards, exclude actors and their interests, and also control the information flow to local communities on avenues to development assistance. He reminds us that 'one cannot assume that agents operating as intermediaries *at the interface* between their community and outside aid donors automatically and actively represent all community members' (D'Exelle 2009:1453, emphasis in original). A key variable for the possibility of aid reaching local populations, the study finds, is whether or not aid is captured in the hands of a small group of intermediaries rather than spread out across a more representative selection of individuals that do not hold themselves accountable only towards each other (see also Wanvoeke et al. 2016). D'Exelle presents a significant conclusion that donors across the spectrum of development intervention should take seriously: 'there is a strong case for a more active role for aid donors in searching and selecting community representatives' (D'Exelle 2009:1455). As this book later shows, those representatives that are easy to access may not be the most influential; nevertheless, they present the easier option when it comes to negotiating how much variation of rule of law understandings a foreign donor can accept.

Foreign actors' reliance on intermediaries was evident in Myanmar. One expression of this influence was seen in the way that intermediaries selected who got to be involved as local counterparts of rule of law assistance. A foreign lawyer and senior legal adviser explained the dilemma she faced when trying to organise development activities:

> He [intermediary] compiled an invitation list for our seminar, which was quite controversial. There were issues of hierarchy, who was on the list, who was there and who was not and so on. There was a perception from one or two that he selected groups of those who kind of . . . that he was biased. The groups and associations for most parts were perceived as not that democratic. I can't say to what extent who it was that selected the people we ended up with. I don't know why he selected these; I don't know the landscape well enough.
>
> (Interviewee #8, 22 May 2014)

A bilateral donor concurred when he complained about losing control over the activities they funded in Myanmar: 'In the beginning, we had a better overview of what was going on, but now there are so many groups, etc. Sometimes we don't even know what Pyoe Pin is doing – we do lots of stuff that we hardly know we are doing' (Interviewee #12, 7 May 2014). What he meant was that even an organisation like Pyoe

Pin that was set up with a lot of donor involvement and headed by foreigners was difficult to keep track of. Another foreign programme manager suggested that the intermediary had 'a lot of influence' in their organisation: 'He set up meetings which led us to hire the people we have' (Interviewee #3, 8 May 2014). The intermediary in question himself suggested that he

> helped many international organizations to find lawyers, who are the best fit for them. I also try to help local lawyers, for example, with their resumes in English (then they can learn more on the job) and also help them to understand the process of human rights ... some are involved in the NLD but not all ... I also like to help young lawyers to go abroad.
>
> (Interviewee #17, 23 Sep 2014)

During one of my visits to the lavish, perfume-scented lobby of the 'Traders' hotel (now Sule Shangri-La), which served as a mobile office for foreigners in need of air-conditioning, a respite from the buzzing of Yangon streets, and a good internet connection, I listened in to a conversation between two foreign lawyers who were the country managers of INGOs, one well known with offices across the globe (A), and one small, with operations only in Myanmar (B) (field notes, December 2014):

A:  He will be in demand when he comes back [from studies abroad].
B:  That's why we have to follow his wishes so that we can keep him away from people like you; we are basically only doing this project so that we can keep him.

The representative from the smaller INGO was happy that the local staff was back with them after having completed a study programme in the USA, but expressed concern that the bigger INGO would offer him a better salary and lure him away. The country representative then suggested that the price of keeping him was his autonomy to design and carry out projects. We can interpret this story as an indication that intermediaries wield influence (more such indications are presented in Table 5.1) that extends to steering the direction of rule of law assistance activities in Myanmar.

Intermediaries may substitute 'local voices' as they become representatives of those at the margins and we see a possible effect of intermediaries' influence: donors design interventions in ways that are beneficial for intermediaries rather than for the intended beneficiaries.

TABLE 5.1 Reliance on intermediaries

**Foreign practitioners describe their reliance on intermediaries**

He [intermediary] is the connection to a lot of different groups; he is the key person to reach out to local groups; it worries me a bit. Not surprisingly, things are very interpersonal. All our work is done through him, and I am a bit suspicious. I try to balance it a bit. Everything I hear from other people is that he is very principled and procedural, I trust him but, for example, he is a former political prisoner and has a lot of connections with the NLD and split up groups of the NLD which means that a lot of our partners relate to that. (Interviewee #3, 8 May 2014)

They became very reliant on one junior lawyer, and I told them this, I am pretty sure he chooses whom to talk with, which gives him a lot of power. They did acknowledge that it is an issue but say it's a necessity and see no other way forward. (Interviewee #41, 11 December 2014)

**Intermediaries explain how they experience their influence**

When it comes to choosing institutions or activities to support my opinion will be influential when it comes to material things, just a bit. (Interviewee #6, 19 May 2014)

First, they tried to do the trainings on their own, but they could do nothing without us. (Interviewee #14, 5 October 2014)

Without us, the [donor] initiative would probably not be as successful. (Interviewee #17, 23 September 2014)

I am much influential, [they] took my advice seriously because they know I know best. They think I do it. (Interviewee #17, 23 September 2014)

They pay 100% attention to my advice; they rely 100% on my knowledge. I really appreciate that. (Interviewee #55, 25 September 2015)

## 5.2 A NEW CULTURAL SETTING

In Myanmar's nascent rule of law assistance field, intermediaries become imperative for foreign development actors attempting to gain traction because they can help them to understand the new cultural setting. One foreign practitioner explained how it was only possible to 'get things done in the country both language- and culture-wise' with the assistance of an intermediary. Otherwise, he suggested, 'You can only scratch the surface' (Interviewee #2, 7 May 2014). The perceived complexity of hierarchical structures and reluctant government coun-terparts (as an effect of an authoritarian culture of secrecy and lack of transparency) caused foreign actors to suggest, anxiously, that they lacked significant information about 'What is really going on ...? How is the current system working? We just don't know' (Interviewee #9, 23 May 2014; see also Interviewee #35, 19 November 2014).

Foreign actors established contacts and networks outside formal channels (Interviewees #3, 8 May 2014; #5, 16 May 2014; #7, 21 May 2014) because they needed 'some internal route to get govern-ment information (for example draft laws) without hurting anyone' (Interviewee #5, 16 May 2014). Many of the foreign actors who arrived in Myanmar to work on rule of law assistance after 2011 had little experience working in similar settings. Save for a few senior consult-ants, many were young and inexperienced when it came to understand-ing authoritarian politics. While some had experience from a Southeast Asian setting (e.g., Cambodia), the positioning of foreign legal experts in that setting has some significantly different features, due to the extraordinary events that caused the creation of the United Nations Transitional Authority (Mayall 1996) and the subsequent Extraordinary Tribunal (Sperfeldt 2013). If foreign practitioners had worked previously during the democratisation periods in Indonesia or in China (prior to its reversion to autocracy under Xi Jinping), perhaps they would not think that hierarchy 'is really complex to understand' (Interviewee #5, 16 May 2014).

Foreign practitioners commonly mentioned a main cultural chal-lenge being communication and, in particular, the Myanmar concept of *anadeh* (e.g., Interviewee #54, 25 September 2015), which, according to one foreign practitioner, relates to power hierarchies and structures (Interviewee #8, 22 May 2014). Myanmar scholar Steinberg explains it as the 'unwillingness to embarrass the leadership (or any social superior) by bringing bad news, or causing someone to be uncomfort-able'. Such unwillingness relates to the 'strong hierarchical system within Burmese society that tends to enhance the authority of the leader and his or her power' (Steinberg 2001:42, 2013:153). Seekins' (2006) *Historical Dictionary of Burma (Myanmar)* describes *anadeh* as involving 'very strong inhibitions against asserting oneself in human relations described as shyness, embarrassment, or awkwardness. This is coupled with a strong sense of consideration for the feelings of others and a desire not to cause them to feel psychological distress or unease'. Examples of the social effects of *anadeh* include students' reluctance to ask a teacher questions for fear of distressing a superior or choosing not to reveal a serious illness to family members for fear of worrying them (Seekins' 2006). The concept thus influences aspects of everyday social life, not only relations with an authoritarian leadership or between subordinate and ruler.

According to intermediaries, it means 'being hesitant to disagree – we will not show it, this makes it a little bit difficult to detect the opinions of feelings and people involved' (Interviewee #6, 19 May 2014). One intermediary suggests that in practice it means that 'the Burmese person is not telling it all, you know *anadeh*' (Interviewee #10, 12 May 2014). A translator needs to understand when this is happening and 'has to be able to ask for more info by themselves – but this is not easy' (ibid.).

As a possible effect, there are challenges in working with foreign practitioners who are too direct in their communication. This was expressed by one intermediary: 'She is sometimes very straightforward and knows what she wants – this can be a bit of a culture clash sometimes' (Interviewee #17, 23 September 2014). Foreign practitioners, themselves, may understand that their directness of communication is an issue that is becoming pronounced in translation or that they choose to ignore to various degrees:

> It was a challenge also how direct we were in meetings, etc. We couldn't be very consultative, would send agenda ahead of time, in our mind they could change it. They got frustrated that they could not talk freely. We had to design for outcomes, but they want more discussion. Our national counterpart acts as interpreter; he is not interpreting only, sometimes there are bigger interpretation issues with a real interpreter, they don't soften things up the appropriate way, as we speak rather direct.
> (Interviewee #8, 22 May 2014)

> There is a fear of change and doing something different here. I tell him to say something direct and to not 'soften up' the message, but he will soften it up. Sometimes I will ask the translator straight away: 'did he soften it up?' and say that 'this needs to be direct.'
> (Interviewee #40, 9 December 2014)

Seekins (2006) suggests that there exists a tension between foreigners who interpret *anadeh* as an obstacle to free discussions about (and thus the development of) democracy and civil society, for example, and local and national actors whose high level of frankness in discussions may be regarded as aggression. The interview excerpts just cited suggest that foreign practitioners may be aware of the complexity of communication that is too direct but refrains from a change of approach. In light of Seekins' suggestion, the strategic ignorance towards such cultural aspects of communication is troubling.

## 5.3 'CUTTHROAT' PROCESSES TO 'GET' INTERMEDIARIES

Because of the difficulties of engaging in rule of law development work in a new setting, foreign actors enter into a competitive struggle to find competent intermediaries in Myanmar. A foreign lawyer and programme manager expressed his irritation with this, and suggested that the search for individuals (or groups of individuals) who could serve as intermediaries had turned into a ridiculous competition by 'internationals': 'There is a huge rush by internationals to get these people. Internationals are stealing each other's staff. It's like cutthroat processes' (Interviewee #2, 7 May 2014). Another foreign practitioner exclaimed that she needed 'to get one of those!' when we discussed the obstacles that her organisation experienced. 'One of those' meant an English-speaking Myanmar lawyer with knowledge and understanding of international ideas of human rights and the rule of law (Interviewee #3, 8 May 2014). A programme manager explained how it was comparatively difficult to set up a local team in Myanmar: 'We just could not find anyone. I hope someone can take over in two years' time. When we say that we want them to take over, they might feel overwhelmed, so much demand for people like them' (Interviewee #4, 15 May 2014). Similar notions were expressed by several foreign development practitioners, who complained, for example, that '[i]t is difficult to find bridging organizations and individuals, all are so busy' (Interviewee #15, 22 September 2014) or that 'there are not many people available, they are overburdened' (Interviewee #5, 16 May 2014).

The frustration that foreign practitioners felt is not unusual in transitional settings where development activities are overwhelming, or where, as in Myanmar, the host government has little previous experience of hands-on interactions with the international community. Carruthers and Halliday (2006:576) show that it can be more difficult to find competent and loyal intermediaries in settings where there are great gaps between the 'global' and the 'local' which might 'lead to competition for intermediaries among international agencies, between global and local actors, and even among local actors'. They are describing Indonesia, but we see a similar phenomenon also in Myanmar.

As a consequence of the competition, a common understanding by foreign practitioners was that most staff would not hesitate to leave their contract when a better offer was made by a competing organisation (Interviewee #2, 7 May 2014; interviewee #3, 8 May 2014):

> He was a practising lawyer, worked for a donor and completed his two-year contract which is very uncommon as these guys get offers from everywhere every day, USAID tries to snatch everyone, so it was a big thing that he stayed through the contract period.
>
> (Interviewee #29, 23 October 2014)

Foreign practitioners' movement between contracts and organisations was, on the other hand, never described as an issue. A follow-up in 2016 suggested that a majority of the foreign practitioners I interviewed in 2014 had either left their jobs in Myanmar or changed employers. Switching between employers and assignments is not surprising because intermediaries might be more interested in building their own social capital than in supporting the specific objectives of foreign organisations (see also James 2011). For example, a foreign practitioner explained his local staffs' unwillingness to take more responsibility for the organisation with reference to the cultural notion of *anadeh*: 'We would all like him to be more assertive and take on more, but it's *anadeh*, he doesn't want to do it. We would like to see him take a stronger role' (Interviewee #48, 10 October 2014). The intermediary himself, on the other hand, suggested that he did not want to take on a leadership role within the INGO because he had other political goals, even though he perceived that what he learned there in relation to access to justice was politically important and thus related to his political work (Interviewee #55, 25 September 2015).

### 5.3.1 'Pick-Ups'

Donor events and conferences provided ample opportunities for foreign practitioners to find local partner organisations, staff, and consultants (Interviewees #19, 25 September 2014; #8, 22 May 2014; #15, 22 September 2014). One foreign practitioner suggested that it was '[after] 2008/2009 you would see people stand up [at events] and speak English' (Interviewee #12, 7 May 2014). A foreign lawyer and practitioner replied to my question about how her organisation enrolled the local intermediary by saying: 'I met [him] through various [laughs] rule of law conferences and trainings' (Interviewee #8, 22 May 2014). Another foreign practitioner described the process of finding local partners: 'We got a snowball connection through several groups. In Yangon, we have just been going to events and conferences. Who else should we meet? Brought us to other people; it is a slow and informal process' (Interviewee #15, 22 September 2014). One foreign practitioner was not sure how they ended up with a local intermediary: 'Somehow he was appointed as the coordinator of the new steering committee – I am not sure how it happened as there were some strange translations going on during that meeting' (Interviewee #8, 22 May 2014).

For local practitioners, donor events provide a novel opportunity to be discovered by foreign actors. A local intermediary, a junior English-speaking lawyer, explains how he got his first job for an international organisation:

> I was 'picked up' during a conference led by a South African NGO, where I was leading one of the working groups. I got a chance to speak and presented on behalf of my group. Probably in that workshop, some people saw me as a potential candidate. [They] came up to me to discuss, they wanted my opinion. They asked if I wanted to be a part of [NGO]. I was their consultant, my first international job.
>
> (Interviewee #14, 5 October 2014)

A similar process of being enrolled as an intermediary was described by another local lawyer: 'I met [foreign practitioner] at a conference I was facilitating and he invited me to Geneva' (Interviewee #17, 23 September 2014). The intermediary then became a legal adviser for the organisation that the foreign practitioner in question worked for. A local practitioner suggested that his previous engagement with pro-democracy work for a foreign organisation meant that he '[g]ot a lot of friends' and that therefore '[t]he donor chased me up' (Interviewee #24, 14 October 2014). The 'pick-up' also extended to one foreign practitioner who had been asked to come for a meeting and then asked to travel to Nay Pyi Taw to support a national rule of law actor (Interviewee #41, 11 December 2014).

De Jong (2018:619) has suggested: 'The ambition to leave a marginal social status could provide the impetus for seeking intermediary roles.' For individuals in Myanmar, opportunities to work for foreign organisations often resulted in opportunities and higher remuneration for junior professionals with English skills than they might otherwise have had access to. However, no local respondents mentioned financial remuneration as a motivation for their work with foreign organisations, even though they were aware that some believed that it was higher earnings that motivated them (see, e.g., Interviewee #17, 23 September 2014).

Local intermediaries who had been picked up by foreign actors continued to work for various donors on different projects and contracts. Intermediaries themselves were reluctant to reveal the extent of the activities and the full range of actors they were entangled with; they were careful in balancing their various roles. For example, one foreign practitioner suggested that when they set up their office in 2012, they tried to hire a local lawyer but the person they had in mind '[w]ould have been a candidate but was too busy; [instead] we hired him as a local consultant, he's a bit sensitive about all his contracts. We started the organization quickly with [him] advising, at that time he wasn't quite as busy with advising everybody, then we hired his friend instead' (Interviewee #48, 10 October 2014).

An effect of the competition to find suitable intermediaries and their resulting parallel engagements also indicates that at this time only a handful of people acted as conduits for much of the initial rule of law assistance to Myanmar. In Callon's (1986:12) terms, relationships had been established with a few who became representatives of 'the masses'; consequently, '[t]hat which is true for a few is true for the whole population'. On that note, a foreign practitioner also addressed the concern that most of the recipients of their assistance were the same people:

> The biggest problem to describing rule of law or justice issues is that we work with the same group of lawyers all the time. It is interesting that it is always the same people ... Some foreigners who have provided training are for example surprised that people understand the basic principles and 'know the answers', but it's always the same people attending all these trainings, and they have learned the answers ... These people know what donors want to hear (i.e., the people who want to rise to the top)[;] some are more controversial.
>
> (Interviewee #3, 8 May 2014)

This dynamic is not unique to Myanmar: Nicholson and Low (2013) find, in the case of Vietnam, that the distinction between roles and agencies was not always clear because the same individuals worked for donors, government legal agencies, or government advisory boards simultaneously. Rodriguez-Garavito (2011:160) in his analysis of judicial reform in Latin America observes that 'actors in one project may simultaneously or sequentially participate in the other's networks'. Halliday and Carruthers's (2009:297) observation that the channel 'through which the global/local reformist encounters flow' is narrow was also an accurate description of Myanmar in the transition period in relation to the aid flows that came in to support the rule of law. The small cohort of intermediaries that were profiting on development influx before the 2015 elections had transitioned by 2020 to other fields of work or had lost reputation, and were seeking opportunities with employers to whom they were less well known. The narrow field had become wider and was filling up with more young and eager interlocutors.

### 5.3.2 The Importance of Personality

Myanmar employers valued people who were 'very likeable' (Interviewee #48, 10 October 2014), had 'confidence', knew 'how to interact with foreigners', and were easy conversationalists and relationship builders (Interviewee #25, 3 October 2014). One programme manager acknowledged: 'It is who we hired that has been important. He [intermediary] gets along very well with our director. It is very personality-based' (Interviewee #3, 8 May 2014). Another stated: '[Y]ou also have to think about who you want to sit in an office with, he is very devoted, we interviewed a lot of people, but he definitely stood out as the best' (Interviewee #29, 23 October 2014). We see that in finding suitable people and organisations to work with in Myanmar, personality matters. These descriptions are similar to Gonzalez's (1972) portrayal of typical development brokers who are educated abroad, have 'cosmopolitan' manners, and are fluent in English, which enables them to instil foreigners with a feeling of ease. That intermediary actors possess certain likeable personalities is inherent in the conceptual definition of an 'intermediary actor', which rests on the condition that they are relationship builders.

However, these attributes may have had a particular significance in authoritarian Myanmar where formal processes are opaque and relationship and trust building among various partners is essential. An NGO tasked with donor co-ordination concurred that local organisations viewed 'relationships with donors and INGOs as a matter of personality' and considered that 'personalities and interpersonal communication style were seen as the determinants of successful funding partnership' (Local Resource Centre 2012:14). That is to say, likeability is not simply a matter of making the workplace a friendlier and more relaxed setting in which to get things done. The importance of personality rests on the intuition that 'a person or corporation with a certain charisma' will be better at conveying ideas about development assistance than someone without it (Rottenburg 2013, cited in Behrends et al. 2014:18).

An effect of this tendency to prioritise intermediaries with likeable personalities is that individuals with local influence can easily be overlooked. Foreign actors sought individuals who were 'easy to work with' (Interviewee #41, 11 December 2014) and they prized this convenience. Those who were 'good at talking' (Interviewee #3, 8 May 2014) rather than those most qualified and senior (Interviewee #48, 10 October 2014) were often prioritised, which led to resentment and anger by those bypassed local actors who, for example, did not possess the same facility with English. I sensed the tension when a senior local lawyer exclaimed: 'They get much attention from the international side, but they are not influential with us ... He is junior but has way too much power' (Interviewee #47, 9 December 2014). Such sentiments might also come as a result of senior lawyers' perception of their own hard struggle for legal development for the past decades, while it is the younger generation of lawyers who are now reaping the benefits and making a substantial living out of development projects after the transition. Resentment follows from the view that the younger generation has not sacrificed but has been rewarded nonetheless. (For a discussion about various notions of 'sacrifice' during decades of democracy struggle in Myanmar, see Mullen 2016.) However, these feelings that were being expressed, in combination with an overview of who was working on rule of law in the transition period, does raise questions about how much impact a young inexperienced lawyer can have on the type of institutions that rule of law actors typically try to engage. So, in this case, intermediaries' influence on the state of rule of law development per se might not have been where their main influence lay; rather, it was their influence as potential agents in the field that managed to stir resentment resulting in poor reception of foreign assistance to the rule of law sector, as compared to what could have been the case if foreign donors chose to work with people with real influence in a hierarchical system. So, while the preference for interpersonal and communicative skills is not surprising, it is potentially an

intricate problem in a setting that is culturally and linguistically difficult to grasp and where interventions require people who can connect
to spaces of power. One consequence of these current approaches is that
they may lead to what Autesserre (2014) frames as a problem of
intermediaries who neglect large groups of communities because they
are, in fact, disconnected from them. Relying too heavily on people
with likeable personalities thus comes with the risk of not lending
support to other networks that can and should be sustained.

### 5.3.3   Personal Qualities in Lieu of Rule of Law Knowledge

Foreign rule of law actors expressed that intermediaries' lack of rule of
law understanding or a legal education could be compensated for by
their personal qualities:

> My previous colleague was excellent; I took him everywhere. He was
> lovely, competent. The fact that he was not a lawyer complicated some
> things, but it did not really matter.
>
> (Interviewee #2, 7 May 2014)

> There is not much domestic experience in this area. Luckily our staff is
> fast learners and good at relationship building. It is difficult to find local
> staff in the areas we work with. Our senior staff was referred to us by
> UNDP, we took a chance as she had not worked much with rule of law,
> but her personal qualities were important. She had other development
> experience instead.
>
> (Interviewee #25, 3 October 2014)

> Staying with us gives him a lot of respect; he is not a lawyer. He was for
> example set up as a facilitator for a conference, local lawyers laughed at
> him, but a lot of people loved him, which gave him some credibility.
>
> (Interviewee #3, 8 May 2014)

The selection of non-lawyers as intermediaries for rule of law development work is interesting in light of the professional status of the actors
at whom foreign rule of law assistance is often targeted: Myanmar
lawyers. Foreign actors seek resemblances to rule of law as it is found
in its original setting, where lawyers are often central to supporting its
ideals. They do this regardless of the fact that a lawyer's work in
Myanmar differs dramatically from much of the work that lawyers
perform in the settings where foreign practitioners originate from
(see, e.g., Cheesman 2015). However, similarly to what Carruthers
and Halliday (2006) find in relation to intermediaries in Indonesia, in

Myanmar's transition setting, intermediaries who could channel rule of law were particularly scarce because opportunities to learn English and gain an understanding of global concepts (e.g., human rights and rule of law) had been limited during military rule. In particular, foreign development actors had a hard time accepting intermediaries who did not believe in universal human rights. This got clearer in the wake of anti-Muslim violence during 2012 and 2013. Many erstwhile advocates of the rule of law and human rights then revealed themselves as Islamophobes and racists. As one foreign lawyer and programme manager explained: '[S]ome national advisers had to leave us as they realized that their goals did not match Human Rights when they realized that the people they don't like (like the Bengalis) should also have Human Rights' (Interviewee #29, 23 October 2014), which underpins the substantive rule of law that the UN definition espouses. But the quote also indicates that intermediaries needed to understand concepts like human rights similar to a foreign well-educated human rights expert and advocate (which was the profile of the foreign practitioner). In effect, when lawyers were difficult to find, intermediaries' lack of rule of law understanding and legal education was compensated for by personal qualities.

## 5.4 STRATEGIES TO CREATE INTERMEDIARIES

When I asked a foreign rule of law consultant about the status of one organisation frequently mentioned by rule of law practitioners – in order to find out if it was a 'local' initiative – the reply was interesting: 'I don't think I can comment on that [smiles], I think you understand the thing, they say they are . . .' (Interviewee #40, 9 December 2014). When suitable intermediaries are not readily available, foreign rule of law development actors create them. They do this through supporting the creation of coalitions and NGOs that can help them channel rule of law in its new setting. Bierschenk et al. (2002) suggest that development actors often prefer associations and organisations over individuals as intermediaries because, arguably, coalitions provide less room for non-transparent and unchecked activity. Within such organisations, actors with outside connections are the ones that usually take on the role as leaders.

In Myanmar's young development setting, the creation of organisations was easily observed: foreign development actors affirmatively gathered individuals to form local NGOs. Some did this in order to fill their need for intermediaries while others based their business model on creating institutions deemed necessary for rule of law.

## 5.5   GATHER PEOPLE WHO SUPPORT RULE OF LAW

The set-up of new coalitions and organisations involved the identification of people who seemed 'to be doing good stuff' whom foreign actors helped 'off the ground' in order to 'facilitate and enable' (Interviewee #28, 22 October 2014; see also Interviewee #24, 14 October 2014):

> We support coalitions of interest; if you pick up the right issues, they will help influence the rules of the game both formally and informally. Coalitions don't necessarily exist ... you identify the actors who have an interest in rule of law; they might be both formal and informal. We have networks through the team. Who has influence where? How do we build both horizontal and vertical relationships?

For example, a well-known programme that worked on rule of law-related issues had been initiated by a small group of people representing foreign humanitarian donors 'during dictatorship' in order to reach civil society (Interviewee #12, 7 May 2014). A programme manager explained the rationale:

> We thought we wanted to do something with rule of law, but not going to court or anything, we don't have any lawyers, we want to develop legal awareness and networks, etc. and see how actors can work together. We are not promoting the rule of law, no one is, we are building capacity so that people can do it.
>
> (Interviewee #20, 30 September 2014)

Another coalition of law firms and lawyers was also created with foreign involvement, established after a sponsored visit to South Africa to study legal aid. A programme manager described it thus: 'We choose people with the idea to build relationships between government and civil society ... [I]t was about finding those key leaders' (Interviewee #24, 14 October 2014).

Instead of creating new organisations, foreign development actors also worked with existing organisations that, as a result of interactions, moved their activities towards rule of law. Michael (2004:171) describes such practice as one of donors positively encouraging 'local NGOs to branch into new areas of development'. A foreign programme manager (Interviewee #20, 30 September 2014) elaborated on their positive encouragement of one local NGO into areas of rule of law:

> They were not an obvious way to work with rule of law, but we respected their work, we are friends with them. The embassy was friendly with them previously ... there was a very small circle back in those days. They operated below the radar, below the surface, getting farmers together which sounds innocent but is not. Back then, they did not describe their work as rule of law. We sat down for three days and considered what we should do; we went through potential areas. The idea of doing something legal, something with the law started to take hold. We started talking about how we could involve lawyers a bit more, how could we get lawyers and civil society together? Seems funny today, but this was 2010. They knew this law firm, had some friends who were lawyers.
>
> I was out with someone from the donor about a month before we submitted the proposal – we had some drinks, and I suggested the local partner. He was a bit dubious about how that would work; he had not seen them in that light before. They were the 'wishy-washy folks', farmers and artists, this would be a bit of a departure for them, but they are an organization that would be able to do such work, it did not need sector expert knowledge. Then all of a sudden they are involved in rule of law.

These examples suggest that foreign development actors looked for supporters of rule of law and when such people were not readily available, they created new organisations to play an intermediary function. Foreign development promoters become invested in particular actors, and they expect certain outcomes (Décobert and Wells 2020). This dynamic is not unique to Myanmar: Halliday and Carruthers's (2009:302) observations from China and Indonesia are that foreign actors struggle to 'find intermediaries who are competent, influential and loyal' and therefore form alliances with local NGOs or, if no appropriate organisation exists, create them to provide an intermediary function. 'However, actors do not always behave in ways that donors expect, and programs may have unforeseen outcomes ... Actors, who were constructed in a particular way, no longer respond or act in that way' (Décobert and Wells 2019:297).

While scrutiny of foreign organisations' support to local NGOs with potential ties to specific spaces of politics and power is imperative, in order to avoid some of the harmful effects of aid (Hilhorst and Jansen 2003), in Myanmar, it was mainly local organisations that pushed back on donor involvement or refrained from working on issues they deemed too sensitive. When doing so, they risked being labelled as inappropriate counterparts (Interviewee #3, 8 May 2014; see also Décobert and Wells 2020). One example of one such sensitive issue that local NGOs wanted to refrain from, but that foreign donors sometimes pushed for, was anything that involved the Rohingya Muslim minority (Interviewee #29, 23 October 2014). According to local respondents, this was a highly contested area to work in that could ruin an organisation's local reputation and lose them respect (Interviewee #33, 11 November 2014). Anderson and Olson (2003) have previously stressed the potential for foreign organisations to worsen divisions among conflicting groups by advocating for and appearing to favour a specific side which is often a marginalised group.

When foreign development actors created new organisations in Myanmar, even when these were presented as local initiatives, they ended up operating with foreign involvement through regular guidance and the sending of 'experts' to advise (Interviewees #14, 5 October 2014; #20, 30 September 2014; #24, 14 October 2014). More direct attempts at steering activities were sustained through the positioning of foreign practitioners who could serve as direct channels of communication from donors to those on the ground. In terms of sustainability and effectiveness, one practitioner expressed annoyance over the fact that the foreign donors who funded the local initiative she worked for repeatedly bypassed senior Myanmar colleagues and asked her for certain information directly: 'The donors are very sneaky, I don't sit above anyone else, I am the local organization's counterpart. Still, donors try to contact me directly as it is an easier and quicker way coming through me' (Interviewee #40, 9 December 2014). Another foreign practitioner who was placed with a local organisation suggested that donors contacted her directly to get reporting, 'probably because I am more responsive and easier to communicate with' (Interviewee #53, 5 October 2015). Hilhorst and Jansen (2003:7) have also suggested that the rationale for such placements by donors may be to minimise mismanagement of funds by having ex-pats 'managing, advising and reporting'. Such strategies for 'implement[ing] programs in a way that fosters dependency on outside "experts" who are constantly brought in to run activities' (Anderson and Olson 2003:26) presented challenges of credibility and legitimacy in Myanmar where foreign organisations, even when fronted by local registration or local consultants, were continuously perceived as 'foreign' and thus less trustworthy (Interviewee #24,

14 October 2014). In illiberal regimes, these forms of NGO activities with foreign support can be perceived as a form of interference in domestic politics (Risse and Babayan 2015). Underestimating sentiments of distrust towards thinly disguised international involvement in 'local' organisations may also pose a risk of increasing that distrust (see Chapter 7). This has been observed in other illiberal settings like China and Russia where strict regulations that target foreign NGOs that conduct development and advocacy activities have been put in place (Blake and Bartlett 2015; Phillips 2016; Wong 2016). In China, foreign NGOs, if at all allowed to exist, are heavily scrutinised and operate under government instruction, thus in practice encumbering them of their influence as mediators between the state and the people (Kellogg 2020). Post the 2015 elections in Myanmar, deemed a democratic victory for the country, foreign practitioners in conversation perceived a narrowed room for engagement in the country, possibly as it started to dawn on them that from the initial optimism of transition towards democracy, what could be expected was rather a hybrid form of authoritarian rule (see Stokke and Aung 2020) as the military continued its grip on power.

Ultimately, when donors sideline existing local organisations through a preference for ones created with foreign involvement, this has implications for development sustainability (Anderson and Olson 2003). Hilhorst and Jansen (2003:6), writing about the neighbouring field of humanitarian aid, suggest that because 'many NGOs are the offspring of INGO operations', special attention needs to be paid 'to … [the] extent [to which] they are rooted in society, and to what extent they really represent the intended target group'. In fragile contexts, such strategies may even have destabilising effects (Anderson and Olson 2003). In their historical overview of international aid to Myanmar, Décobert and Wells (2020:295) argue that aid promoters from abroad have made shifting 'decisions about who are legitimate socio-political actors and agents of change' or 'illegitimate pariahs' throughout different times in history. Such strategies, they argue, 'can have significant impacts on long-term development and peace'. The set-up of new organisations also matters in light of repeated calls for 'local ownership' of development processes (Bosch 2016) because constructing such ownership on behalf of foreign interests, coupled with intermediary organisations that respond to donor objectives, may result in distorted understandings of local-level grievances.

## 5.6 OPPORTUNITIES IN THE RULE OF LAW ASSISTANCE FIELD

Local actors also drew on their established capital and new connections to set up organisations or shifted prevailing focus, to work on rule of law-related issues. They reinvented themselves as development consultants, local staff, or NGO leaders parallel to the processes of enrolment that donors engaged in.

Bierschenk et al. (2002:24) suggest that development brokers enter their career as opportunities present themselves, rather than after careful planning to obtain such roles. Therefore, they say, the nature of existing development configuration results in situations where brokers are more likely to 'respond to the dynamics of "project availability" than to "sell" initiatives originating "at the bottom"'. The result of this, they suggest, is that, as local development brokers intervene in existing systems that change due to the influx of aid, they may disrupt the existing political balance, by aggravating antagonisms or forming biases to their own benefit (gaining monopoly) through the use of certain strategies that create patron–client relations. Cohen and Comaroff (1976), on the other hand, find that local leaders build careers by constructing the need for intermediary roles and services.

In Myanmar's emerging rule of law assistance field, it seems that NGOs and coalitions have been able to mobilise if not fully transparently then at least more so than was possible for NGOs operating during military rule (Liddell 1997; South 2008). This coalesced with their increased 'discovery' by foreign organisations that offered them funding. Local NGOs thus transformed from working on pure advocacy activities into being positioned as intermediaries for foreign actors.

### 5.6.1 Reinventions

Foreign practitioners experienced 'an uprising of [local rule of law] organizations – everything has just expanded' (Interviewee #9, 23 May 2014; see also Interviewee #12, 7 May 2014). These local organisations had 'charismatic leaders', took 'a lot of funding' (Interviewee #3, 8 May 2014), and were 'popular with international organizations' because 'they are young and switched on' (Interviewee #8, 22 May 2014) according to foreigners that were around to work on rule of law at the time. Reflecting on the change, one foreign practitioner suggested that it had been in the period post the 2010 elections that many rule of law groups, made up of former pro-democracy people, sprang up, which led to rings on the water for others to feel more comfortable in advocating (Interviewee #53, 5 October 2015). Another practitioner reflected on the change she saw:

> The first time I came [to Myanmar] was in 2009. Then there were few names you would always go to, now that pool is expanding. When people learn how to play this game, I think the roles that people play also change. My impression would be that I have met some people or groups ... my impression is that they change roles, for example, one organization I see has changed from being mainly engaged in information giving to positioning themselves for funding, and then they change ...
>
> (Interviewee #7, 21 May 2014)

The leader of one local NGO suggested that the organisation's focus on strengthening civil society had changed after the 2010 elections, so that it now, as he explained, had become a pioneer organisation for rule of law: '[W]e realized that rule of law is needed for democracy. The government understanding is very different from the one by people; the government wants rule by law. There was a big change after 2010. There was little space to mobilise before' (Interviewee #30, 24 October 2014). This NGO leader was, however, not entirely positive about the increased amount of funding that they had managed to attract after the arrival of foreign donors in Myanmar; in his view, he had to struggle to carry out the organisation's own agenda while pushing back on foreign funders. A similar suggestion came from a local project manager in Myanmar who commented: '[R]ule of law is now on everybody's mission and vision but then they do all these different things and assume that they work on it' (Interviewee #46, 9 December 2014). The same interviewee was concerned by the fact that so many local NGOs had sprung up 'really overnight, you would be surprised' to work on 'prefabricated donor programmes' that oftentimes involved data collection. She elaborated:

> It's supposed to be rule of law in a very down to earth way, with farmers, all of a sudden they become NGOs. You can't turn a farmer into a researcher all of a sudden. All of a sudden many little civil societies and rural-based organizations are doing legal awareness training then they collect data. Bringing those data back together and getting their conclusions worry me, it doesn't mean their data is valid. They don't

apply data collection methods. There is no objectivity; they have already determined what they want to find.

Other examples of organisations that reinvented themselves in the rule of law field included a law practice that was established in 2010 but by 2012 had moved into NGO work focusing more on legal aid and awareness training (Interviewee #17, 23 September 2014). The same year the leader of the NGO had met a foreign scholar who called 'to ask many questions [about rule of law] . . . there was more talk about Human Rights before that' (ibid.). He suggested that it was after his conversation with the scholar from abroad that he had got into rule of law-focused work. Two local practitioners and NGO leaders concurred: 'Before 2013 we were not interested in rules of law [sic], but now we are interested in connecting rules of law and human rights, we will incorporate rules of law in future training' (Interviewees #22 and #23, 2 October 2014). The NGO leaders explained that they had started some rule of law training based on a 'rule of law checklist' they had got from a foreign lawyer. Another NGO was established after a study tour abroad to learn about opportunities for rule of law development. The organisation's leader explained the rationale for setting up the new NGO: 'I learned a lot during the trip, after I went back and founded the [NGO] . . . [with a] colleague I know from the human rights training at the British Council' (Interviewee #33, 11 November 2014).

One important implication emerging from this overview is that, even if we see local actors who 'reinvent' themselves within the rule of law assistance field so as to emerge as intermediaries, much of the work targeted especially at the rule of law assistance industry is often inspired to some extent by foreign involvement or influence. For some intermediaries, the influx of foreign development actors, however, results in burden rather than opportunity.

### 5.6.2 Intermediaries on the Government Side

Due to the continued complexities of the country's authoritarian politics with most government staff residing in the isolated capital, Nay Pyi Taw, where they have their daily moves monitored and opportunities to meet foreigners except at formal government meetings are few opportunities to leave a government job to gain better-paid opportunities with foreign actors in Myanmar circa 2014 were limited. Out of my local respondents, only one was a former judge who had left a government job to work for a foreign donor. The respondent suggested that such a move had been possible for her because people knew what stance and opinions she had had towards the government (Interviewee #27, 7 October 2014). Thus, based on her critiques of the previous government and the limits of her job, she was taken for someone sufficiently trustworthy to work on questions of rule of law improvement. I was also handed a business card of a judge who allegedly searched for opportunities with foreign actors. I was, however, never able to get in touch with him: emails bounced back, and his mobile was switched off.

As I sought to speak with government agencies as counterparts in rule of law programming, I also found their intermediaries. In the case of Indonesia, Carruthers and Halliday (2006) observe that, while foreign development actors will seek intermediaries who are invested in their ideologies and global models, national actors will seek intermediaries who serve their national interests. While this may also be the case in Myanmar in the longer term, in this start-up phase for rule of law assistance, what seemed to matter most was the extent to which the intermediary had any English language skills. It is often the few who speak English who are put in positions to 'deal with the internationals' (Interviewee #47, 9 December 2014). As in other young development settings, these intermediaries are 'bombarded' with meetings (Interviewee #5, 16 May 2014): the influx of international rule of law development actors put pressure on government actors, who faced an increase in requests for meetings and collaborations as well as being the target of direct critique. Intermediaries' positioning provided a way to buffer direct demands from foreigners. One foreign intermediary suggested that sometimes government actors requested the assistance of trusted international consultants to help explain the difficulties and challenges they faced to other internationals (Interviewee #41, 11 December 2014):

> They [Union Attorney General's Office] had asked me to come on my own. I was a bit nervous. Would they arrest me? Throw me out of the country? . . . I was taken to a room to meet with them. At the meeting, they said: 'we know what you do . . . we are tired of the internationals being upset with us all the time, can you help us explain to them?' I told them that if they have their reasons for doing things in a certain way, then they should explain to the internationals why. They were a bit afraid to do this, so I did it with them.

What differs here from the intermediary actors who reinvent themselves to find more lucrative opportunities in the new development field is that the position as government intermediary was less appreciated. Government staff were often put in an intermediary position on an involuntary basis. One such person, for example, told me about the ambivalent feelings he had towards such work: 'It torments me a lot, I don't feel like I am qualified for the task, I feel trapped in this role … At the moment I am stuck here, they need me, but I am hoping to move on someday' (Interviewee #34, 18 November 2014). The quote reflects the complex situation that government employees were in as they reluctantly had to accept their position, in contrast to the more enthusiastic non-government intermediaries, who were able to make a good living out of their positions.

## 5.7 CONCLUSION

The reforms in Myanmar and the resulting development assistance reopened or created fields of action for intermediaries. This chapter asked questions about how certain actors are transformed into intermediaries and why. I argued that intermediaries gain and exert influence in the rule of law assistance field because actors from abroad, who lack cultural and linguistic knowledge, are reliant on them to carry out their development activities.

The chapter illustrated the way that intermediaries emerge in periods of societal transformation and governance transition, which was possible to observe in real time in Myanmar due to its recent and unique transition. I showed how international, national, and local structures gradually connected as development intervention escalated after 2010. In response to the transition, young lawyers, seasoned NGO activists, consultants, and government officials became established in positions as intermediaries, either by drawing on their own capital to gain such positions or through their enrolment as part of foreign actors' frantic search for individuals that could help them navigate unfamiliar systems and connect them to counterparts.

Observing intermediaries' emergence provided deeper understandings of the structure of development assistance. I argued that foreign development actors do not anoint intermediaries in an indiscriminate way and that they look for intermediaries who understand their aims and objectives to function as suitable representatives. I suggested that, as a result of high demand but limited supply of suitable intermediaries, foreign development actors compete for individuals who possess valued characteristics such as wide networks and likeable personalities. To bolster the lack of supply, they support the creation of coalitions and invest in NGOs that can serve as competent intermediaries.

The chapter showed why development actors from abroad seek intermediaries and why they view them as essential. It also presented the intermediaries' perspective to show how they compete for a part of the development space and acquire their interface positions. Such revelations are fundamental for understanding aspects of structure and agency in the development sphere: for example, who gets to be included, who gets to exert influence, and why.

I suggested that the tendency of donors from abroad to seek individuals with likeable personalities who are easy to work with has implications for rule of law assistance because it indicates that foreign actors choose people to work with out of convenience rather than influence. In addition, the inclination of foreign donors to work with the same group of intermediaries who move between donors and assignments resulted in the perception that a lot of people supported foreign-funded initiatives while in fact, at the time, only a handful of people with significant capital channelled much of the rule of law assistance to Myanmar.

# CHAPTER SIX

# INTERMEDIARIES: BACKGROUND, CAPITAL, MOTIVATIONS

Becoming an effective intermediary requires social capital of the kind envisaged by Bourdieu (1986) – resources linked to a sustainable network, including resources accessed through connections to other actors (Lin 2001). Equally important is their access to foreign capital which – following Dezalay and Garth (2002) – is made up of contacts, knowledge, and education accessed through actors from abroad. Intermediaries accumulated both social and foreign capital during the period of military rule before political transition after elections in 2010.

When the field of rule of law assistance opened up following political transition, both types of capital were central for intermediaries' positioning as actors 'in between' foreign, national, and local development counterparts because connections to 'internal' and 'external' spaces of knowledge are a prerequisite for carrying out an intermediary function (Gonzalez 1972; Mendras and Mihailescu 1982). Intermediaries' success in what they do springs from a combination of personal 'charisma' (see Lidholm 2018), the possession of large networks, and the control of knowledge. Intermediaries have 'development skills, English skills, confidence, [and] knows how to interact with foreigners' (Interviewee #48, 10 October 2014). This is a theme that runs through the history of intermediation.

Intermediaries accumulate social capital via their engagement in local-level politics, which forms the basis for their countrywide networks. Linkages to political activities contribute to some individuals being identified as 'reform-minded', which leads to them catching the attention of actors from abroad who offer their support in the form of contacts with actors outside the country's borders, new knowledge, foreign education, and more. Donors from the outside thus apply 'international strategies' (Dezalay and Madsen 2012) to instil local change through individuals who strategically use their social capital as a means to attain other purposeful goals (Lin 2001).

Ma Thida Aye is one such person. Around the time of political transition, she had recently returned from studying for a Master's degree in international relations and human rights in the USA. She was excited to tell me about her diverse background, and the different places her social and political engagements had taken her in life. Not long before we met in 2014, Ma Thida Aye had been offered a place on an exposure trip to learn from other transitional settings, arranged by a foreign rule of law donor. The opportunity to learn from other settings, lawyers, and examples, she told me, inspired her to start her own legal aid-focused NGO.

'Having the voluntary spirit' had always been Ma Thida Aye's key motivation in life, she recounted with a smile. As a junior lawyer, she spent most of her time defending farmers in her local village. She laughed as she remembered how she would upset local officials when she offered poor farmers her legal services free of charge. Already, as a university student, Ma Thida Aye was engaged in student politics and supported the National League for Democracy (NLD). She also studied English at the American Center in Yangon during her student years. The English classes, however, involved 'a lot more than English' and, after a while, Ma Thida Aye also joined a political book club. It was via her engagements with that foreign institutional presence in Myanmar that she was later able to study abroad with a scholarship. Ma Thida Aye made a lot of friends through her political engagements and English studies. She told me that the people she met at the American Center now worked 'all over the place' for different development organisations.

In addition to running her own legal aid NGO, Ma Thida Aye also works for a foreign organisation that supports judicial reform and legal aid development. She explained that she is well suited to work with a foreign organisation because she was in America for a long time, which, according to her, means that she knows 'how to deal with their nature ... I don't have a problem to deal with *them* [foreigners]'. Ma Thida Aye also explained how she capitalises on her exposure to international concepts of law and justice: 'From what I learnt abroad, I can bring knowledge back home, like a bridge.'

The story of Ma Thida Aye illustrates the characteristic background of rule of law intermediaries who are from Myanmar and who work for foreign organisations as local staff or lawyer consultants (a full overview of the categories of research participants is provided in the Appendix). They reveal similar characteristics in relation to their trajectories, the way they accumulate foreign and social capital during military rule, and their motivations. Ma Thida Aye's personal history is one example of how exposure to external ideas, manners, and ways of living, etc. (Lewis and Mosse 2006; Gonzalez 1972) can facilitate being able to later carry out an intermediary function between development counterparts from different places. Her story shows how intermediaries are able to capitalise on foreign capital accumulated from connections to 'global' actors to further build 'power at home' (cf. Dezalay and Garth 2002; Hammerslev 2006).

In this chapter, I focus on intermediaries who reveal similar backgrounds in relation to the accumulation of foreign and social capital. Their backgrounds tell an interesting story about how capital was accumulated during military rule in a country often described as having been 'completely isolated' from foreign ideas and connections (see, e.g., Turku 2009).

Intermediaries' trajectories also provide important insights into the rule of law assistance field in Myanmar after political transition as certain practices 'emerged on the basis [of their] common capital and ideas' (Dezalay and Madsen 2012:448–9). An exploration of intermediaries' backgrounds is important for understanding who they respond to as well as what their own motivations are (Dezalay and Garth 2002). These are factors that will arguably influence their actions and decisions, negotiations, and interactions (Halliday and Carruthers 2009) and ultimately the way they translate rule of law to the Myanmar setting.

This chapter first presents an overview of rule of law intermediaries' social capital, as interlinked to their political engagements and personal motivations. Then, I illustrate how intermediaries accumulated foreign capital during a time in Myanmar's history that posed many challenges for reform-minded and politically engaged individuals. I analyse how intermediaries' social and foreign capital were reinforced as they became engaged in the rule of law assistance field. This chapter concludes with a reflection of how foreign capital helped or hindered intermediaries to build social influence. While access to foreign capital helped 'amplify' intermediaries' work on rights-related issues at home (e.g. by drawing on their networked resources to channel aid money or development activities to local levels in order to gain political influence), linkages to actors from abroad were not solely to their benefit in light of the existing distrust of foreign interests which affected the value of such capital.

## 6.1 RULE OF LAW INTERMEDIARIES' SOCIAL CAPITAL

The most central component of rule of law intermediaries' social capital is their links to a sustainable network (Bourdieu 1986) within which they are experts, have time to foster, and are willing to use for personal profit (Boissevain 1974; see also Gonzalez 1972; Seeley 1985). Resources in the network are often 'acquired', for example through intermediaries' educational efforts, rather than 'ascribed' (Lin 2001) because intermediaries were not born to beneficial positions as 'elites' in Myanmar society. More often they came from poorer families, from the country's different regions of which some were conflict-ridden.

Intermediaries were frequently described in relation to their networks. For example, one foreign programme manager suggested that his local staff was an invaluable resource because '[s]he knows everybody in the country' (Interviewee #25, 3 October 2014). A foreign lawyer expressed his gratitude about working with a specific intermediary: 'He is a great guy – he has all the connections' (Interviewee #29, 23 October 2014).

Rule of law intermediaries' networks could be observed in different ways. For example, a comment from a foreign programme manager was suggestive of how intermediaries were interlinked: 'They know each other from back in the dark days ... Some people we lost track of; the others are all over the place' (Interviewee #20, 30 September 2014). The programme manager was referring to the fact that intermediaries knew each other from the political activities that they were engaged in when Myanmar was under military rule, during the 'dark days' which commenced when General Ne Win took power in 1962 (Turnell 2011), continuing as the State Law and Order Restoration Council (SLORC) acquired rule in 1988 (Guilloux 2010) only to officially end in 2011 when a civilianised government was sworn in.

The genuine nature of intermediaries' access to networks is likely difficult for foreign actors to assess; however, as Lin (2001) suggests, it might suffice to let others know about one's network in order to further build one's influence. My own observation from attending workshops and conferences and my meetings with intermediaries in the field confirms that many interviewees were connected to each other in some way. When I asked them, they told me that connections dated from shared activities during the period of military rule. I review such activities in detail in the rest of the chapter.

## 6.2 INTERMEDIARIES' POLITICAL ENGAGEMENTS

Intermediaries in Myanmar have a history of social and political engagement, a shared 'sentiment' as they gathered around 'activity' (Homans 1950) during military rule, which further strengthened their network ties. In Myanmar, the common sentiment was explained by one participant as one of a shared 'voluntary spirit' (e.g., Interviewee #33, 11 November 2014; Interviewee #17, 23 September 2014) which eventually was capitalised on in favour of a shared cause (Lin 2001) of rule of law development.

Intermediaries' political and social engagements stretched from providing legal defence for farmers – as in Ma Thida Aye's example – an activity that in Myanmar does not come without risk (Cheesman and Kyaw Min San 2014) – to human rights advocacy, documentation of human rights violations, involvement in student politics, and engagement as (primarily) NLD party members. At the time of military rule, these activities constituted risky undertakings. Student activism has a long history in the country, dating to the colonial period, and has often been crushed by disproportionate violence by the government. For example, in 1962, student protests against the revolutionary Council's closing of independent political organisations were met with a bomb being detonated to blow up the student union building and shootings that resulted in several casualties (Steinberg 2001). Political opposition (including any sort of politically deemed work) was declared illegal by the 1964 Law to Protect National Solidarity. Reminiscent of the way in which 'political and social forces' were crushed during colonial rule, classified as criminal under the mantra of internal security (Callahan 2004:22), the 1964 law targeted forces rivalling the state for removal (Taylor, R. H. 2009). Some intermediaries' political involvements led to prison sentences, for example, for spreading flyers and other written material at the university (Interviewee #14, 13 May 2014). Under the SLORC's rule, opposition politicians were often charged with criminal offences under the 1950 Emergency Provisions Act that criminalised the spread of false news and the disrupting of morality or security, or under section 122–1 of the Penal Code, the British drafted India Act from 1860, which criminalised high treason and had the effect of nullifying opposition politicians' elected status (Diller 1997).

In the transition period, intermediaries perceived that they were able to obtain influence because of the social capital they had accumulated from the political engagements during military rule. An effect of their social and political work was thus that intermediaries could access local areas more easily to promote rule of law reform. For example, intermediaries described how local actors knew them from that time which facilitated the activities they later carried out while working on rule of law assistance. A local lawyer who was a member of the NLD, and had been so during military rule, suggested that because he had travelled extensively during his political engagements – for example to document human rights violations – people across Myanmar knew him, and therefore it was easy for him to locate lawyers across the country: 'Today, in every state I just call the local NLD office; often there is someone there that I know, and then I can get to the other people' (Interviewee #14, 5 October 2014 and 13 December 2014). In Myanmar, he suggested, with a big smile, that knowing means trusting: 'That's also why all the internationals come to see me' – because of his trusted connections at local levels (see Chapter 7). Another intermediary believed that her country-wide travels had taught her how to recognise different cultural traits among Myanmar's many ethnic groups, thus providing her with the necessary understanding to be able to act as a 'cultural broker' (Geertz 1960), a skill that foreigners lacked (Interviewee #10, 12 May 2014). This ability that intermediaries had to travel around Myanmar where they had established networks mattered because for foreigners it was still difficult to tour the country freely; some local areas remained classified as restricted (see Myanmar Ministry of Hotels and Tourism n.d.) and sometimes they were afraid of exposing their activities to the government if they left Yangon's urban disguise. Sometimes, they recognised that they lack the cultural and linguistic understanding to comprehend the social and political dynamics of rural areas. A foreign lawyer and INGO programme manager reflected on these difficulties: 'I am a foreigner so there are a lot of places where I can't go. Rural areas are very hard – you don't know what's going on . . . glad we did not go in' (Interviewee #3, 8 May 2014).

Political engagements also influenced intermediaries' personalities. For example, I learned that Aung Thura Ko, a Myanmar lawyer whose confidence is a striking feature, had previously been in trouble with the authorities for his political involvements. However, he told me he had always responded to the government's involvement with a fearless and progressive approach. According to Aung Thura Ko, this also influenced the work he was involved in with development actors from abroad after the political transition. For example, after Military Intelligence – a structure of intelligence and specialised security agencies and a common feature of military rule that put anyone, from members of the general population to proclaimed political dissidents, under its surveillance in the quest to abolish opposition (Selth 1998) – showed up at one of the rule of law trainings I was observing, he exclaimed that he was not afraid to talk to them, or to the police, nor to the military: 'We don't see any barriers' (Interviewee #17, 23 September 2014). This fearlessness was common to other participants – they were not only likeable but, in many cases, also brave and seemingly confident about taking on confrontations that others would not. The importance of this elaboration on personalities rests on the intuition that 'a person or corporation with a certain charisma' will be better at conveying ideas about development assistance than someone without it (Rottenburg 2013, cited in Behrends et al. 2014:18; see also Santos 2006). In settings like Myanmar, the conveying of rule of law ideals to unwilling or hostile counterparts also requires some level of persistence and courage, which can be boosted by support from outside sources.

## 6.3   RULE OF LAW INTERMEDIARIES' FOREIGN CAPITAL

During military rule in Myanmar, some individuals were able to accumulate 'foreign capital' through their connections to actors from abroad, which later helped position them on a path towards becoming intermediaries (see also Gonzalez 1972). At the time, being associated with foreign organisations was a risky undertaking, and many such organisations were either expelled or put under strict regulation. For example, in the wake of the 1962 coup, public information libraries of embassies, private foreign aid organisations – like the Ford Foundation, the British Council, the Asia Foundation, the Fulbright programme, and British and American language training initiatives – had been forced to leave the country (Taylor 2009a). In addition, contact with foreigners was not encouraged, and media control meant that the country was cut off from foreign influence (Steinberg 2001). When foreign organisations were allowed to return to Myanmar and take up some language training activities, intermediaries studied English at the British Council or the American Center and became engaged in some affiliated political activities. Such activities helped build intermediaries' networks with actors both inside and outside of Myanmar.

Foreign actors suggested that the purpose of their previous interactions with 'reform-minded individuals' (Interviewee #20, 12 November 2014; Interviewee #28, 22 October 2014) was to sensitise them to foreign ideas and knowledge and to prepare them for future transition. So what they were preparing through their initiatives was, in Hammerslev's (2006:75) words, people 'who were able to take "power away from the previous regime"' and 'who agreed on the priorities of the development of law'. Next, I present some of the activities that helped build intermediaries' foreign capital in more detail.

### 6.3.1 Training at Foreign Institutions

Rule of law intermediaries gain competitive advantages in the rule of law assistance field because of their English language skills, especially because communication is of strategic importance in linking actors who do not share the same language or culture (see Chapter 8). Many intermediaries studied English (and received some political training) at the American Center or the British Council. A foreign programme manager explained:

> They all went through English training and some more political training. We had the safe space to train the cadre of well-connected and well-trained individuals, averse in an understanding of international institutions, knowledge and skills to get things moving when the country was going to open.
>
> (Interviewee #20, 12 November 2014)

The quote suggests that one of the objectives of training was to prepare individuals for future transition and to support potential agents for change. Indeed, educational institutions are effective in transmitting and passing on 'social capital in the form of social rules and norms' (Fukuyama 2000:10); in this case, foreign educational institutions rather promoted norms that were inspired by liberal systems and international law.

As a result of their English training, in combination with having completed a university education at home on topics that included law or economics, individuals were able to apply for education abroad and scholarships to support them (see, e.g., British Council 2016). One local lawyer, for example, suggested that everyone who was engaged in one of the political book clubs 'got' foreign education (Interviewee #14, 13 December 2014). He was not claiming that it was an easy process but recalled that application requirements were hard and that a lot of pocket money had to be spent on taking the courses. Thereafter, students needed to secure permission to leave the country – which at the time was nothing but an easy process. One intermediary recalls the worry he felt the first time he was on a plane: not until the plane took off did he feel complete relief (Interviewee #17, 23 September 2014). After having overcome such challenges, intermediaries studied topics including international law, international relations, human rights, development, politics, and transitional justice, in the United States or the United Kingdom or in places closer to home, like Hong Kong, Japan, Thailand, or Singapore.

### 6.3.2 Previous Contact with Foreign Development Actors

Intermediaries' foreign capital was accumulated through their previous work on aid projects. Such contact with development actors, where individuals get to learn about industry expectations and 'development lingua', has been identified as key for becoming a successful intermediary (Bierschenk et al. 2002:20–1). In the case of Myanmar, a majority of rule of law intermediaries (save some of the most junior intermediaries) had previous contact with development actors from abroad through projects within the country, a few in the United Kingdom or the United States, and on both sides of the Thai–Burma border.

The range of jobs varied from UN agencies, youth development programmes, embassy jobs, or Christian, livelihood, or health organisations. Even if their previous development practice involved topics other than rule of law, these experiences taught intermediaries about development industry expectations, codes, procedures and resources, as well as possibilities (see also Massoud 2015).

### 6.3.3 Exposure Trips

Intermediaries' accumulation of foreign capital was also enhanced through exposure trips, sometimes offered as an activity of development assistance, often as a reward for 'good behaviour' (see, e.g., Gibson et al.

2005). We see such formulations of recompense in the rule of law assessments that were drafted in the transition frenzy, for example, the US Agency for International Development (USAID) suggests: 'Following a demonstrated commitment by Burmese judicial leadership through investment in political will, time, money or human resources, study tours to appropriate jurisdictions in the region may be considered' (United States Agency for International Development 2013:9).

Exposure trips were offered, if possible, before transition, but accelerated thereafter. The trips often went to countries that had been through (allegedly) similar transition (e.g., Cambodia and South Africa); ones that hosted global conferences (e.g., Japan and Switzerland); or where exchange programmes in the form of shorter study tours were offered (e.g., the USA, Australia, and New Zealand).

The aim of such trips was to provide exposure to different ideas, systems, and working procedures. They were also used as an opportunity to build personal relationships between key leaders within the government and civil society who sometimes attended the trips together. One rule of law programme manager described the rationale: 'You identify people who seem to be doing good stuff ... then take them on an exposure trip' (Interviewee #28, 22 October 2014). Another suggested: 'We choose people with the idea to build relationships between government and civil society ... it was about finding those key leaders' (Interviewee #20, 12 November 2014). Intermediaries commented that they learned a lot and established important relationships during such trips; sometimes they were even inspired to initiate their own rule of law-focused work back home (e.g., Interviewee #33, 11 November 2014; Interviewee #17, 23 September 2014; Interviewee #55, 3 October 2015). Nevertheless, foreign practitioners sometimes complained about the lack of interest shown by participants on such trips, or about the fact that they did not seem to 'get' the purpose of the trips. For example, one practitioner expressed disappointment when travelling with a group from Myanmar to Cambodia to meet with lawyers who had been involved in the transitional justice movement. The Myanmar lawyers allegedly showed no interest in talking to the Cambodian lawyers and remained largely quiet since they did not want to criticise their own country during what was described as an awkward meeting about transitional justice. There is also the vexed issue of which countries' aid recipients are comfortable being compared with or analogised to – foreign observers may see points of connection between Cambodia and Myanmar, but Myanmar actors may not.

## 6.4 INTERNATIONAL STRATEGIES TO BUILD INFLUENCE AT HOME

Intermediaries' strategies of using both foreign and social capital to further their aims were not without difficulties. Mixed perceptions of intermediaries and their motivations spring from the inherent nature of the role as one that exhibits a dual quality (Stovel and Shaw 2012). While intermediaries can facilitate social interactions and relationships where these are absent, and with positive benefits for all involved, intermediation is also considered as having a negative side because the work has the potential to foster exploitation and personal gains to strengthen intermediaries' own position (Seidel 2017). This is the moral ambiguity of the intermediary, an actor who carries out fine-tuned navigation in between, potentially in order to maximise individual gain (James 2011).

Foreign practitioners perceived intermediaries as being motivated by both 'vested' and 'common' interest (Interviewee #24, 14 October 2014) that included 'career opportunity and a strong desire to contribute to the transition in their country' (Interviewee #31, 10 November 2014; also Interviewee #25, 3 October 2014); '[being] genuinely [interested in] support[ing] justice, promot[ing] legal aid, etc.' (Interviewee #9, 23 May 2014); 'being happy to help' and 'extremely interested in legal practice' (Interviewee #8, 22 May 2014); and 'working with internationals and being exposed to international practices' (Interviewee #2, 7 May 2014), 'money' (Interviewee #2, 7 May 2014), and 'politics' (Interviewee #25, 3 October 2014). Overall, intermediaries' own motivations for working for foreign donors relate more to their attempts to build social capital and further their own interests, which are sometimes political. One programme manager said of his key intermediary: 'He has political aspirations and was open about it from the beginning. He wants to start his own political party. If he leaves us, it will be for that reason' (Interviewee #3, 8 May 2014).

In Myanmar, intermediaries' application of both forms of capital is observed. They are able to gain benefits from their association with organisations from abroad, for example, by accumulating aid resources to local levels, providing links to foreign actors, or by signalling their importance by being selected to travel abroad – activities that could help them further their social and political interests. One intermediary elaborated on the way he was able to assist both foreign and local lawyers because of his connections to spaces of capital:

> I helped many international organizations to find lawyers who are the best fit for them. I also try to help local lawyers, for example, with their resumes in English (then they can learn more on the job) and also help them to understand the process of human rights ... some are involved in the NLD but not all ... I also like to help young lawyers to go abroad.
>
> (Interviewee #17, 23 Sep 2014)

Another example: intermediaries participated in exposure trips not only because it allowed them to travel abroad but also because it signalled to the broader public, which made up their potential political constituency, that they were selected and thus special (Interviewee #40, 9 December 2014). The earlier example of Ma Thida Aye, who decided to start her own legal aid NGO after one such exposure trip, is telling of the way in which intermediaries make use of the 'foreign capital' gained to further 'amplify' work on rights-related issues at home (Risse-Kappen et al. 1999).

That the chosen few felt proud to be selected for activities abroad was apparent, while the frustration from the ones who were left behind was also voiced. One local lawyer complained that foreigners often picked the same junior lawyers for exposure trips (Interviewee #49, 11 December 2014). That comment also connects to perceptions by intermediaries themselves: that their linkages with foreign actors were not always seen in a positive light and their work was contested by a range of counterparts and beneficiaries. We find some explanation for such sentiments in the ingrained distrust towards foreign engagements – a long-term feature of Myanmar's history and part of contemporary politics (reviewed in detail in Chapter 7). In effect, intermediaries not only use strategies to benefit from but also try to conceal their engagements with organisations from abroad.

One area where the reluctance to be associated with foreign organisations became evident was when intermediaries sought broader political engagement. One local intermediary explained that he had ambivalent feelings towards his work with organisations from abroad because he was worried about his reputation in the larger community. He told me that he had a feeling that he had to 'get out of this business' and expressed an urgent need to be 'free-float next [election] year' if he was to be able to fulfil his political dreams. The main reason, he suggested, was because 'people' lacked trust (see Chapter 7) in foreign organisations:

> You get some criticism here. People think that if your project got six million, it means that you personally got the money; they will tell

me, 'Hey, you're rich now!' They don't trust foreign-funded organizations, and they don't like it – I have to get out of this business if I want to
be in politics ... they don't think any foreign organizations do it only
because of good will.

(Interviewee #14, 13 December 2014)

The intermediary further explained that, because of such complexities
and his political motivations, he was 'not attached to any organization'.
Another intermediary also expressed frustration over the way his work
for foreign organisations was perceived:

> Some people really hate me, but for most, I am just misunderstood, they look
> at me, and most think 'Who is this guy?' I am their junior, and I am telling
> them about human rights and democratic values ... but by now they
> appreciate me, they know my intentions ... I do this for the younger
> generations.

(Interviewee #17, 23 September 2014)

In addition to the dynamics of facing criticism and distrust for being
affiliated with organisations from abroad, intermediaries also comment that being independent is a national cultural trait and that they
need a degree of freedom in their work life. However, we can assume
that many of their foreign colleagues consider them attached to their
organisation. Another example was the intermediary who was repeatedly encouraged into taking on a leadership role within a foreign
organisation. The intermediary did not want to do so because he
had other political goals, even though he perceived that what he
learned there in relation to access to justice was politically important
and thus related to his political work (Interviewee #55,
25 September 2015). Foreign practitioners seem quite oblivious to
this dynamic of distrust and to the extent to which intermediaries
perceive their association with organisations from abroad as being
damaging for social promotion.

Intermediaries' political involvement (primarily in NLD or
split-up groups) was characterised by a sense of modesty. This
might be so because the intermediary role requires the showcasing
of being an 'insider', at the same social level as the constituency,
and a genuine will to help people without personal interest, while
reluctantly donning the 'mantle of leadership' in recognition of
public political duty (Paine 1971). For example, instead of stating
that political office was his main objective, one intermediary and
local lawyer commented that he would 'go [into public office] if

they [the NLD and Aung San Suu Kyi] called for him' (Interviewee #17, 23 September 2014). The same intermediary confessed that being an insider was sometimes a constraining part of his political work, for example, because in his local area he had to blend in by wearing traditional clothing (*lunghi*) while in Yangon he was able to wear 'more Western clothes', which he preferred. On the other hand, intermediaries knew to be careful about revealing too much of their various engagements as it could lead to criticism from their foreign employers who provided the finances.

Criticism related to intermediaries' connections to specific political parties, as expressed by one programme manager from abroad, describing an intermediary: '[H]e is a former political prisoner and has a lot of connections with the NLD and split-up groups of the NLD which means that a lot of our partners relate to that' (Interviewee #3, 8 May 2014). She perceived these political linkages as potentially excluding other important beneficiaries of their rule of law assistance. One foreign practitioner elaborated in depth on her scepticism about intermediaries' political motivations:

> So many of them [intermediaries] are involved in politics … all are in it for politics … which of course makes you wonder about their own interests … their interests are not in the work they do for foreign donors. The donors turn on a sort of wilful blindness … they don't want to see what might be happening as it is not going to advance their development agenda.
> (Interviewee #40, 9 December 2014)

What will happen with rule of law assistance activities after the 2015 elections 'if all … go into politics?', she asked. Moreover, intermediaries were described as spending too much time 'attending conferences' or meetings (field notes, May 2014) while not carrying out the 'real' (i.e., technical legal) work they are hired to do (field notes, December 2015). Such comments are suggestive of de Sardan's (2005) argument that intermediary competences do not receive much recognition from the institutions they belong to, contrasted with the utmost significance that foreign actors ascribe to intermediaries' networks, which are fostered through such social events.

Intermediaries' motivations are thus influenced by ambivalence: the trajectory of their social promotion can be facilitated through foreign capital, but they need to constantly balance this against societal distrust of foreign interests and their perceived loyalties.

## 6.5   CONCLUSION

In this chapter, I explored how intermediaries accumulated foreign and social capital during military rule: capital that was central for their ability to operate as intermediaries in the rule of law assistance field in Myanmar after the political transition. That overview also revealed commonality in the backgrounds of rule of law intermediaries: for example, many were politically engaged, studied English during military rule, gained access to foreign education, and worked for foreign organisations.

After political transition, intermediaries mobilised the foreign capital they accumulated during military rule within the rule of law assistance space that emerged. This was evident, for example, in the way that intermediaries used their networks to select who got to be included in rule of law activities, in the way they were able to travel more freely across Myanmar and thus became the satellites for new ideas and the rule of law model, and in the way they used their foreign language skills to serve as knowledge brokers, channelling information and being able to communicate with actors on 'both sides'.

Access to intermediaries' networks is imperative for foreign actors and their rule of law assistance efforts. The networks that intermediaries accumulated during military rule stretched beyond the formal and informal channels that foreigners were subsequently able to access. Foreign rule of law promoters express an urgent need to access intermediary networks; they realise that they are reliant on these in order to achieve the influence necessary for rule of law assistance efforts. At the same time, they have ambivalent feelings about using informal channels. Some are concerned over too much in the country being done through charismatic personalities and personal networks – especially when those networks entail political obligations or aspirations.

I argued that intermediaries' 'international strategies' of using foreign capital to build their influence at home have been supported by foreign actors in preparation for democratic transition. However, in a perverse way, the well-intended efforts of international organisations and embassies, during the years of unmediated military dictatorship, to identify 'reform-minded' people whom they could cultivate (Interviewee #20, 12 November 2014; Interviewee #28, 22 October 2014), by offering them opportunities to study abroad, for instance, or enlisting them in local classes that would inculcate certain values, sometimes backfired. One problem for rule of law projects encountered in the early 2010s was that they met with candidates whose statements fit idioms matching foreign organisations' commitments a little bit too well for their liking. Intermediaries demonstrated 'scenographic competence', showing that they could talk up the rule of law, without revealing their actual objectives.

The use of foreign capital was not only to intermediaries' benefit, because of existing distrust of foreign interests (discussed in Chapter 7). This also created ambivalence for intermediaries, who apply different strategies to hide their connections to foreign actors. While access to foreign capital helped 'amplify' intermediaries' work on rights-related issues at home (e.g. by drawing on their networked resources to channel aid money or development activities to local levels in order to gain political influence), linkages to actors from abroad were not solely to their benefit in light of the existing distrust of foreign interests which affected the value of such capital.

CHAPTER SEVEN

# INTERMEDIARIES AS TRUST BUILDERS

In Myanmar's emerging rule of law assistance field, intermediaries broker influence as they build trust between newly arrived development actors from abroad and national and local counterparts. During one of my trips with a local NGO to Myanmar's western Rakhine state, I met a foreign rule of law practitioner who regularly travelled across Myanmar to meet with local lawyers. He told me that his organisation arrived in 2012 and had had little previous engagement in Myanmar. He went on to express his anxiety over some of the questions he received from local lawyers with whom he met in different parts of the country:

> These local lawyers ask me about [organisation's] interests with our work in Myanmar; they tell me that they know about foreign interests. I don't know what to tell them. I mean, I know what my own interests are and that I believe in the work that we do. But I don't know how to convince them about [foreign organisation's] interest.
>
> (field notes, October 2014)

The local intermediary who worked alongside the foreign practitioner suggested that these were issues that related to distrust; local people did not trust foreign-funded organisations and did not think that foreign organisations were engaged in the country because of good intentions. However, the intermediary suggested that the local lawyers trusted him because they knew and liked him: 'That's how our society works' (Interviewee #14, 5 October 2014).

This foreign practitioner's experience of being questioned and the intermediary's explanation hint at a central aspect of development co-operation in Myanmar, namely, the distrust that remains towards foreigners and foreign interests (see also David and Holliday 2018) and the importance of interpersonal relations built on trust – 'confidence in one's expectations' (Luhmann 1979:4) for effective results in rule of law assistance. In the example here, the intermediary views his role as key for building trust with local counterparts because foreign actors are distrusted (Hardin 2001).

Development studies have previously highlighted the importance of relationship building and trust between foreign and local actors as key factors for development success (Anderson, Brown, and Jean 2012; Diallo and Thuillier 2005; Moore 2013). In her exploratory book on development aid in Cambodia, McWha (2011:37) finds that the creation of '[a] relationship based on trust and respect may be essential for the success of capacity-development initiatives'. Developing such relationships between foreign and local counterparts was dependent, for example, on opportunities to chat informally with colleagues and to develop friendships outside of work (ibid.). Studies have also collected the voices of local counterparts to rule of law assistance who find that donors' short-term approaches constitute an obstacle to trust- and relationship building with foreign practitioners (International Council on Human Rights 2000; United Nations Development Programme 2011). A key theme that is missing from these analyses is the role that intermediaries play in building relationships and trust among development counterparts. In order to understand how intermediaries influence rule of law assistance in Myanmar, we thus need to understand: how trust functions as a key indicator for development success; why ideas of distrust exist in the Myanmar setting; how trust is gained; and what kinds of matters intermediaries are trusted with.

This chapter commences with a discussion about interpersonal and institutional trust and distrust in Myanmar and seeks historical explanations of how past regime practices, including national policies of isolation and the external sanctions regime, resulted in widespread distrust of foreign actors and ideas. Thereafter, I address why intermediaries were pivotal in this regard for foreign actors' rule of law development efforts and how foreign actors, both consciously and unconsciously, made use of intermediaries' agency for their aims of working on the rule of law. The section outlines the expressed need for a trusted link between foreign practitioners and local and national counterparts and analyses the role that intermediaries play in becoming trust and relationship builders with effects on rule of law progress.

This chapter concludes that trust and relationship building can be seen as a prerequisite for successful rule of law assistance. It is the focus of much donor effort in attempts to build trust with local counterparts in Myanmar. However, because foreign actors cannot supply prior proof of trust, it is the known actors, such as intermediaries, who instead take on the role of trust builders. While doing so, however, intermediaries, as figures 'of moral uncertainty' (James 2011, 319), are repeatedly criticised for being too close to foreigners and their interests.

## 7.1 INTERPERSONAL AND INSTITUTIONAL TRUST AND DISTRUST IN MYANMAR

Levels of institutional trust (perceptions of fair processes and institutional identities) and interpersonal trust (relationships between individuals) (Hardin 2001) are low in Myanmar (Asia Foundation 2014), where for decades a system of military rule promoted fear, power, and control rather than trust (Fink 2001). The distrust stretched from personal interactions to the law that was, and remains, an 'object of avoidance and distrust' (Crouch and Lindsey 2014a). In 2014, Asia Foundation's survey on 'civic knowledge and values in a changing society', which included face-to-face interviews with more than 3,000 respondents across Myanmar's 14 states and regions, illustrated that trust in Myanmar society was 'astonishing[ly]' low, towards both institutions and 'people' (Asia Foundation 2014). According to the survey report:

> When respondents were asked whether, in general, most people can be trusted, an astonishing 77% said that most people cannot be trusted. Only 21% believed that most people can be trusted. Social trust was lower in urban areas, where only 15% of respondents believed most people can be trusted, compared to 23% in rural areas. Levels of trust were also lower in the regions (18%) than in the states (27%).
>
> (Asia Foundation 2014:87)

When respondents were asked to rate the integrity of institutions, 'few were rated highly, and the large number of respondents answering "don't know" underscores the general lack of knowledge about key governance institutions in the country' (Asia Foundation 2014:90). Central rule of law institutions gained the lowest positive response:

The police, in particular, received the weakest positive response – only 2% of the public felt the police had 'very high integrity' – and the strongest negative response, with 21% of respondents believing the police to be of 'low integrity,' and 10% of 'very low integrity.' The courts received similarly low positive ratings and high negative ratings, though more people said they did not know when asked about the courts (26%).

(Asia Foundation 2014:91)

The survey findings provide indications of the state of trust in Myanmar at the time of development activities that sought to strengthen rule of law institutions and enhance people's trust in them. However, they are not surprising: trust in institutions in authoritarian or totalitarian settings has been identified repeatedly as a rare phenomenon (Latusek and Olejniczak 2016). As the workable alternative, societies with weak institutional trust ('low trust societies') (Fukuyama 1995) rely on interpersonal trust, which can be quite high. In their study of Russia and Poland, Latusek and Cook (2012:514) show how trust networks '[i]n societies that lack reliable institutional framework … may emerge to fill the void left by the demise of these institutions'. This is common, the authors suggest, drawing on their cases, in countries that have experienced totalitarianism where 'the excessive reliance on close circles of family members and friends, combined with distrust of the authorities and the law, was forged by decades of experience with totalitarianism'.

Consistent with the survey findings in Myanmar, other scholars find a correlation between low institutional trust and low interpersonal trust among individuals in a society (see Khodyakov 2007 for an overview of such debates). Hardin (2001:513) suggests that authoritarian policies to erode protection under the law can lead to a lack of confidence in both the state and other individuals 'because the state cannot be relied upon to prevent the worst possible outcomes from various joint endeavours and contractual relations'. State policies that ruin relationships of trust are also a good way to crush potential mobilisation for opposition (ibid.), a phenomenon that was seen in British colonial policies of 'divide and rule' applied to impair trust between Burma's ethnic groups as a strategy to prevent mobilisation for political opposition and resistance (Taylor, R. H. 2009). In effect, low interpersonal trust in authoritarian settings is damaging to the accumulation of social capital, which stems from trust and is crucial to democratic systems (Mishler and Rose 2001; Park 2012).

161

Foreign practitioners concurred that trust was low in Myanmar, and they perceived the country as more 'distrusting' than other settings where they had previously worked. The distrust they observed included that of the legal system (Interviewee #4, 15 May 2014) and the government (Interviewee #53, 25 September 2015) that for decades oppressed rather than served its citizens; as a result, 'people have little trust' (Interviewee #20, 30 September 2014; see also Denney et al. 2016). In addition to this, xenophobia – the fear and distrust of that which is perceived to be foreign or strange (see Callahan 2010 for a discussion about the sometimes sweeping understandings of xenophobia in Myanmar, and the military's role in fostering xenophobic ideas) – was seen as deeply rooted and contributed to general views of distrust of 'foreign interests' (Interviewee #35, 19 November 2014), perhaps not always 'obvious to newly-arrived development actors who don't always recognize how things work here' (Interviewee #3, 8 May 2014).

This last comment was from a discussion with a foreign lawyer and rule of law practitioner who had worked in Myanmar for three years when I first met her in 2014 (a relatively long time when compared to many other foreigners). She went on to explain how she was worried about staying in the country too long, because '[t]he longer you stay here, the more you realise you don't know what's going on'. The practitioner was referring to the distrust that she had experienced from government actors; from 'the locals' she had met in her work; and also from local NGOs that her organisation tried to co-operate with for purposes of rule of law assistance. In addition to a lack of personal and institutional trust, distrust towards foreigners and their interests was prevalent.

### 7.1.1 The Politics of Distrust in Myanmar

In Myanmar, colonial history and decades of isolation under military rule have contributed to distrust towards foreigners, which affects relationship building between development organisations and local and national counterparts in the transition period.

Nationalist sentiments took root in Burma when the country struggled for independence from British rule (Callahan 2004). An independence movement supported by the Burmese press, student activists, Buddhist monks, and emerging Burmese political parties (Hobbs 1947) gained popular support (Maung Maung 1989). Nationalist politicians, like U Aung San, U Saw, and U Ba Maw, focused on issues that involved increased opportunities for higher education (Callahan 2004) and representation on the Legislative

Council (colonial interventions of the legal sector had especially contributed to anti-imperialist sentiments). By the end of British colonial rule, anti-imperialist and leftist thoughts (Trager 1959), seen as the opposite to British capitalist and liberal rule, were common (Taylor, R. H. 2009) and would come to influence political events in the decades to come. Dissatisfaction with later Japanese rule was equally rampant (Taylor, R. H. 2009). The Anti-Fascist People's Freedom League (AFPFL) arose as an anti-Japanese resistance movement that came to emerge as the key political group after the war (Silverstein 1977). The new leaders of Burma had little interest in promoting liberal democracy as such was the system associated with the British colonisers; rather, they were embracing a nationalist, anti-imperialist, anti-capitalist, and 'utopian socialist project' (Callahan 1998:52).

Nationalist sentiments were sustained in a quest to keep the country independent from foreign exploitation as Ne Win took power in 1962 (Shwe Lu Maung 1989). Nationalism, xenophobia, and isolationism aligned under the military's goal of protecting the state from destructive elements and preserving culture and tradition under its new socialist ideology (cf. Callahan 2010). The *Burmese Way to Socialism* (1962), published within a month after the 1962 coup, mixes Buddhism, Marxism, and humanism to provide a state ideology intended to influence popular support for the state (Taylor, R. H. 2009). In 1963, as *The System of Correlation of Man and His Environment* (Burma Socialist Programme Party 1963) was published, it became the philosophical and intellectual foundation for the country's approach to society and socialism (Steinberg 2001). Cheesman (2015:80) suggests that, under the 'socialist banner', 'the new government could situate itself in a historical narrative of anti-imperial and anti-capitalist struggle while creating opportunities to target adversaries through new legal and administrative measures couched in ideological terms'. Laws 'became vehicles [with which] to implement' the new 'radical and socialist developmental plans' based on ideology, and courts became both its instruments and its implementers (Myint Zan 2014:160). Thus, the socialist ideology came to rest on many of the legislative and institutional reforms that had been, and were to be, undertaken and that helped create the nationalistic and isolated nation that Burma was to become (Turku 2009).

Increased isolation and xenophobia resulted in the forced departure of all public information libraries of embassies and private foreign aid organisations (Taylor, R. H. 2009). Xenophobic propaganda became manifest (see, e.g., Turku 2009). And through a Printers' and Publishers' Registration Act, the state began to isolate its culture from external influences (Taylor, R. H. 2009). Books from the outside were screened for political content, and domestic expressions of opinion were highly censored through the Press Scrutiny Board; contacts with foreigners were not encouraged; and there was a restriction on imports of consumer goods (Steinberg 2001). Eventually, speaking with a foreigner could, and did at times, lead to jail terms (Skidmore 2003). According to Steinberg (2001), xenophobic propaganda was effective because the Burmese started to believe that foreigners were unsympathetic and that they held views that opposed those of Burmese society, which were Buddhist and socialist rather than 'Western mainstream'.

In the socialist Buddhist unity that Ne Win was promoting, ethnic minorities were perceived as a threat. Not long after the 1962 coup, individuals with Indian heritage were expelled (Steinberg 2001) and, gradually, other minorities were marginalised as members of the majority ethnic group the 'Bamar' were increasingly influenced by the idea that the country was full of potential enemies ready to destroy the union (Steinberg 2001). Nationalism was enhanced by the perception that ethnic minority groups wanted independence and that they maintained close ties to foreigners (ibid.). Burman-Buddhist nationalism continued to thrive in Myanmar after 2010 (Cheesman and Farrelly 2016; Walton and Hayward 2014). Horsey (2015) even argues that it increased after the country's 'opening' (also shown by David and Holliday 2018). He illustrates such increase with reference to the strong support there is for nationalist monks and groups including the organisation for the protection of race and religion (*ma ba tha*) and a package of new legislation which encompasses the regulation of polygamy, religious conversion, inter-faith marriage, and unequal population growth intended to protect Myanmar Buddhism (see also Looi 2015). International concern was voiced towards the passing of the legislation, due to its discriminatory features in violation of international human rights (United Nations Office of the High Commissioner for Human Rights 2015).

Writing about the subsequent military rule, Skidmore (2003:8) suggests that the regime maintained a system where they promoted 'fear of the other' as a temporal strategy with which to uphold control. 'The other' could consist of a foreigner, a traitor, or a neocolonial presence whose threat one should be extra vigilant against. Through various strategies, the regime kept a tight grip of control on the population. For example, Military Intelligence managed to control the population through 'a range of national security laws enforced by a pliant judicial system' (Pedersen 2008:152). Through an extensive surveillance network (including the monitoring of telephones, mail, and fax) and local wardens and police making sure people's moves were registered, a sense of societal distrust and fear was successfully sustained (ibid.). Skidmore (2003:16) concludes that trust eroded in society due to this heavy intelligence apparatus: 'The military dictatorship thus effectively manages to isolate Burmese people into small knots of friendship. The sense of isolation people feel is commonly expressed as ("they [Military Intelligence] are always listening; you can't trust anyone").' Skidmore (2003:16) illustrates the breakdown in interpersonal trust that was put into effect during military rule leading ultimately to what she describes as 'a nation of individuals unable and unwilling to trust each other'. In addition to regime strategies, such as wiping out currency and closing banks, this, she argues, resulted in 'the complete lack of trust Burmese people have in their institutions'.

In effect, foreign development actors interested in supporting the rule of law as an ideal and the institutions that provided it intervened in a setting where nationalist sentiments had prevailed for decades and where foreign ideas and interests were met with suspicion. In addition, they experienced the legacy of Myanmar having been cut off from the outside world as a result of the decades-long rigid sanctions regime imposed by foreign states on the country.

### 7.1.2 Foreign Sanctions

Western sanctions that applied to Myanmar from 1988 cut it off from both international ideas and advances in knowledge as possibilities to build linkages with actors in-country remained largely unexplored (Pedersen 2008). It was the regime's disrespect for human rights and its refusal to hold elections, coupled with Western governments' agenda for a 'new world order' based on democratic governance as well as international admiration for Aung San Suu Kyi (who had recently won the Nobel Peace Prize), that resulted in one of the toughest sanctions regimes towards a country ever instituted. Grassroots campaigns by human rights activists and Burmese exiles worked together with (primarily US) lawmakers to introduce laws targeting companies doing business in Burma, consumer boycotts, and lawsuits (Pedersen 2008). Some of these were granted NGO status and able to speak about military atrocities at the UN Human Rights Commission, invited to visit European foreign ministries, and thereafter went to the USA to lobby for support and recognition (Silverstein 1997).

The international community's human rights concerns, which led to the imposition of strict sanctions, included the government's mistreatment of minorities, especially the use of extensive violence against non-combatants in the long-standing civil conflicts in breach of the Geneva Conventions of 1949 to which the government was a signatory (Silverstein 1997). In 1989 Myanmar was brought to the attention of the United Nations High Commissioner for Human Rights which appointed special rapporteurs to report on the situation in the country; however, these were granted only limited access to areas and places of interest to inspect (Silverstein 1997). It was especially the aftermath of widespread student protests in 1988 that had highlighted the grave human rights violations. Protests had escalated in the capital as a response to state failure (Taylor, R. H. 2009) and economic disparity following decades of economic mismanagement and regulatory changes, the most infamous perhaps being three cases of demonetisation (Steinberg 2001), leading to the country being classified by the UN as a Least Developed Country (United Nations Development Policy and Analysis Division 2015). The protests had quickly escalated to unprecedented proportions and large parts of the general population as well as civil servants joined in (Pedersen 2008). Observing journalist Lintner (1989) provides a detailed account of how protesting students were shot, raped, and arrested over several months, which sparked further protests, an escalation of violence, and harsher attempts at restoring 'law and order'. A new military government, under the banner *State Law and Order Restoration Council* (SLORC), took over power with the promise to maintain 'rule of law', a term it had quickly come to hijack as its slogan for upholding law and order (Cheesman 2009).

The military's violent crackdown on protestors (Steinberg 2001) made the outside world conscious of the human rights violations taking place inside the country's closed borders. West Germany and the USA terminated their aid programmes to show their disapproval of the new regime and Britain and main donor Japan voiced the need for a Burmese solution of democracy (Lintner 1989). As long as the SLORC continued to avoid holding elections, which it vaguely declared would be held as soon as the people's standard of living had been improved, the transport network had been upgraded, and law and order had been restored, foreign donors stayed out of the country as this was their condition for renewed aid (ibid.).

The rigid sanctions regime imposed on Myanmar was lifted after the political transition in 2011. Thus, while other countries in Myanmar's vicinity co-operated with foreign actors on rule of law and economic development, Myanmar remained isolated and remained in little contact with foreign knowledge and ideas before the transition period. The international sanctions regime demarcates the pre-2011 conditions and the transition setting in which foreign actors wanted to support rule of law reform.

## 7.2 FOREIGN-FUNDED RULE OF LAW ASSISTANCE AS A SOURCE OF DISTRUST

Foreign actors' attempts to promote rule of law in Myanmar brought in unfamiliar elements in the form of new ways of explaining rule of law, assessments and critique of current legal practices, institutions, and systems, through workshops, research briefs, and legal awareness campaigns. In an authoritarian country with low levels of trust, dealing with such intervention by 'anonymous strangers' can be viewed as a risky undertaking (Latusek and Cook 2012).

An NGO tasked with donor co-ordination explored how xenophobia and distrust matter when it comes to 'bridging the gap between the donor community and local organizations in Myanmar' (Local Resource Centre 2012) and concurred that foreigners were generally mistrusted but also that local organisations felt that they were being discriminated against and not trusted. Such views held against both 'sides' led to damaged relationships between foreign and local organisations. I found that in Myanmar, foreign practitioners were well aware of the distrust towards them and their intentions; this was perceived as constraining their work (e.g., Interviewees #10, 12 May 2014; #53, 5 October 2015; #14, 5 October 2014). One programme manager acknowledged that local counterparts stopped talking when she entered a room because they did not 'trust her the same way they trust local staff' (Interviewee #19, 25 September 2014). Another practitioner felt as if her national counterparts kept significant information from her about their common interests (Interviewee #35, 19 November 2014).

The lack of trust sometimes led to damaged relationships. A foreign practitioner described how a local partner organisation 'might have been worried that we asked too many questions', which eventually led to them becoming 'very hostile . . . then I heard [that] one of the lawyers had told someone about us; [s/he said:] "Why does it matter[?] [T]hey are foreigners, just make something up, write anything"' (Interviewee #3, 8 May 2014). Such sentiments also explain why the intermediary organisations eventually 'applied to do [project activity] themselves based on our model' (Interviewee #3, 8 May 2014). Foreign practitioners were irked about the way that intermediaries sometimes took all the credit for the work. Some intermediaries insisted on removing any trace of transnational involvement in projects, because, they said, local people distrusted foreigners. 'They present it as the [local organisation's] rule of law project, they talk about the [local organisation's] approach to rule of law', said one programme manager. 'It really got a bit much after a while. They did not recognize any international support' (Interviewee #20, 30 September 2014). The irony of this grievance is that project appropriation is necessary for success: if rule of law is to come to anything at all, it has to strike roots in local soil. But foreign rule of law actors still have a felt need to brand and label their assistance (see Taylor 2016), and are annoyed when they do not get the recognition that they think they deserve. Amid this backdrop of mistrust, gaining trust becomes a central focus for rule of law assistance actors from abroad.

### 7.2.1 Attempts to Gain Trust

For foreign practitioners, whether or not they were 'trusted' mattered a lot. One consultant said that because his organisation had worked in the country for more than thirty years, in the Golden Triangle, it was 'very trusted, that matters here, it's all about levels, many levels of trust – between civilians and the military and between the military and the police' (Interviewee #1, 6 May 2014). Luhmann (1979) maintains that a decision to trust requires previous experiences, present experiences, and reliance on future experiences. For newly arrived foreign development actors, accumulating such past and present experiences for future trust was difficult.

In Myanmar, some practitioners were acutely aware of the relevance of building personal relationships and thus focused much of their work on trust building. They recognised that trust building was a timely (Interviewee #35, 19 November 2014) and difficult process (Interviewee #54, 25 September 2015) since '[i]t's all about relationships, who knows who and what' (Interviewee #40, 9 December 2014). Especially difficult was the process of gaining enough trust so that local staff felt comfortable to interact with, and express dissenting opinions towards, their foreign employers (Interviewee #40, 9 December 2014; Interviewee #3, 8 May 2014). Interactions with government actors were also reliant on relationship building. A foreign practitioner told me that government actors where she worked 'are used to me now, I can go to the court and other places without any issues. In Myanmar, once they know you on a personal level, it is all much easier' (Interviewee #31, 10 November 2014).

Gaining trust was experienced as a burdensome task because relationships with local and national actors were difficult to build. The difficulties were experienced at work as well as outside work. When I visited the UN office, foreign and local staff sat in separate sections, and foreign practitioners suggested that they seldom spent time with 'locals' in their free time.

Foreign practitioners described how it was particularly difficult to build relationships with the government actors whom they sought as counterparts. They were perplexed by the political sensitivities they encountered in Myanmar that were coloured by lack of transparency and military-style hierarchy structures. In this situation, intermediaries became two-way translators of political sensitivities: 'upwards' because foreign practitioners 'wanted to ask about political things' but were concerned that they 'pushed it too far' (Interviewee #8, 22 May 2014; see also Interviewee #48, 10 October 2014) and 'downwards' because they filtered messages from the actors who were being asked questions deemed too political (Interviewee #8, 22 May 2014).

A variable that contributed to the distance between foreign and local counterparts was the location of key government ministries in Nay Pyi Taw: most rule of law practitioners who worked for major donor organisations live in Yangon (on the question of distance between development counterparts, see Verma 2011). Still, even those who were placed in the capital experienced the city's regulatory effects as hampering interactions. For example, comparing his work in Cambodia with Myanmar, a foreign practitioner who lived in Nay Pyi Taw explained that he found it 'difficult to spend time with officials outside of work [to build up relationships]' (Interviewee #39, 22 November 2014). Another practitioner said that it had taken her

169

organisation (which is a major multilateral donor) 'two years to even have a conversation with the government' (Interviewee #35, 19 November 2014). As a comparison, a local acquaintance of mine who worked for a foreign-funded initiative in another field of development explained how it had taken her one full year of friendly visits just to be able to initiate any form of substantive activities. The problem with a long-term approach was expressed by one practitioner: 'We tend to stay a longer time, we get criticised that we are too slow, but time is the most important thing to make assistance effectively' (Interviewee #39, 22 November 2014).

Foreign practitioners' eager attempts to build trust can be contrasted with development efforts that focus on institutional trust building (see, e.g., International Development Law Organization 2016; World Bank 2017) rather than interpersonal trust (Mawdsley, Townsend, and Porter 2005). Theories of how trust is developed in 'low-trust societies' (Latusek and Olejniczak 2016) position a four-stage model where the starting point is found in relational trust, transformed into organisational trust, that contributes to institutionalised trust, and finally leads to a situation of generalised trust (the last transformation has been studied in detail by Braithwaite and Levi 2003). The paradox of this is an aid industry where practitioners are expected to contribute to the development of trust in national rule of law institutions while they themselves are often the subject of mistrust, and the structure of the industry hampers possibilities of spending enough time in one specific setting to build the trust necessary for a close partnership with local actors.

### 7.2.2 Contract in Lieu of Trust

As a parallel process to foreign practitioners' attempts to build trust with local counterparts, the structure of the aid industry pressures them to bring in their learned models of formal contracts and technocratic donor systems of evaluation and control in part to compensate for trust deficits. Such strategies to build trust that is based upon economic assumptions are often incomplete (Stern 2008) and problematic in developing settings, where 'impersonal procedural rules' are met with suspicion because they 'operate without regard for the person' (Rottenburg 2009:62). While the introduction of 'contract' is intended to replicate characteristics of 'trust', it adds aspects of formality and regulation that might not be well received in a 'country without contracts' (Interviewee #29, 23 October 2014). Thus, not surprisingly, the introduction of formal reporting requirements and even applications for funding from major donors did not always sit well with local actors. A foreign programme manager, for example, suggested that when the time came for audits as part of compliance requirements, relationships between the donor and local NGOs often deteriorated:

> I feel awkward sometimes with compliance requirements when we run robust audits on local organizations. It's been awkward, feels like Nazi concentration camp, like I am just following orders [even though I know it is damaging for relationships]. I don't want to brutalise a successful and well-perceived organization. Afterwards, I have to re-establish those relationships.
>
> (Interviewee #20, 30 September 2014)

As stressed earlier, local counterparts of rule of law assistance were bothered by donors' focus on money and monetary compensation because, as one local intermediary claimed, 'Myanmar people generally care very little about money' (Interviewee #17, 23 September 2014). A local intermediary concurred: 'These senior lawyers don't care about money, they care about the personal connection[;] trust and respect are key in Myanmar, more than money' (Interviewee #14, 5 October 2014). Correspondingly, one foreign practitioner suggested: 'Civil society doesn't trust anything that comes from official sources; many NGO's won't accept foreign funding' (Interviewee #35, 19 November 2014). Another foreign practitioner exclaimed with some irritation: 'You can't just bring money, they will say "No" if they don't know you' (Interviewee #29, 23 October 2014). In Myanmar, relational trust (Latusek and Olejniczak 2016) was prioritised in lieu of organisational and institutionalised trust based on formal contract and reporting requirements.

## 7.3 INTERMEDIARIES AS TRUSTED LINKS

Perceptions of the trustworthiness of intermediaries, of their being fair and honest in their dealings with local populations, were cited by interviewees as a consistent predictor of relationships. Thus, in enhancing local perceptions of foreign-funded rule of law development initiatives, demonstrating cultural respect, interacting personally and informally, and performing duties consistently and professionally mattered more than generous grant-giving.

Because it was 'difficult to gain trust as an outsider' (Interviewee #3, 8 May 2014), intermediaries were utilised to 'create trust and opening [*sic*] the doors' (Interviewee #5, 16 May 2014) to 'help ... build relationships and respect' (Interviewee #56, 26 September 2015). Trust in interpersonal relations is especially needed in 'complex' societies where trust 'serves to overcome an element of uncertainty in the behaviour of other people' (Luhmann 1979:22). Intermediaries were able to build trust because of interpersonal qualities in an environment coloured by institutional distrust and xenophobia. In addition, local intermediaries remained in Myanmar on a more permanent basis while foreign practitioners left for assignments in other countries; they were sometimes previously known for reasons I shared in Chapter 6; and they possessed at least some level of understanding of the country's various cultures, which contributed to their chances of building relationships.

Rule of law intermediaries frequently defined 'trust' as 'knowing someone' or 'knowing me'. Similarly, Luhmann (1979:39) makes such linkages to 'personality' central for interpersonal trust:

> Trust is extended first and foremost to another human being, in that he is assumed to possess a personality, to constitute an ordered, not arbitrary, centre of a system of action, with which one can come to terms. Trust, then, is the generalized expectation that the other will handle his freedom, his disturbing potential for diverse action, in keeping with his personality – or, rather, in keeping with the personality which he has presented and made socially visible.

Following Luhmann (1979), interpersonal trust consists of four conditions: mutual commitment; participants' knowledge of the situation they are putting trust in; the offer and acceptance of trust (not demand); and the earning of trust. In fulfilling these conditions, communication and action play important roles in building interpersonal trust because they say something about the individual and their behaviour. This means that whoever wants to win trust must take part in social life and be in a position to build the expectations of others into their self-presentation rather than distancing themselves (ibid.).

Following such reasoning, it is no surprise that foreign rule of law actors have a harder time building trust in Myanmar when they are unapproachable – often located in Yangon at a distance both from government actors in Nay Pyi Taw and from local actors in regional areas – lack means of communicating effectively (they do not speak local languages), lack mutual commitment (foreign and local counterparts have different aims and objectives with rule of law reform), and lack knowledge of the exact situation that local and national counterparts are putting themselves in as a result of their work following foreign organisations' aims and objectives.

Rational and social explanations of trust are also applicable to the case of intermediaries (Braithwaite and Levi 2003; Hardin 2001). The former suggests that trust is largely based on expectations of reciprocity while the latter suggests that trust can alternatively be based on social connectedness or perceptions of shared identities, characteristics, values, or experiences, or open and respectful communication. Perceptions of intermediaries' degrees of cultural understanding, receptiveness to local input, and social connectedness are most powerfully associated with social explanations of trust. Because of their familiarity with a wide range of people, we can suspect that they were trusted because they provided some reciprocity in the past. Such reliance on networks and close circles of friends can be seen as a result of societies with little trust in institutions (Latusek and Cook 2012), which is observed also in Myanmar where intermediaries are primarily connected through 'friendship associations' and invite people they already know to rule of law events (Interviewee #53, 5 October 2015; see also Interviewee #14, 5 October 2014).

It has previously been shown that intermediaries are put in a privileged position because of their trust, knowledge, and contacts (de Jong 2018). Intermediaries themselves suggested that it is because of their trustworthiness and respect that people 'come to them' (e.g., Interviewee #14, 5 October 2014; Interviewee #42, 5 November 2014). When we discussed success factors in his work for a foreign organisation, one intermediary, with a big smile on his face, confidently told me that local counterparts

> know me, that means, they trust me ... [L]ocals do not trust foreigners, they know about foreign policy and that donors have their own interests [however] they trust the local staff a bit more and also me even if I have a political background it does not matter because they like me, that's how our society works ... they [local counterparts] ... come to us. They say 'we respect you'.
>
> (Interviewee #14, 5 October 2014)

Another intermediary similarly suggested: 'I have trust from the [local] organizations' (Interviewee #42, 5 November 2014). Intermediaries who were themselves foreigners suggested that it is possible to gain some level of trust through a continued illustration of alignment with the Myanmar 'side':

> We are in a very good position between Myanmar and the [donor] side, we can choose our standpoint in accordance with the situation, we are using our positions as mediators, we are always situated in the office, so we feel more attached to the Myanmar side, we always fight [the donor], that might be one of the reasons the Myanmar side trust us. We don't report the whole thing, like personal relations with officials within the ministries or which people don't get along. These are important aspects that affect the work, relationships between people.
>
> (Interviewee #39, 22 November 2014)

The practitioner speaking in this way happens to be Japanese. A practitioner in a similar position, but attached to a Western donor, expressed his role, by contrast, as one where he represented 'the international community' (see also Autesserre 2014) and explained that he did not feel as if he was able to build any significant relationships with government actors. Such instances of indication that different approaches to relational aspects of aid might influence development success and sustainability have been more rigorously suggested by ethnographers (Fechter and Hindman 2011). Also Nicholson and Low (2013:38), in comparing foreign rule of law donor approaches in Vietnam and Cambodia, find that Japanese donor JICA was perceived as being better at winning the government's trust because the organisation used 'pools of common consultants ... in a way that the current practice of tender and contracting used by most Western donors does not' and because JICA staff devoted time to counterparts outside of work where they tried to build personal relationships (see also Nicholson and Hinderling 2013). This approach indicated more positive outcomes and these examples hint at the possibility that donors that invest in long-term engagement, with staff that stay with their assignments for extended periods, have the potential to be more sustainable.

Intermediaries are also entrusted with information that foreign counterparts, on the one hand, and local or national actors, on the other, would not reveal to each other. One intermediary explained that 'people tell me things and ask me not to tell them, because they trust me so much', which led him to conclude that he 'should be as honest as possible' (Interviewee #55, 26 September 2015). But the question of being honest was not an easy one: 'Sometimes there is a space we should not open up, for both sides, it depends on the issue. But it is good to keep confidentiality sometimes', another intermediary suggested (Interviewee #27, 7 October 2014). We get a better understanding of the difficult middle position that intermediaries sometimes find themselves in by contrasting the views of a local intermediary who explained that 'people tell [her] things they would not tell each other' (referring primarily to what local and national counterparts would say about her foreign employer) and that only in some cases did she see 'a need to breach confidentiality' (Interviewee #11, 14 May 2014), while her foreign employer was confident that she, in her role as 'national staff',

> will tell us everything the [counterpart] tells her. I think it would be different if she had had relationships with them before. But now, we built up the relationship with her first. To be honest, I do not think that the [counterpart] will ask them [local staff] things about us [smiles] that they would not ask us directly.
>
> (Interviewee #25, 3 October 2014)

Such different perceptions of trust, and who has the strongest relationship, again indicate foreign practitioners' understanding that interpersonal trust is a key factor for successful rule of law development co-operation.

But then again, as we have seen so often, the intermediary became the object of criticism: '[Y]ou get some criticism here ... people ... don't trust foreign-funded organizations' (Interviewee #14, 5 October 2014). Another explained the double nature of his role as he moved from being a trusted facilitator to being a mediator because '[s]ometimes hostilities are very big' (Interviewee #14, 5 October 2014). The intermediary role was compromised as, on the one hand, she is expected to embody and build trust in a setting permeated by distrust while, on the other hand, she is responsible for mediating the conflicts that arise when counterparts do not understand each other or when they hold different perspectives. The issue of 'mixed loyalties' is a common theme that runs through the history of intermediation (de Jong 2018:620). The ambiguity expressed by the rule of law intermediaries in this study indicates that they need to know 'both sides' in order to carry out an intermediary function, while at the same time having to face many challenges because they are seen as having mixed loyalties, which leads to the questioning of their allegiance (James 2011). The trusted intermediary thus also runs the risk of being viewed as not trustworthy and amoral if she is seen to diverge from one group's value system (Stovel and Shaw 2012).

## 7.4 CONCLUSION

In this chapter, I illustrated dimensions of distrust that exist between local and foreign counterparts of rule of law assistance in Myanmar and analysed the role that intermediary actors take on to mediate such distrust. I outlined how notions of distrust in Myanmar have historical roots that can be explained in relation to past regime practices that boosted nationalism and xenophobic sentiments. Foreign development actors thus intervene in a setting where nationalist sentiments had prevailed for decades. This situation is exacerbated by Myanmar having been cut off from the outside world as a result of the decades-long sanctions regime. We can assume that these are factors that influence the way that foreigners are perceived.

Whether issues of distrust are more prevalent or particularly evident in the rule of law field in Myanmar is not considered in this book; I make no comparisons with other fields of international development. However, when reviewing the general distrust that exists towards law and justice institutions, foreign interests, and intervening actors, it could be hypothesised that foreign rule of law development attempts face particular challenges, especially if they risk boosting the power of already distrusted authoritarian institutions (Moustafa 2008).

A lack of trust was identified as a key constraint on foreign practitioners' experience of rule of law work in Myanmar: whether or not they were 'trusted' mattered a lot to them. Because trust is perceived as a prerequisite for successful rule of law assistance, building it or finding someone who can serve as a trusted link becomes a focus of donor efforts. Gaining trust was, however, experienced by many of my interviewees as a comparatively burdensome task because relationships with local actors were difficult to establish. Because foreigners lack prior demonstrated trustworthiness, known actors such as intermediaries instead take on a role as important trust builders. Trust is earned through processes that involve establishing friendships outside and within the workplace. Claiming kinship (*swe-myo-set-deh*) and spending time together through 'friendly visits' were seen as prerequisites for earning trust. In some spaces, such as the regulated capital Nay Pyi Taw, involvement in trust-building activities was hampered by the difficulties of spontaneous outside-work interactions. My own process of trust building was facilitated by 'knowing someone' or by showing engagement and following people on their travels, dining together, visiting pagodas, and having tea. Sceptical glares were exchanged for conversation once it was established whom I knew and who I was. Often the requirement was to spend full, or several, days together with people once they considered you someone to trust, a sister or next of kin.

Intermediaries are primarily able to build trust because of their interpersonal qualities. However, intermediaries' roles as trust builders are not without complications; they have to navigate perceptions that they are too close to the 'foreign' side, which could be damaging for their reputation. They also have to mediate conflicts because they are often trusted with important and confidential information. Perceptions of the trustworthiness of intermediaries, of their being seen as fair and honest in their dealings with local populations, are seen as a consistent predictor of relationships. Thus, for foreign-funded rule of law development initiatives to enhance positive local perceptions of their work, demonstrating cultural respect, interacting personally and informally, and performing duties consistently and professionally matters more than generous grant-giving.

# CHAPTER EIGHT

# INTERMEDIARIES AS TRANSLATORS

At one of Yangon's many Japanese cafés, I caught up with Aung Ko, a local intermediary, whom I had interviewed many times before. As in my previous conversations with him, I asked how he understood and translated rule of law. I remembered that Aung Ko often liked to discuss the importance of the concept and that he had told me previously that he considered 'accountability' an important aspect of this because he believed in the importance of 'doing good' and 'showing loving kindness' (*metta*). At the time of this meeting, he was three years into his work as an intermediary for foreign rule of law organisations, and Aung Ko was more frustrated about the topic. He explained that he preferred not to use such terminology. The reason? 'You can't talk about rule of law when the laws we have are so outdated like they are now ... I don't want [rule of law] in Myanmar.' Instead, Aung Ko told me: 'I say rule of *fair* law ... I talk about the role of civil society in Myanmar, legal reform, better modernized law, modern values; I can't say "rule of law".'

Aung Ko's frustration exemplifies some of the issues that arise when foreign actors attempt to translate a global model to a setting that lacks the institutional and cultural rationales for successful adaptation. In this case, the rule of law's 'substantive' characteristics (Tamanaha and Krygier 2005) have stayed behind. Instead, in Myanmar, influenced by existing political and societal understandings, the term was interpreted in its formal version, or rule by law. As a consequence, in his position as an intermediary, Aung Ko draws on his own capital and experience (reviewed in Chapter 6) to translate the rhetoric of the global model to better fit local circumstances.

In this chapter, the role of intermediaries as rule of law translators is conceptualised at the intersection of Law and Society scholarship on justice reform and legal anthropology. I draw on Sally Merry's (2006a) framework of 'vernacularisation' – 'the process of appropriation and local adoption of globally generated ideas and strategies' (Levitt and Merry 2009:441) – to analyse how intermediaries as actors in 'the middle' translate rule of law in Myanmar (see also Chua 2019). According to Merry, which resonates with findings from Myanmar, intermediaries draw on their knowledge to appropriate foreign norms while relating them to their own understandings of the situation into which they are immersed (see also Carruthers and Halliday 2006; Halliday and Osinsky 2006; Seidel 2017). Vernacularisation is a core part of rule of law norm translation (Berger 2017; Zimmermann 2017), although seldom analysed in relation to the 'diffusion' that take place during attempts to adapt global legal norms to a dynamic national context (Zürn et al. 2012) or considered by rule of law reformers (Channell 2006).

This chapter illustrates the way in which intermediaries reframe the rule of law by steering away from a language brought in by foreign promoters, easily interpreted as 'law and order' or 'rule by law' in the Myanmar locale. Unintentionally, in authoritarian and semi-authoritarian settings like Myanmar, the work of foreign actors risks supporting illiberal versions of rule of law when the political reality is oversimplified (Décobert and Wells 2020). While Myanmar's political history and reality have produced an authoritarian form of rule of law (see also Hurst 2018; Rajah 2012), associations with formal aspects of the concepts were initially enhanced by foreign promoters who brought in their versions of a concept they deemed modelled on international standards that were universal and non-negotiable. Seidel (2017) similarly finds that promoters from abroad, in this case those that were experimenting in South Sudan's constitution-making, brought in their preferred global 'technologies' in attempts to establish rule of law. It was intermediaries that had to adapt these to local circumstances and, in that process, some manage to translate inter-national instruments in ways congenial to their own power interests (see also Dezalay and Garth 2011, 2012; Hammerslev 2006).

In the case of Myanmar, as we saw in the frustration experienced by Aung Ko at the start of the chapter, 'rule of law' as a term without further unpacking was simply not a good match for either local or national understandings. While the term may sit comfortably in the international forum (from which NGOs get their funding), and with Burmese elites, who read it as 'law and order', for the same reason, it is mistrusted by ordinary people who are used to the term being used to coerce rather than represent. This is the reason why Aung Ko, and many other intermediaries like him, repeatedly stressed a language that refrained from the term foreign promoters propagated.

Before I turn to an analysis of vernacularisation as it has played out in Myanmar, the first part of this chapter highlights the main translation challenges that rule of law promoters from abroad experienced when they arrived in Myanmar in the transition period. Then, I introduce the divergence between international and domestic ideas about rule of law, mainly a result of the way that military governments have conflated the term lexically and subordinated it semantically to law and order (Cheesman 2015).

Thereafter, I present intermediaries' insider perspectives on how they translated rule of law in Myanmar. They adjusted and simplified the definitions as applied by foreign practitioners because they were perceived as too technically complicated or politically and socially inept. Frictions thus appeared at the interfaces of the rule of law concept that they tried to further. Here the effect of intermediaries' work shows the incongruence between foreign ideals and local realities. While intermediaries seemed to understand their work as calling on them to interpret ideas in culturally relative ways, their counterparts from abroad were more insistent on the universality of the concepts and approaches with which they came and over which they claimed expertise (see Tungnirun 2018).

The chapter shows how intermediaries are significant in their role as translators as they manage to broker influence: they do not just mobilise their contacts and use their local language skills – they also buffer conversations in which the speakers are mutually incomprehensible and substitute content where they consider this necessary. This highlights that the choice of intermediary is important – as is understanding their motivations and the pressures that they experience because those influence their performance. The chapter highlights that the translations of rule of law that occur in Myanmar are not without friction, because of the gap between the global ideal and values and understandings in the locale. Intermediaries' involvement in translation is compromised as they struggle to balance their allegiance to such diverging values. They influence translation activities by infusing them with their own values and understandings, grounded in personal and political motives.

## 8.1 'THE CONCEPTS CAN GO TOTALLY UPSIDE DOWN': ISSUES IN TRANSLATION

'Translation' happens in the direct communication between rule of law counterparts; when foreign actors contracted local researchers to help them make sense of the new setting; and through strategies to disseminate 'foreign' material to local and national actors (e.g., producing handbooks and cartoons, or digital media, such as a TV show). In the last case, one NGO, for example, wrote handbooks in 'laymen terms, easy to understand Burmese' (Interviewee #16, 22 September 2014). Another INGO translated international rule of law documents and handed them to local groups as part of its rule of law promotion strategy (Interviewee #29, 23 October 2014). Translation of rule of law also happened through attempts to develop cartoons (Interviewee #3, 8 May 2014; Interviewee #16, 22 September 2014). Oral translation (interpreting) took place at conferences and workshops that became important sites of 'mediated communication' (Levitt and Merry 2009). Within the confines of these meetings, intermediaries translated ideas and messages of rule of law (Interviewee #24, 14 October 2014; Interviewee #55, 26 September 2015).

Foreign practitioners experience translation a main challenge in their rule of law assistance work: they suggest that much of their work involved aspects that were 'lost in translation' (Interviewees #8, 22 May 2014; #29, 23 October 2014; #39, 22 November 2014; #40, 9 December 2014), for example the contents of a meeting or discussions at a conference (Interviewee #8, 22 May 2014). In relation to official documents and their translation, one foreign practitioner suggested that English language translations (in this case she was discussing the national land use policy) 'is not reflecting the Myanmar version' but rather 'appeases the foreigner', for example because 'the English version mentions women, but the Myanmar [version] doesn't' (Interviewee #40, 9 December 2014). An added variable that complicated this work was the prevailing assumption that loan words, for example 'democracy', had the same meaning as in the West, while the way that terms were understood by a foreign practitioner would differ from local interpretations (see Fuller 2015a; Wells and Walton 2015). The same goes for terms like 'justice', which, also in Burmese, would be referred to firstly as 'justic' or 'justice' rather than one local version such as *tararrmyahatamhu*. When I visited the national parliament in Nay Pyi Taw in 2014, I passed a wall where several English words that I recognised as typical development lingua (e.g., 'local ownership') were accompanied by lengthy explanations in Myanmar script. Acknowledgement of the fact that direct translation of words does not always exist is seen in International IDEA's 'English–Myanmar Glossary of Democratic Terms', which is presented as 'more than just a translation of key terms. In some cases where no direct translation into Myanmar exists, the glossary [thus] provides a brief explanation or contextualization of concepts and, where possible, draw links to Myanmar's existing legal system and traditional governance concepts' (Institute for Democracy and Electoral Assistance (International IDEA) and Local Resource Centre 2015:3).

My own experience tallies difficulties in daily interactions due to language difficulties: I was confused as I attempted to enter a local court in Yangon when I was stopped by two security guards who blocked the entrance. They looked approachable, sitting on their small, rugged plastic chairs. Behind them, I could see a decaying colonial building and frantic activity going on. The old wooden staircase looked rotten, but at the same time it seemed to majestically move lawyers, clients, the accused, police, and sundry other people from the ground floor up to their hearings. I asked if I could enter, and both guards looked at me, one slightly smiling, the other, not so much. In reply, one shouted: 'No problem!' As I was about to enter, the other shouted: 'No! Problem!' so I stopped. Slightly confused, I asked again if I could enter and got the same answers from both guards. I interpreted this to mean either 'There is no problem for you to enter' or 'No, you cannot enter – that would be a problem.' After asking one more time with the same outcome, I decided to withdraw in order to avoid any potential 'problem', for both myself and the guards.

This is a comparatively simple example of the type of misunderstandings that frequently arise among individuals who do not speak the same language. But for purposes of development aid, which involves not only hefty sums of money but also grand aims and objectives of improving people's conditions, the difficulties that arise from translation challenges can be severe (Autesserre 2012, 2014; Hanks and Severi 2014).

Language knowledge deficits have posed challenges for efficient development work, and the way in which translation issues impact the success of development interventions is an issue that has attracted surprisingly little attention in the field of rule of law assistance. As of the mid-2010s, few foreign practitioners in Myanmar spoke local languages, and fluency in English among potential local partners, let alone other internationally used languages like Japanese, Chinese or French, was limited. A foreign practitioner who was reliant on her co-operation with local lawyers considered that she had surrendered to the language difficulties and admitted with some disappointment: 'I don't spend time talking to lawyers; there are language barriers' (Interviewee #9, 23 May 2014). A government employee in Nay Pyi Taw described as being an issue bringing in English-speaking foreigners who did not have any Burmese language skills to work in government agencies:

> In the beginning, most would come with their English-speaking experts and provide trainings in English. Then they started realizing that this approach did not really work. More and more started to recruit their own Myanmar staff. We have one foreigner working in here, and now after a couple of months she is getting a junior Myanmar colleague . . ., it is needed.
>
> (Interviewee #36, 19 November 2014)

For rule of law promoters in Myanmar, translation challenges excluded them from key conversations and led them to work in an environment where they could not read key documents (Interviewee #2, 7 May 2014); meet counterparts (Interviewee #5, 16 May 2014); or communicate directly with local staff (Interviewee #4, 15 May 2014). A foreign programme manager explained:

> Language is an issue and translation is a big problem. For example, the drafting of the [deleted] law, I supported the drafting process that became such a mess; no one knows if concepts are still there or lost in translation. Myanmar and English are so different from each other. How do you, for example, translate 'accountability' or the many jargon words you use? They just don't translate very well. When I contact people, they are shy to communicate in English. If you want to hire a translator – many are crappy freelancers – you don't know what they are translating. The concepts can go totally upside down.
>
> (Interviewee #5, 16 May 2014)

A foreign consultant similarly suggested:

> It is surprising how limited the English language skills are among the local people, and I don't mean anybody; I mean people with education and quite important positions within NGOs, political parties, etc. Translation is very important for rule of law implementation, but it is

not easy to deal with, they don't know English well enough. This goes well beyond translation problems. Burmese is a difficult language to translate; it's a constant problem.

(Interviewee #18, 24 September 2014)

The comments indicate the difficulty inherent in translating concepts that circulate in global development discourse. The fact that development practitioners from abroad do not speak local languages is nothing new, but the expectation by foreign promoters is that their counterparts will learn and adapt to the foreign language rather than vice versa: the attitudes towards translation and language learning sustain the hegemony of English as the dominant language in the field (Roth 2019). Misunderstandings that arise between development counterparts that do not share the same language and 'cultural codes' affect cross-cultural communication with detrimental effects for development assistance (Autesserre 2014; Coles 2007). These ambiguities of translation appear most evident when things are not going the donors' way, and their interventions result in unintended consequences (Behrends et al. 2014). This is seen, for example, in local reinterpretations of terms and concepts that foreign organisations introduce in ways that do not fit their intended aims and values. This is the topic I turn to next, as, in Myanmar's illiberal setting, 'rule of law' was commonly interpreted as 'law and order'.

## 8.2 RULE OF LAW AS LAW AND ORDER

When asked to define 'rule of law', foreign promoters in Myanmar often-times referred to the former UN Secretary General's definition, which also sometimes features in transnational projects' operational statements. It states that 'all persons, institutions and entities, public and private, including the State itself, are accountable to laws that are publicly promulgated, equally enforced and independently adjudicated, and which are consistent with international human rights norms and standards' (S/2004/616 23 August 2004). This definition stresses both procedural guarantees and the substantive goals associated with them. It also emphasises general principles to eliminate arbitrariness and protect rights, rather than more legally pluralistic and culturally contingent approaches to law and justice for which some researchers advocate, particularly for culturally diverse countries like Myanmar (see Denney et al. 2016; Kyed 2017).

Rule of law promoters from abroad everywhere encounter local counterparts whose understandings of the concept diverge from the contents of international law, and so it is not at all surprising to find that they do in Myanmar too. There, military governments in the 1990s and 2000s conflated the rule of law lexically and subordinated it semantically to law and order (Cheesman 2015). These are concepts that are opposed to each other, as the former is based on defined values of procedural justice and rights, while the latter is primarily concerned with administrative and coercive measures to keep control in society (Cheesman 2014a). Into the 2010s, policy statements in Myanmar continued to convey ideas about the rule of law not as a panacea for arbitrariness but as a mode of social control (Cheesman 2014b).

Adaptation of the term had already begun when General Ne Win took power in 1962 (Cheesman 2009). Coercive legal and regulatory reform had been a key feature of British colonial rule, and Ne Win did little to improve progress towards a justice system that was based on the premises of actually providing 'justice' (for some interpretations of that concept in Myanmar, see Denney et al. 2016). Instead, judicial and executive powers were placed in the hands of 'rule by man', and the parliament was suspended (Taylor, R. H. 2009). At regional levels, military-led administrative bodies took over responsibility from state governments. As a result of these reforms, a system arose that reduced 'the rule of law to the process of enacting and enforcing law' (Cheesman 2015:81), that is, law that was, and to this day, in many instances, remains, repressive.

The idea of 'rule of law' as a substantive concept was further appropriated when a new configuration of military leaders took power in 1988 (Cheesman 2009). The State Law and Order Restoration Council (SLORC), as Cheesman, puts it, 'declined to adhere to any coherent set of principles' and instead 'conflated the rule of law with the "law and order" of its title and pronounced this to be its objective' (Cheesman 2015:101). The SLORC's various changes to the law and justice system caused observers to denounce its regime as one of persistent arbitrariness, disregard of procedure, and protection of the powerful rather than the weak (Pedersen 2008).

The divergence between international and domestic ideas about the rule of law was perhaps thrown into sharpest relief during 2016, when Aung San Suu Kyi, the Nobel Peace Prize laureate who for years harped on the topic, in her new role as de facto head of state suggested that violence in Myanmar's Rakhine state, which had by then already forced hundreds of thousands to flee to Bangladesh (see Cheesman 2017), was being handled according to 'principles of the rule of law' (Funakoshi

2016). Whatever game Aung San Suu Kyi, whose rhetorical use of the rule of law has varied with time and audience (see Cheesman 2014b), may have been playing at here, clearly her reference to principles of the rule of law was a long way removed from those principles that foreign organisations want to espouse.

The issue of local reinterpretations of the term 'rule of law' was experienced by foreign practitioners. One consultant suggested, with evident fatigue, that while there was a constant discussion about it and 'rule of law is everywhere', due to its historical legacy, 'it absolutely translates as law and order, not just linguistically but also conceptually' (Interviewee #35, 19 November 2014). Such understandings stretched from the local to the national level, as expressed by a local intermediary: 'The government does not want to do it; they have no concept of duty to the people; the government is a distant military force. It is quite difficult then to organize this rule of law idea. The judiciary is the last place you go to solve a dispute. Everything is local justice' (Interviewee #29, 23 October 2014).

Lack of trust in government institutions generally and especially in the courts meant that these were spaces that people rather stayed away from, unless they had powerful connections. Instead, people would entrust local actors, for example wardens, to help them resolve disputes or protect their interests. The interesting paradox here is that the warden is, in fact, a prolonged arm of the state and a former part of the military, as the lowest level General Administration Department administrator (MyJustice 2018).

Local reinterpretations pose a challenge for foreign promoters because when they speak about 'rule of law', it is heard as 'law and order'. A foreign programme manager explained: 'You can meet government representatives who are very enthusiastic about rule of law, but then you realize he is talking about law and order' (Interviewee #29, 23 October 2014). Such appropriation of the concept implies that foreign and national development counterparts come together around a common rule of law 'metacode' (Rottenburg 2005) and achieve consensus about whatever is being discussed and agreed upon because the actors around the table believe that they are talking about the same thing. Yet 'rule of law' for one party means 'law and order' to the other. In this case, the programme manager, himself comparatively immersed in Myanmar society, language, and culture, discovered that the 'metacode' was, in fact, a 'cultural code' already during such meetings. In many cases, however, the realisation will not dawn until agreements are about to be implemented. I was told by a foreign programme manager: '[T]hey say they understand the rule of law, but when it comes down to practice you see that that's not the case [E]ven if the law on paper is OK, practice is so different' (Interviewee #40, 9 December 2014). Gibson et al. (2005) explain this phenomenon as one of 'perverse incentives' that structure 'interactions between or among the key corporate and individual actors involved in development cooperation' (Gibson et al. 2005:63) with potential impact on development success. In practice, the recipient government decides on a strategy of (A) accepting all projects but not committing to any of them, (B) accepting all projects but committing only to those it wants to support, or (C) accepting only projects that are consistent with what it wants. In authoritarian settings, Gibson et al. (2005) find, the most likely choice will be strategy A; in some cases, it is B. Because information about incentives can be extra challenging to obtain in an authoritarian setting intermediaries get tasked with more challenges at the interface of negotiation and implementation.

Local actors were also described as understanding the concept differently from the meaning intended by their foreign interlocutors. An American lawyer reflected on his experience of discussing questions of rule of law with local activists around the country:

> Most people have no idea of what they are talking about, or they have a very narrow focus of their understanding of it. They know it is important but can't go very far in expressing an understanding of what it is. The Burmese have for 60 years been so mistreated by the military, and they are very sceptical. Oh boy, will they raise questions if you tell them that a law should be applicable to everybody, the military, government, etc. – not a single person says that they believe in this. I would say they are starting below zero in developing it. You have to try to work with those factors to bring a correct picture of rule of law.
>
> (Interviewee #18, 24 September 2014)

Judging by this, the potential for substantive rule of law understandings in Myanmar is constrained by larger structural forces that in the end will contribute to rule of law understandings that in the best case fall somewhere in between liberal and illiberal (see David and Holliday 2018). Similar depictions were heard across the spectrum of foreign practitioners. One complained that 'people say: "Yes, we agree – the rule of law – the people should obey the laws" . . . People always roll their eyes; the term doesn't mean that much, it can be used to hide behind' (Interviewee #48, 10 October 2014). The demeaning tenor of these remarks is part of a narrative suggesting that people in Myanmar do not understand a concept like rule of law. Yet this ignores the potential of other ideas with roots in Myanmar culture and society, for example Buddhist values (see Walton 2016), that were often stressed by local intermediaries but that most foreigners shied away from. Only one participant, who happened to be one of the few foreign practitioners from a non-Western country, suggested that '[p]eople might know what the rule of law means, but they express it a bit differently – accountability is often expressed as being important' (Interviewee #7, 21 May 2014).

Local staff who worked for foreign rule of law organisations were also described as lacking knowledge and understanding of the rule of law. One foreign practitioner explained how when she worked on a project that attempted to illustrate the rule of law in an accessible way, it became evident that her staff '[h]ad no idea of what we were talking about – the concept was not the same, they referred to the law books, we ended up not doing the [project]' (Interviewee #3, 8 May 2014). Another foreign programme officer exclaimed: 'They really don't get what the rule of law is. [E]ven my staff in Yangon come to me and say – "We really don't get this, please explain it to us"' (Interviewee #35, 19 November 2014). 'They' in the quote refers to a very broad category – everyone – and the suggestion is supported by the evidence that *not even* the local staff, who worked on rule of law issues, understood the model. I got a sense in this discussion that the category 'local staff' (those who did work on rule of law assistance) was used to stress the foreign practitioner's emphasis that *really* 'no one' understood what the rule of law meant.

Foreign practitioners, however, reserved utmost amazement for their experiences with local lawyers whom they suggested understood neither substantive aspects of the rule of law, for example the importance of impartiality (Interviewee #2, 7 May 2014), nor the fundamentality of law beyond the criminal justice system, for example for purposes of good governance and division of powers (Interviewee #35, 19 November 2014). The following quotes make graphic their surprise:

> I had lots of contact with local lawyers. There are problems. I was very pleased of the interest of local lawyers to learn about rule of law. You would sort of think that a group of lawyers in Yangon would be quick to pick things up, but it's not.
>
> (Interviewee #18, 24 September 2014)

[Lawyers'] understanding of the rule of law as we know it and how things should work is just so different. I mean, somewhere in their minds they seem to know that things are different in other places, but for them, they don't know any other way ... It's like they know things should be done in other ways, but they are so used to their system.

(Interviewee #2, 7 May 2014)

The fact that lawyers understood rule of law differently from their foreign counterparts is not surprising in light of the history of marginalisation of the legal profession during military rule. Nevertheless, foreign practitioners arrived in Myanmar with the perception that institutions there, like the legal profession, would perform in ways that were familiar to them, save for the need of some 'development'. While we find explanations of practitioners' lack of preparation and the disregard for country knowledge in the larger structures of the development field (Simion and Taylor 2015), they are too important to continue to disregard. When foreigners could not demonstrate sufficient grasp of Myanmar history and political and legal context, much less the local 'mentality', their technical legal expertise was disregarded (local lawyer, informal conversation, December 2014). Ultimately, misinterpretations of the country context pose risks of unintended consequences that may subvert the intentions of development promoters. In the worst case, they can result in development promotion that strengthens the authoritarian characteristics of rule of law institutions (Moustafa 2008) rather than fostering the values and ideals that rule of law promoters wish to convey.

## 8.3 RULE OF LAW ADAPTATION

Because the rule of law was appropriated by Myanmar actors to signify 'law and order' or 'rule by law', intermediaries became responsible for creating different interpretations and steering away from such preconceptions in their translations. Intermediaries take on roles as translators and interpreters because they are multilingual. They already have skills that lend themselves to communicating between different languages and cultures (see, e.g., de Jong 2018; Meehan and Plonsky 2017). They have mastered both local and transnational linguistic codes, and have become accustomed to their respective cultural worlds (see de Sardan 2005). Additionally, where transnational organisations are trying to build the rule of law in settings that call for professional and high-quality interpretation services, but where such services are scarce, as in

Myanmar (see Dolinska 2017), they have little choice but to rely on intermediaries to help in this respect as well.

During Myanmar's transition period, a significant part of intermediaries' work involved cultural and conceptual translation, to make foreign concepts 'make sense in Myanmar' (referring to both the country and the language, which is also referred to as 'Burmese') (Interviewee #3, 8 May 2014; Interviewee #31, 10 November 2014). Following Merry's (2006a) framework of 'vernacularisation', intermediaries brokered influence over rule of law translation by drawing on their own background, knowledge, and motivations (see Chapter 6). A representative example is provided by a local intermediary, educated partly in the USA, who explained how, for the former Union Solidarity Development Party-led government, the rule of law meant '[b]eing quiet under the law, that the people are obeying the law ... We have a vocabulary in international law for this – "rule by law"' (Interviewee #55, 26 September 2015; see also Interviewee #24, 14 October 2014). By expressing his understanding of international law and aligning himself with the 'we' of the 'international', the local intermediary distanced himself from local interpretations. He drew on his foreign capital and was able to reflect on the way the term was interpreted in the national context. Another intermediary similarly explained how he wanted to 'stress access to justice':

> Increasingly, I have tried to avoid using the term [rule of law] ... We are staying away from it more and more. The term has been taken up by *ma ba tha* [Association for the Protection of Race and Religion] during the recent weeks, it almost carries potential for someone who is on the wrong side.
>
> (Interviewee #20, 30 September 2014)

One term can indeed carry a plethora of interpretations and variations, and this is well recognised in global rule of law debates (Kleinfeld 2005; Shklar 1998). In Myanmar, introducing the term 'rule of law' was equally perplexing. In a process that often involved ruling out the suitability of the rule of law terminology and models used by foreign promoters, because these were 'confusing' and 'counterproductive' (Interviewee #26, 6 October 2014; also tallied by the quote from the intermediary in the introduction to this chapter), intermediaries explained how they had to 'localize the concepts and bring them to people's daily lives' (ibid.). Local intermediaries repeatedly mentioned the need to distract listeners from language that contained the misinterpreted term 'rule of law' (Interviewee #26, 6 October 2014), to instead emphasise labels such as 'justice' and 'just' (Interviewee #24, 14 October 2014), 'fairness' (Interviewee #14, 5 October 2014), 'accountability' and 'trust', because those were terms that they perceived as 'easier to talk about' (Interviewee #53, 5 October 2015). Foreign intermediaries with some local buy-in explained the process as one of navigating challenges to 'see what works' without enforcing anything and by facilitating Myanmar actors 'to analyse issues themselves' (Interviewee #25, 3 October 2014). They variously reflected on the way that they 'vernacularised' the concept and term:

> I tend to talk about rule of law in a broader context. Our mandate is to promote rule of law globally. Access to justice and legal side of development included. It is a bit tricky with local stakeholders with the connotations of rule of law when translated into Myanmar, a bit authoritative. I try to focus on what is rule of law beyond translation and what is the difference between 'rule of law' and 'rule by law.' We don't start with the assumption that they would interpret it the way we see fit. The Government understands it different than civil society. They might initially have a negative view, but once they know about the principles and the aims of people's attitudes change.
>
> (Interviewee #54, September 2015)

> Rule of law is everywhere, constant discussion. Usually, I put it in terms of what do we mean by these ideas. It often comes down to fairness. A senior government counterpart shared a term with me: 'living under the framework of the law leads to a just and peaceful life'. The concept is also Buddhist infused. Applies to the people- the civil servants don't see it so much as applying to them.
>
> (Interviewee #35, 19 November 2014)

> I explain it as the opposite to have a person's sense of injustice resolved, rather than a set off institutional processes. Institutional arrangements are still not working, limited and need tweaking, quite obvious that there is political engagement and entrenched elite that has got a very firm grip.
>
> (Interviewee #20, 30 September 2014)

I experienced one example of adaptation when I met with one of the intermediary NGOs that had attracted significant donor funding for rule of law-related activities since the country's opening. A webpage listed its work as focusing on 'rule of law and human right-based [sic] democracy' (Namati: Innovations in Legal Empowerment n.d.). When I spoke with one of the NGO leaders, he repeatedly described their work in terms of 'democracy' and 'accountability' with little reference to 'rule of law' (Interviewee #30, 24 October 2014). Such reference illustrates the possibilities of the creative reinterpretation and mobilisation of rule of law language that happen in Myanmar. In this case, the idea might have been to emphasise the importance of human rights and rule of law for democracy and to stress the term's substantive sense, which is easily lost in translation when the model merges with existing understandings in Myanmar. For the organisation's later activities, 'justice' was stressed as a way to '[avoid using the] term rule of law', even though the previous use of the term had emphasised a 'substantive definition, tweaked with human rights' (Interviewee #20, 30 September 2014).

Often, terms used by foreign promoters did not even find a match in the Burmese language, which meant that intermediaries adopted a strategy of listing words with lengthy explanations, trying to get anywhere near capturing the essence of the promoters' objectives (Interviewee #3, 8 May 2014; see also Wells and Walton 2015). These adaptations are important to acknowledge because they indicate that foreign promoters push forward terminology and concepts that are problematic in their ambiguity as to the fundamental basis of their intervention. While perhaps it is the ambiguity of the global rule of law ideal that makes it at all promotable, what the Myanmar case rather shows is that well-meaning development actors from abroad become unintentional promoters of a concept that in the locale is associated with illiberal values.

The multifaceted Myanmar interpretations of the term 'rule of law' eventually dawned upon foreign promoters who began to use terms like 'access to justice' (Interviewee #12, 7 May 2014) because it was easier 'to identify with' (Interviewee #56, 26 September 2015). A foreign lawyer suggested: 'Some people say that we should not use the term "rule of law"[;] better to use "access to justice"' (Interviewee #19, 25 September 2014). Such 'recursive' – or multidirectional 'back and forth' – translation (Scribner and Slagter 2017) happens when intermediaries feed domestic adaptation 'upwards' (Halliday and Carruthers 2007) in processes that involve responsive, multidirectional, and mutual influence that flows among the actors participating in the development process. In practical terms this means that the global rule of law concept, as well as the term, unfolds recursively, rather than in a 'global' to 'local' fashion (Berger 2017), and changes meaning through local and intermediary influences (see also Seidel 2017;

Zimmermann 2017). Nevertheless, while rule of law promoters in the field had the scope to steer activities towards discourse they deemed more suitable, often based on the insights or wants of the local intermediary, they are criticised for not being able to adhere to idealised conceptions of the rule of law – either those put forward by scholars (see, e.g., Santos 2006) or those pushed for by foreign 'clients' and the working definitions used within their organisations (Interviewee #25, 3 October 2014). In their role as intermediaries, however, they broker influence by stressing the way things have to be adapted to the local context.

Eventually, the way foreign promoters discussed rule of law also shifted more towards a language that focused on 'trust', which extended to the framing of rule of law activities, often after a realisation that neither 'rule of law' nor 'access to justice' was a suitable term to use because they were misunderstood by 'people' (Interviewee #53, 5 October 2015). A focus on establishing trust in rule of law institutions is indeed a common component of and a key goal for many rule of law projects (British Council 2016). However, in addition to a focus on trust building as part of a broader agenda to establish trust in the justice system, what stood out in the recursive translations going on in Myanmar was the tendency to replace 'rule of law' terminology with 'trust'. For example, a local organisation framed one of its rule of law projects as 'building support for justice' under the banner 'access to trust' (presentation slides, 4 October 2015, on file with the author). Two foreign practitioners explained the rationale behind their project's focus on trust:

> We present this project as building trust because it is quite critical, a good 90 percent of the people have little trust. The trust-building element is critical. It is a way of saying that you are going to work with a lot of actors but slightly empty in a way.
>
> (Interviewee #20, 30 September 2014)

> Many people talk about trust, so we pick this terminology/focus- it's especially important in relation to the police and courts, it's a better term than rule of law that people can misunderstand. Access to trust, looking at it from different angles. The basis of trust with the authorities is the law; if you obey the law, you have their trust. My observation after two years in this country is that there is no trust, especially between the government and public. It is easier for some to talk about trust rather than rule of law.
>
> (Interviewee #53, 26 September 2015)

Another practitioner from abroad suggested that they often worded their rule of law reform efforts as 'trust' when working with the government because '[i]n a place where law is seen as a transactional discipline – the emphasis on building trust is a two-way stream. Institutions must improve, and people be sensitized on the role of those institutions' (Interviewee #54, 26 September 2015). What these examples hint at is that the rule of law has little real traction in Myanmar. What matters, instead, is to what extent projects build trust. The paradox of such foreign-supported efforts to build trust in Myanmar's justice system is that the foreign-funded initiatives and foreign interests currently prevailing are handicapped by the lack of trust towards them (see Chapter 7).

## 8.4 INTERMEDIARIES' ALLEGIANCE TO SOURCE OR TARGET

Intermediaries' involvement as translators of rule of law is not without friction because of the perceived gap between the global ideal and local understandings, and so they struggle to balance their allegiance to different actors and values. On the one hand, they try to convene the message of their foreign employers by stressing words that steer away from the misinterpreted term 'rule of law', while, on the other, they deal with local counterparts who do not approve when intermediaries seem too aligned with their foreign employers.

Scholars have previously found that intermediaries' commitments to either the 'source' or the 'target' have implications for how they operate as translators. Table 8.1, for example, captures Merry's suggestion that '[t]ranslators committed to the target produce more

TABLE 8.1 Replication and hybridisation (per Merry 2006a)

| Intermediaries closer to the global source | **Replication** • Source relatively dominant • Superficial adaptation • Import remains largely unchanged |
|---|---|
| Intermediaries committed to the local target | **Hybridisation** • Target more powerful • Influenced by local institutions and structures • Merges the import with local institutions and symbols |

hybrid transplants, whereas those closer to the source create replicas' (Merry 2006a:8). Also, it has been found that intermediaries who are more loyal to the nation-state than to a global organisation are more likely to justify objection or resistance to global norms (Halliday and Carruthers 2009).

While intermediaries often raised the need for local and national adaptation, foreign promoters stressed the need for replication, as they repeated allegiance to international standards and human rights regulations, which thus far have had little traction in Myanmar. A foreign practitioner explained:

> We base all our work on international standards on rule of law. Justice officials here equals rule of law with law and order, so they think that is really good. Always when we engage, we do it within the framework of international standards, human rights, etc.
>
> (Interviewee #31, 10 November 2014)

Another foreign practitioner concurred that 'we have our ideas of international best practice. In this field, there is a pretty good consensus of what an independent judiciary is' (Interviewee #25, 3 October 2014). The practitioner's reference to the judiciary echoes the argument presented in Chapter 2 that promoters in the field share common understandings of specific aspects that rule of law carries. In the national context, this sort of replication that the practitioner is referring to as the standard is difficult because the role of international law in Myanmar was, and remains, ambiguous (Booth 2016). A local translator explained that some of the main difficulties of his work derived from the fact that 'the international law concepts are not coherent with Myanmar custom; people do not understand what they read' (Interviewees #57 and #58, 30 September 2014). A government representative similarly suggested that international law had little means of being adapted to Myanmar's culture and that instead '[t] hey [the international community] should change the international law so that it fits the Myanmar context' (Interviewee #37, 20 November 2014). Such adaptation is, of course, a central feature of vernacularisation (Levitt and Merry 2009); however, for foreign practitioners the idea of abandoning their allegiance to international standards is unthinkable, unless it involves particularly 'sensitive issues' such as war crimes prosecution or global standards for citizens' rights (Interviewee #2, 7 May 2014; Interviewee #3, 8 May 2014).

A telling example of how international law is met with suspicion was provided by a local intermediary who explained that local counterparts [in this case, local lawyers] expressed distrust towards international law and international interests: 'Many think that international law is just nonsense, 70% don't care about international law; they don't have the legal knowledge about the supremacy of international law over national law. They don't know the basic fundamental international laws. Sometimes we hear that we need to abandon certain things, universal rights for national interests' (Interviewee #55, 26 September 2015).

A local human rights activist, however, argued that concepts that relate to universal human rights were rooted in Myanmar's Buddhist culture and that the common understanding of international law as something foreign was deceiving: 'It is not about bringing something foreign to our culture even if that is what the regime wants us to believe' (Interviewee #26, 6 October 2014). Reference to Buddhist culture as an entry point to justice or human rights was not often mentioned as a way of interest or awareness by foreign promoters. Neither was a mediating role for monks reflected upon which might seem strange in a country so obviously connected to the authority of the *Sangha*. This was likely a result of the uneasy relationship foreign promoters developed with a religion that did not reflect the ethnic diversity in a country where the recognition and respect of such values were becoming a key aspect of the rule of law work and where monks took on roles as active promoters of its opposite non-democratic values. Gil's 2008 suggestion that 'in Burma, it would be difficult to find better mediators and respected authorities than the members of the sangha and their voice could be valuable and beneficial for both the authorities and the people' (Gil 2008:11) had by 2015 developed to a realisation that the monkhood could indeed be a powerful but perilous voice (Than 2015).

Intermediaries who worked for foreign organisations and who were invested in international law were closer to 'the source' rather than 'the target', and they drew on their 'foreign capital' to gain social capital at home. However, intermediaries' commitments sometimes became a source for conflict between development counterparts who were influenced by different understandings of what rule of law means. Overlaid on such conflicts was local and national actor distrust of foreign interests. An example of the intermediaries who worked on a project involving local lawyers as counterparts is telling. The intermediaries were criticised by local counterparts for 'twisting' messages in meetings, for being in favour of 'international ideas' rather than local ones, and for getting 'too much attention from the international side' (Interviewee #47, 9 December 2014). One of the intermediaries' replies to that criticism indicated how he saw his role in the processes of translation: 'I try to show how international and national law can align ... try to show them how to think what is the best option for them' (Interviewee #17, 23 September 2014). A similar explanation was provided by another intermediary:

> I explain the local context to the internationals and the international framework to the locals. They say: 'Hey – don't stand in the way.' They think it is my view and that I am more on the international side, but I am just explaining the framework- they say 'They don't understand the Myanmar context' – I say 'You don't understand [me and the inter-national framework]'. I don't want to be there in the middle.
>
> (Interviewee #14, 5 October 2014)

These comments suggest that intermediaries take on the role of explaining a system of international law that appeared 'foreign' but that intermediaries understand because of their previous experiences and current work. Also, the implementation of processes that have the potential for reconfiguring structures for the exercise of social power will inevitably result in conflict and contestation. Groups and individuals involved in carrying out programmes for social change are in a position to influence who become the winners and losers in those contests, which is why it should not be surprising that self-interest plays a part in the exercise of contestation and influence.

## 8.5 SELECTIVE TRANSLATIONS AND MORAL ENTREPRENEURSHIP

Intermediaries everywhere use opportunities to translate between transnational actors and local counterparts to their advantage, craft-ing communications so as to make everyone happy. They also pitch ideas from abroad in ways that they think will resonate with their listeners (see Levitt and Merry 2009). Translators often have bonds to various interests and quest for 'opportunities for wealth and power' that affect the processes of vernacularisation (Merry 2006a:40). The broker is a 'professional manipulator' who receives her power by facilitating transmissions of messages through a sequence of complex manoeuvres involving manipulation and self-interests (Boissevain 1969:382). Those in Myanmar are no exception to any of these practices. One with whom I spoke said that in his role as 'translator' he did more than just 'ordinary' translation. Rather, he said, he infused translations with his own values when he helped explain concepts: 'Sometimes I also do something like a translator, but not just a translator, it is not only word translation but also concept translation, an ordinary translator cannot do this … I feel like I am helping the process. It is good to put some of your own values in the translation' (Interviewee #17, 23 September 2014). Based on the intermediary's motivation to 'help people in need', he perceived this act – what we might call a form of 'moral entrepreneurship' (Becker 1973; Finnemore and Sikkink 1998) – as an important part of his work in trying to influence actors around him to understand rule of law. The 'middleman role' also involves the dissemination of a person's 'own value system' because he may be 'concerned about the kind of exposure that is made … of western values which may impinge upon his domain' (Paine 1971:6–7).

In Myanmar, intermediaries infuse translations with their own values to protect local-level interests from 'foreigners' (Interviewee #3, 8 May 2014; Interviewee #34, 18 November 2014) and 'they want to protect the other side from looking bad' (Interviewee #10, 12 May 2014). Intermediaries confess that they 'tailor' (Interviewee #29, 23 October 2014) and 'filter' (Interviewee #8, 22 May 2014) messages, sanitise 'dirty info' (Interviewee #6, 19 May 2014), use 'many language tricks' to make meanings more pleasant, and 'give many options for interpretation' (Interviewee #14, 5 October 2014): 'I want them to know what this all really means – I am like a bridge … You can hire an interpreter, but they can make a lot of problems, they don't understand all the concepts and how to keep the different actors satisfied. So this is part of what I do' (Interviewee #14, 5 October 2014). Selective communication by intermediaries is inherent in the role itself (Paine 1971) and the capacity to manage meanings is an essential aspect of how intermediaries are able to broker influence by strategic-ally manipulating 'transactional relationships' (Cohen and Comaroff 1976:89).

However, intermediaries' strategies for infusing translations with their own values led to tensions with foreign practitioners who recog-nised that 'things happen often. It's a shame that things get lost in translation – to prevent it, both sides need to be more responsible' (Interviewee #6, 19 May 2014). The 'things' that happened included 'filtering' of messages because there was 'a lot of trust involved in these

Myanmar language things and how messages are being conveyed' (Interviewee #8, 22 May 2014). One foreign practitioner described the situation of translation as one where the intermediary knew how to 'tailor messages to the audience' but, as the practitioner explained:

> I recognize it, but I have seen many organizations that don't recognize that the guy is saying something else. It is not an issue in our organization, but I do think it is an issue. Not everyone gets human rights, so he has to be careful and make sure the message comes out the right way. You have to really start at the beginning, at the basics and not with high-level concepts. Even the basics were illegal until a couple of years ago.
>
> (Interviewee #29, 23 October 2014)

One foreign respondent suggested that tensions arose with local staff when 'they have a translation role but also want to make their own point' (Interviewee #4, 15 May 2014). Respondents described how intermediaries did not 'just translate' but also did 'something else' (Interviewees #6, 19 May 2014; #7, 21 May 2014; #31, 10 November 2014). Intermediaries were seldom perceived as neutral translators. One foreign practitioner reflected on the fact that many of them had 'extraordinary personal histories' which they brought into their work which she believed could 'be much more important than being a "neutral" translator', but then she went on to reflect on 'the issue of bias – do they bring their own views and meanings into the interpretation? . . . They tell us sometimes if it is their own view we get' (Interviewee #7, 21 May 2014). Another foreign practitioner concurred that the local intermediary employed by their project was 'not interpreting all for me but gives his opinion on things and paraphrases a lot[;] this does not necessarily give accurate information' (Interviewee #8, 22 May 2014). This illustrates the tension in working with people that are able to adjust and adapt meaning to the locale while foreign promoters are stuck to international concepts and a culture where bias is perceived as something that compromises rather than facilitates processes to move forward.

Rule of law intermediaries' selective translations not only affected communication between development counterparts but also influenced local receptions of rule of law. Intermediaries in Myanmar seemed to have come around to the view that the definitions of the rule of law to which their foreign counterparts often referred were too encompassing, too difficult to discuss, let alone to propose to implement. Intermediaries found it necessary to protect local interests from foreign development actors' tendency to view their knowledge as the most advanced (Rottenburg 2009) in a setting where '[n]ot even the lawyers are so strong on the topic' (Interviewee #27, 7 October 2014).

By using strategies of substituting the content of translation with their own views and values, and claiming to know best, intermediaries were also able to displace linguistic experts. Professional interpreters were sometimes dismissed as being unsuitable for the task of working on rule of law, yet intermediaries were not performing the interpreting role to the ethical standards that would be required of a professional interpreter. The relative absence of professional, high-quality interpretation services in Myanmar at the time (Dolinska 2017) might have contributed to opportunities for intermediaries. However, the frequent suggestions by foreign practitioners, and even more frequent suggestions by intermediaries, that the field involved such complex translations that no ordinary interpreter or translator could suffice are striking. In effect, intermediaries' interpreting and translation could not possibly be neutral, yet international employers tried to manage intermediaries – and their tendency to deploy themselves to further their own ends. However, because of their acute need for intermediaries and the scarcity of professional legal interpreters in Myanmar, foreign practitioners became even more reliant on these actors. While intermediaries' moral entrepreneurship and selective translations embody the ambiguity of their loyalty and commitments (Merry 2006b), they remain perhaps the most central components of rule of law assistance to Myanmar.

## 8.6 CONCLUSION

This chapter showed that intermediaries draw on their experiences to convey ideas from one context to another, adapting and reframing them from the way they attach to a source context to one that resonates with the new location. I illustrated some of the issues that arise when foreign actors attempt to translate a global model to a setting that lacks the institutional and cultural rationales for successful adaptation. In this case, rule of law's 'substantive' characteristics had stayed behind and were interpreted as a formal concept, influenced by existing political and societal understandings. The overview thus illustrated that 'authoritarian rule of law has foundations and facades that must be penetrated in order to be analysed' (Rajah 2012:280) through the story of local redefinitions of the rule of law as 'law and order'.

This chapter highlighted the main translation challenges that rule of law promoters from abroad experienced when they arrived in Myanmar in the transition period. I argued that unintentionally, in authoritarian and semi-authoritarian settings like Myanmar, the work of foreign promoters may have unintended consequences of promoting illiberal versions of rule of law when they bring in a concept to a political reality that they oversimplify (Décobert and Wells 2020). While Myanmar's political history and reality have produced a semi-authoritarian form of rule of law (see also Hurst 2018; Rajah 2012), rule of law as a term without further unpacking was simply not a good match for either local or national understandings. While the term may sit comfortably in the international forum and with Burmese elites, who read it as 'law and order', for the same reason it is mistrusted by ordinary people who are accustomed to the term being used to coerce rather than represent. This is the reason why intermediaries stressed a language that refrained from using the term in the sense that foreign promoters propagated.

The chapter illustrated how intermediaries broker influence as translators in a process in which they are seldom neutral: they put their own values into translations and filter messages as 'moral entrepreneurs', thus protecting local-level interests. In their translations of rule of law, they move away from the discourse used by global actors to avoid connotations of 'law and order'. The chapter revealed how intermediaries frame rule of law in ways more suitable for the national and local settings by abandoning references to aspects of a global language that they see as being unfit for their purposes. I presented intermediaries' insider perspectives of their work as translators. While intermediaries seemed to understand their work as calling on them to interpret ideas in culturally relative ways, their counterparts from abroad were more insistent on the universality of the concepts and approaches with which they came and over which they claimed expertise.

The chapter showed how intermediaries are influential in their role as translators as they manage to broker influence: they do not just mobilise their contacts and use their local language skills – they also buffer conversations in which the speakers are mutually incomprehensible and substitute content where they consider this necessary. This highlights that the choice of intermediary is important – as is understanding their motivations and the pressures that they experience because these influence their performance. Intermediaries' involvement in translation is compromised as they struggle to balance their allegiance to diverging values, influencing translation activities by infusing them with their own values and understandings, grounded in personal and political motives.

Even when the linguistic translation problems are 'solved' (e.g., local interlocutors become better at English), the collision of concepts and priorities, and the appropriation of the new concepts for local uses (both benign and less benign) are likely to continue. We can see that one outcome of foreign intervention in a country like Myanmar is likely to be 'rule of law' with a very authoritarian cast.

# CHAPTER NINE

# INTERMEDIARIES' INFLUENCE, FOREIGN ACTORS' DEPENDENCE

This book posed the question – how do intermediaries broker influence of foreign-funded rule of law assistance in Myanmar? By answering the research question together with a set of sub-questions relating to intermediaries' emergence, backgrounds, motives, methods, and activities, this book has established that intermediaries convey ideas from one context to another, adapting and reframing them from the source to one that resonates with the new location (Levitt and Merry 2009) because 'rule of law' travels through processes of 'translation' to new sites where its institutional conventions, knowledge, and practices are lacking (Berger 2017; Berger and Esguerra 2017; Zimmermann 2017). In Myanmar, the emerging field of rule of law assistance was shaped, in part, by intermediaries who came to possess influence through brokerage and mediation (see also de Jong 2018; Meehan and Plonsky 2017; Stovel and Shaw 2012).

This book illustrated that development actors from abroad often relied on intermediaries who were charismatic, fluent in English, and had been educated abroad (see also Gonzalez 1972). Many had a background in social or political engagements and some previous experience of working for foreign development actors. Some intermediaries capitalised on these new opportunities, as they reinvented themselves as consultants or started their own NGOs or law firms. Intermediaries had motives and goals that stretched beyond the work they did for their foreign employers – which had implications for how rule of law project activities came to be planned and implemented, the way rule of law was translated, and ultimately development sustainability.

The central finding of this book was that intermediaries broker influence in the rule of law assistance field in that they steer the direction of development interventions, translate global concepts selectively, and mediate and buffer complex disagreements among development counterparts who do not share the same values and understandings. Foreign development actors who lack cultural and linguistic knowledge are reliant on intermediaries to carry out their development activities, which yields them influence. Throughout this book, I showed that, because of their central importance, intermediaries influence project allocation, deliver diffused messages of 'local needs', and have the influence to decide who will, or will not, be included in development activities (D'Exelle 2009; Wanvoeke et al. 2016).

Although critique and a need for reinvention have been voiced in relation to rule of law assistance, the examination of the ideological underpinnings of the field has remained static (Desai and Woolcock 2015). This book provides a critical perspective on the attempts to transplant Western principles to new settings (DeLisle 1999): I provide illustrations of how those processes require intermediation because they are part of development models rather than universal norms (Remadji and Behrends 2014).

I advanced current theory in the scholarly field of rule of law assistance by introducing an actor who has remained largely silent in the literature on rule of law assistance: the intermediary, a known figure of development practice that remains under-analysed (Bierschenk et al. 2002; Lewis and Mosse 2006). This focus relates to debates that stress the importance of sociological understandings of the law because it centres on the individuals who are responsible for various forms of legal translation and appropriation (Chua 2015; Halliday and Carruthers 2007; Krygier 2009b).

This book highlighted the effect of intermediaries' activities during a historical moment of political change in Myanmar (Mullen 2016; Pedersen 2014) and thus shed light on challenges of translating rule of law to a regime transitioning from military rule (Cheesman 2014b). The case of Myanmar highlights that donors need to adjust their strategies to political realities because development 'on paper' looks different from development in practice (Crewe and Harrison 1998).

This book demonstrated how donors could gain an understanding of what is happening in the confined spaces, places, and meetings that are inaccessible to them, or that official reporting fails to capture, by accessing the insights of intermediaries (de Sardan 2005). The challenges faced by rule of law intermediaries also point to what is going 'wrong' in the field of foreign-assisted rule of law reform in settings such as Myanmar, because intermediaries are also repositories of knowledge about the challenges that their counterparts face (Hasegawa 2009).

## 9.1 ETHNOGRAPHIC ATTENTION TO INTERMEDIARIES

Research that involves charting intermediaries' careers and activities is a strategy with potential because it reveals ethnographic insights that remain largely unreported form formal accounts of rule of law assistance. Seeking the vantage point of those in the middle revealed that intermediary actors are pivotal to rule of law development efforts.

This book sought to show that rule of law practice needs to move away from viewing intermediaries as neutral facilitators or natural, indispensable features of the field in the shape of 'that guy', 'the translator', or the 'local contact'. Instead, we should regard them as worth studying and understanding in some depth (Lindquist 2015b) as people and as actors whose capabilities and choices often steer the direction of rule of law development assistance. While we may be tempted to predefine who intermediaries are, such an approach limits our socio-legally informed understanding of active agents around and in between the law (see also Moore 1973) in the same way as a formal, rather than pluralistic approach limits our understandings of what law *is* (see, e.g., Calavita 2010). A broadening scope is particularly important in a setting such as Myanmar, where foreigners continue to be excluded from both psychological and physical spaces of local and national power.

By analysing intermediaries' influence in rule of law practice, we can see how their roles are created, why actors seek them out, and how they affect development processes, and this opens up the potential to better understand how rule of law implementation in transitional settings can be improved. If the donor community is willing to move away from the current predominant tendency to privilege international 'expertise' and knowledge and to consider intermediaries' accounts of rule of law interventions, it may be possible to design assistance in ways that better benefit people who live in societies where a well-functioning system of rule of law is lacking.

## 9.2 A TYPOLOGY OF RULE OF LAW INTERMEDIARIES

This book provided a typology of rule of law intermediaries: the local lawyer, the local NGO, the local staff, the international consultant, and the government employee. The inductive approach to the study of intermediaries refrained from attempts to predefine these actors. Instead, I discovered who was an intermediary through ethnographic study. Such ethnographic attention to intermediaries showed that their role is fluid: intermediaries often oscillate across assignments and institutions which enable them to obtain multiple influences at different levels. Because the most sought-after intermediaries worked for several donors simultaneously, it sometimes made it look as though several actors supported the rule of law model, when in fact only a handful of people were channelling much of the field's assistance. Foreign actors were not always aware of the many involvements of the intermediaries, who carefully balanced their multiple roles and identities.

The search for intermediaries was made within the field of rule of law assistance that emerged in Myanmar after the political transition in 2011. I provided a description of that field and illustrated how foreign development actors sought to promote rule of law in various ways. I also presented responses to this process by local actors as they became development counterparts. I suggested that the initiation of rule of law assistance in Myanmar meant that international, national, and local structures were brought into contact in ways that would have been unthinkable during the preceding decades of military rule. It was a setting where relationships between development counterparts were still emerging and where intermediaries, I argued, thus became important for shaping processes of rule of law development.

## 9.3 INTERMEDIARIES INFLUENCE PROCESSES OF RULE OF LAW DEVELOPMENT

In this book, I showed that foreign actors become reliant on intermediaries for carrying out development intervention. When rule of law assistance took root in Myanmar, this led to contestation. Local participants questioned what they saw as a divergence between their motivations for engaging in rule of law development work, and those of their foreign counterparts. Asymmetries in the knowledge of the local setting and imbalances in power relations also fuelled complaints that donors were pushing their own agenda. Competitive and contested ideas and approaches needed careful balancing by rule of law intermediaries, who had to mediate between – and co-ordinate – counterparts. Intermediaries were necessary because there was a 'clash' of objectives and approaches when the rule of law model hit the ground in Myanmar. Intermediaries emerged to navigate between the different values and motivations of international, national, and local actors. Reforms in Myanmar and the resulting development assistance, in turn, reopened or created new fields of action, to which an increasing number of intermediaries were attracted.

Intermediaries thrive in the rule of law assistance field because foreign development actors need backing from individuals who understand their aims and objectives, can help them navigate unfamiliar systems, and can reach out to potential counterparts. This book showed that as a result of the influx of foreign development actors, individuals drew on their personal social capital in order to carve out a space in the rule of law assistance field. In doing so, they reinvented themselves as consultants, NGO leaders, and employees for international organisations. The demand for intermediaries prompted individuals to do so as a result of opportunity or 'discovery' of new openings that enabled increased access to power and economic resources. On the government side, intermediaries also emerged, although this was less because of 'opportunity' and more because of 'burdens' that must be carried out dutifully.

As a result of high demand but limited supply of suitable intermediaries, development actors compete for individuals who possess valued characteristics. To bolster the lack of supply, foreign development actors also support the creation of coalitions and invest in NGOs that can serve as competent intermediaries. Such approaches have implications for development sustainability and local ownership. The demand for intermediaries creates opportunities for these actors to influence the direction of rule of law assistance. While foreign practitioners in the field have the scope to steer activities towards topics or areas they deem necessary or possible to focus on, in practice such decisions are often based on the insights or wants of the local intermediary.

### 9.3.1 Personalities and Networks

Intermediaries' identities are important because their agency shapes the processes of rule of law development (Dezalay and Garth 2011, 2012). This book revealed some commonality in the backgrounds of rule of law intermediaries: they are politically engaged, studied English during military rule, had access to foreign education, and worked for foreign organisations. I argued that after political transition, intermediaries mobilised the foreign capital they accumulated during military rule within the rule of law assistance space that emerged. This was evident, for example, in the way in which intermediaries used their networks to select who got to be included in rule of law activities, in the way they were able to travel more freely across Myanmar and thus became the satellites for rule of law, and in the way they used their foreign language skills to serve as knowledge brokers, channelling information in the languages of actors on 'both sides' (see also Bierschenk et al. 2002; de Sardan 2005).

This book also suggested that the tendency by foreign actors to seek individuals with likeable personalities who are 'easy to work with' and have large networks has implications for rule of law assistance if it means that foreign actors choose to work with intermediaries out of convenience, rather than making an informed decision about those with the most influence.

### 9.3.2 Trusted Links between Counterparts

Foreign development actors intervened in a setting where nationalist sentiments had prevailed for decades and where foreign influences and interests were met with suspicion. I detailed the problems pertaining to distrust that exist between local and foreign counterparts in Myanmar. Foreign practitioners experienced lack of trust as a key constraint on their rule of law work in Myanmar, and they understood that whether or not they were 'trusted' mattered. Because trust was perceived as a prerequisite for successful rule of law assistance, it became the focus of much donor effort. Gaining trust, however, became a comparatively burdensome task because relationships with local actors were difficult to build. Because foreigners lacked prior proof of their trustworthiness, known actors such as intermediaries instead took on the important role of trust builders.

Intermediaries are able to build trust because of interpersonal qualities (Braithwaite and Levi 2003; Luhmann 1979). However, intermediaries' role as trust builders is not without complications. They continually have to navigate the perception that they are too close to the 'foreign' side (Carruthers and Halliday 2006), which can be damaging for their reputation and they are drawn into mediating conflicts because they are trusted with important information. Perceptions of intermediaries as being trustworthy and fair and honest with local populations were a consistent predictor of the success of their networked relationships. Thus, in enhancing local perceptions of foreign-funded rule of law development initiatives, being able to demonstrate cultural respect, interact personally and informally, and perform duties consistently and professionally tends to matter more than generous grant-making (see also Stern 2008).

## 9.4 DONORS APPLY MODELS REGARDLESS OF POLITICAL REALITY

The analysis of intermediaries and their role as translators in this book revealed that foreign donors continue to apply development models regardless of the political reality of the country of intervention. This leaves little room for alternative conceptions of rule of law. Instead, such alternatives emerge when intermediaries translate rule of law to the local context in Myanmar. Donors in the rule of law field will continue to apply global development models in settings beyond Myanmar, especially in light of the acceleration of even more advanced technologies of measuring that accompany the SDG's (Arajärvi 2017; Bergling and Jin 2015; Desai and Schomerus 2018).

This book showed that the history and dynamics of authoritarianism in Myanmar have an impact on the way that rule of law has been locally adopted and appropriated (Cheesman 2015). I illustrated how intermediaries translate the rule of law model to the Myanmar setting and argued that they are seldom neutral translators because they put their own values into translations and filter messages, either as 'moral entrepreneurs' (Becker 1973) or to protect the local level from foreign interests. I found that global actors in Myanmar seek to disconnect their contemporary work from earlier 'law and order' associations with rule of law used by the military leadership. Intermediaries frame rule of law in ways more suitable for the national and local settings and will abandon references to aspects of the global language when they judge these to be unfit for their purposes. In this way, the global rule of law model is reframed to match multiple existing ideologies and understandings.

Intermediaries influence foreign actors recursively with their translations from the 'middle up'. While the themes and structure of rule of law promotion were similar to those found in other settings, a more detailed examination of activities showed that different forms of translation happened, often through the influence of key intermediaries. Translation from the 'middle up' occurred when intermediaries shifted foreign practitioners' approaches to how to frame 'rule of law' (Berger 2017). This is an expected part of the process of translation, yet practitioners are continuously criticised for not being able to adhere to idealised conceptions of the rule of law (whether those put forward by scholars or the working definitions used within their organisations; see, e.g., Santos 2006).

By analysing the strategies that intermediaries use, it becomes evident that they are significantly relied upon to carry out development work and that they become influential in the role as translator because they do more than mobilise their contacts and use local language skills. In practice, they buffer conversations in which the speakers are mutually incomprehensible, and they often substitute the content of their own in those encounters, where they think the substitution would work better. This means that the choice of intermediary becomes important – and understanding their drivers and motivators and the pressures that they experience is important because it, in turn, shapes their performance. From this we can understand that even when the linguistic translation problems are 'solved', e.g., local interlocutors become better at English, the collision of concepts and priorities, and the appropriation of the new concepts for local uses (both benign and less benign) is likely to continue. Thus one outcome of foreign intervention in Myanmar must inevitably be 'rule of law' with an authoritarian cast (cf. Rajah 2012).

## 9.5 IMPLICATIONS BEYOND THE RULE OF LAW IN MYANMAR

Several implications for the field of rule of law development practice beyond Myanmar emerge out of this book's central enquiry: the importance of long-term engagements and relationship building; the risks of preferencing personality over influence when selecting intermediaries; the effects of a continued donor preference for foreign 'expertise' when structuring rule of law interventions; and the importance of understanding why fostering social capital matters for those interventions and for the intermediaries who work with and within them. While these observations may be familiar ground for seasoned development practitioners, the donors, head offices, and policymakers who structure that field seem slow to apply them and instead continue to promote global prescriptions (Desai, Isser, and Woolcock 2011).

The findings presented in this book also challenge some of the assumptions about power relationships in the development field: for example, the idea that international knowledge, expertise, and values are favoured or dominant (Rottenburg 2005) is challenged by the empirical finding that, in fact, rule of law development interventions rest on actors with local knowledge, networks, and the incentives and ability to adjust messages to fit local values (Crewe and Fernando 2006; Roth 2015). Technical skills and 'getting the job done' continue to be stressed as important by international actors, yet local access and knowledge – fostered through intermediaries' abilities to network and accumulate social capital – are regarded as vital. We also see that donors' use of formal reporting and evaluation technologies leads to disagreements that erode, rather than build, trust. This matters because trust is repeatedly identified as a key variable for relationship building among counterparts (Diallo and Thuillier 2005). Donor discourses and global regulatory instruments that stress local ownership and participation (Bosch 2016) are disregarded in practice in this setting: foreign development actors quite deliberately screen the group that they regard as legitimate 'local owners'. Intermediaries too are not appointed indiscriminately: donors are particularly cautious not to engage actors too closely connected to the military, or those who do not share their ideas of what human rights constitute.

This book argued that a methodological focus on intermediaries as central units of analysis is a productive way of unlocking ethnographic knowledge of the rule of law assistance field (Baylis 2015). The study of rule of law intermediaries can be applied in other settings to explain how rule of law making at new sites involves – and requires – contestation, translation, and adaptation. Arguably, intermediaries are pivotal to rule of law development efforts, yet their influence is little acknowledged. We can also apply this knowledge to the way we understand the myriad justice actors found in the literature on legal pluralism (Tamanaha 2008, 2011) because the creation of, and reliance upon, intermediaries means that a new layer of actors and norms has been introduced in settings in transitions where new institutions and legal and paralegal roles have become a quasi-permanent feature of that host legal system or have stimulated local system responses. The advent of rule of law assistance in Myanmar is so recent that it is too early to make such predictions, but the phenomenon itself is worthy of attention because it alters our understanding of legal pluralism as an occurrence in underdeveloped settings that foreign-assisted rule of law interventions aid to systematise.

Rule of law assistance in Myanmar was a comparatively new phenomenon at the point at which this research began, but its prospects for inducing sustained change were increasingly questioned against the backdrop of the political and humanitarian events that played out as I concluded this project. Regrettably, as participants often cautioned, the political climate seemed to be chilling towards, rather than warming to, rule of law norms. In Myanmar in 2020, policy statements continue to convey ideas about the rule of law not as a panacea for arbitrariness but as a mode of social control. Endless foreign funding and initiatives for legal and institutional reform have highlighted problems of access to justice, corruption, and institutional constraints, yet everyday experiences of rule of law and justice remain much alike. The most contrasting aspect of rule of law development in the country remains that of a perhaps general increase in justice provisions for the majority citizen, while some areas of the country are still undergoing heavily armed violence, ethnic discrimination, and crimes against international law. Knowing what we now know about the country (and particularly the backlash against Aung San Suu Kyi's approach to the Rohingya question), Myanmar's 'transition' is looking more delayed.

In many ways, this book is about a time in history that has vanished. A time of cautious but unprecedented optimism in the immediate era of liberalisation after the 2010 elections up to those of 2015. Nevertheless, its main findings on how rule of law intermediaries broker influence remain relevant for any setting where foreign aid has become an ingrained way of life. The trajectory of Myanmar's political transition is unpredictable, but this book is evidence of how intermediaries came to play a vital role in the field of rule of law assistance in Myanmar, and why they emerged with enthusiasm, at such a moment of transition. With the country potentially closing again under yet another military leadership, intermediaries will remain fundamental links between the outside world and development on the inside. Future insights may consider the tangible results that flow from a wider variety of intermediaries who capitalise on new opportunities to promote change in the field of rule of law development in Myanmar and beyond.

# Appendix

## OVERVIEW OF RESEARCH PARTICIPANTS

| Respondent | Category | Type of organisation | Gender | Date |
|---|---|---|---|---|
| #1 | Foreign | Multilateral | Male | 6 May 2014 |
| #2 | Foreign | INGO | Male | 7 May 2014 |
| #3 | Foreign | INGO | Female | 8 May 2014 |
| #4 | Foreign | INGO | Female | 15 May 2014 |
| #5 | Foreign | Multilateral | Female | 16 May 2014 |
| #6 | Local | Multilateral | Male | 19 May 2014 |
| #7 | Foreign | Multilateral | Female | 21 May 2014 |
| #8 | Foreign | INGO | Female | 22 May 2014 |
| #9 | Foreign | Multilateral | Female | 23 May 2014 |
| #10 | Local | Bilateral | Female | 12 May 2014 |
| #11 | Local | Bilateral | Female | 14 May 2014 |
| #12 | Foreign | Bilateral | Male | 7 May 2014 |
| #13 | Local | NGO | Male | 9 May 2014 |
| #14 | Local | NGO | Male | 5 Oct 2014 |
| #15 | Foreign | INGO | Female | 22 Sep 2014 |
| #16 | Local | Bilateral/NGO | Female | 22 Sep 2014 |
| #17 | Local | NGO | Male | 23 Sep 2014 |
| #18 | Foreign | INGO | Male | 24 Sep 2014 |
| #19 | Foreign | Donor | Female | 25 Sep 2014 |
| #20 | Foreign | Donor/bilateral | Male | 30 Sep 2014 |
| #21 | Local | Donor/bilateral | Male | 30 Sep 2014 |
| #22 | Local | NGO | Male | 2 Oct 2014 |
| #23 | Local | NGO | Male | 2 Oct 2014 |
| #24 | Local | NGO | Male | 14 Oct 2014 |
| #25 | Foreign | Donor/bilateral | Male | 3 Oct 2014 |
| #26 | Local | NGO | Male | 6 Oct 2014 |
| #27 | Local | Donor/bilateral | Female | 7 Oct 2014 |
| #28 | Foreign | NGO | Male | 22 Oct 2014 |
| #29 | Foreign | INGO | Male | 23 Oct 2014 |
| #30 | Local | NGO | Male | 24 Oct 2014 |
| #31 | Foreign | Multilateral | Female | 10 Nov 2014 |
| #32 | Foreign | Donor/bilateral | Male | 30 Nov 2014 |
| #33 | Local | NGO | Female | 11 Nov 2014 |
| #34 | Local | Government | Male | 18 Nov 2014 |
| #35 | Foreign | Multilateral | Female | 19 Nov 2014 |

(*cont.*)

| Respondent | Category | Type of organisation | Gender | Date |
|---|---|---|---|---|
| #36 | Local | Government | Female | 19 Nov 2014 |
| #37 | Local | Government | Male | 20 Nov 2014 |
| #38 | Local | Government | Male | 20 Nov 2014 |
| #39 | Foreign | Donor/bilateral | Male | 22 Nov 2014 |
| #40 | Foreign | NGO | Female | 9 Dec 2014 |
| #41 | Foreign | Government | Male | 11 Dec 2014 |
| #42 | Local | NGO | Male | 5 Nov 2014 |
| #43 | Local | Donor/bilateral | Male | 1 Oct 2014 |
| #44 | Foreign | Donor/bilateral | Female | 30 Sep 2014 |
| #45 | Foreign | Donor/bilateral | Female | 30 Sep 2014 |
| #46 | Local | NGO | Female | 9 Dec 2014 |
| #47 | Local | NGO | Male | 9 Dec 2014 |
| #48 | Foreign | INGO | Male | 10 Oct 2014 |
| #49 | Local | NGO | Male | 11 Dec 2014 |
| #50 | Local | NGO | Male | 8 Dec 2014 |
| #51 | Foreign | University | Male | 12 Dec 2014 |
| #52 | Foreign | University | Male | 12 Dec 2014 |
| #53 | Foreign | NGO | Female | 5 Oct 2015 |
| #54 | Foreign | INGO | Male | 25 Sep 2015 |
| #55 | Local | INGO | Male | 26 Sep 2015 |
| #56 | Foreign | Multilateral | Female | 26 Sep 2015 |
| #57 | Local | NGO | Male | 30 Sep 2014 |
| #58 | Local | NGO | Male | 30 Sep 2014 |
| #59 | Local | Government | Male | 15 Dec 2015 |
| #60 | Local | INGO | Female | 3 Dec 2014 |
| #61 | Local | INGO | Female | 3 Dec 2014 |
| #62 | Foreign | INGO | Female | 1 Dec 2014 |
| #63 | Local | Parliament | Male | 14 Sep 2014 |
| #64 | Local | Parliament | Male | 16 Sep 2014 |

# REFERENCES

AbouAssi, Khaldoun. 2013. 'Hands in the Pockets of Mercurial Donors: NGO Response to Shifting Funding Priorities'. *Nonprofit and Voluntary Sector Quarterly* 42 (3):584–602.

Acharya, Amitav. 2004. 'How Ideas Spread: Whose Norms Matter? Norm Localization and Institutional Change in Asian Regionalism'. *International Organization* 58 (2):239–75.

Action Committee for Democracy Development and Progressive Voice. 2018. Grassroots Democracy: Analysis of the Ward or Village Tract Administration Law.

Aguirre, Daniel, and Vani Sathisan. 2016. 'Rule of Law Depends on Reform of Union Attorney General's Office'. *Myanmar Times*, 27 January.

Ahsan Ullah, A. K. M. 2016. 'Rohingya Crisis in Myanmar: Seeking Justice for the "Stateless"'. *Journal of Contemporary Criminal Justice* 32 (3):285–301.

Aljazeera. 2016. 'The United Nations: UN: Rohingya May Be Enduring "Crimes against Humanity"', 30 November.

Amnesty International. 2018. 'Myanmar: Aung San Suu Kyi in Shameful Defence of Reuters Journalists' Conviction'. www.amnesty.org/en/latest/news/2018/0 9/myanmar-aung-san-suu-kyi-in-shameful-defence-of-reuters-journalists-conviction/.

Anderson, Mary B., and Lara Olson, with Kristin Doughty. 2003. *Confronting War: Critical Lessons for Peace Practitioners*. Cambridge, MA: CDA (Collaborative for Development Action).

Anderson, Mary B., Dayna Brown, and Isabella Jean. 2012. *Time to Listen: Hearing People on the Receiving End of International Aid*. Cambridge, MA: CDA Collaborative Learning Projects.

Andrews, Matt, Lant Pritchett, and Michael Woolcock. 2013. 'Escaping Capability Traps through Problem-Driven Iterative Adaptation (PDIA)'. *World Development* 51:234–44.

Andrews, Matt, Michael Woolcock, and Lant Pritchett. 2017. *Building State Capability: Evidence, Analysis, Action*. Oxford: Oxford University Press.

Antons, Christoph, ed. 2003. *Law and Development in East and South-East Asia*. London: Routledge.

Arajärvi, Noora. 2017. *The Rule of Law in the 2030 Agenda*, edited by Berlin Potsdam Research Group: KFG Working Paper Series.

Ashford, Chris, and Paul Mckeown, eds. 2018. *Social Justice and Legal Education*. Newcastle: Cambridge Scholars Publishing.

Asia Foundation. 2014. Myanmar 2014: Civic Knowledge and Values in a Changing Society.

Association of Southeast Asian Nations. 2008. The Charter of the Association of Southeast Asian Nations.

Atkinson, Rowland, and John Flint. 2001. 'Accessing Hidden and Hard-to-Reach Populations: Snowball Research Strategies'. *Social Research Update* 33 (1):93–108.

Aung San Suu Kyi. 1991. *Freedom from Fear*. New York: Penguin.

2002. 'Misrule of Law: Burma Government Leaps Over Legal Process'. *Asian Tribune*, 10 November.

Autesserre, Séverine. 2012. 'Dangerous Tales: Dominant Narratives on the Congo and Their Unintended Consequences'. *African Affairs* 111 (443):202–22.

2014. *Peaceland: Conflict Resolution and the Everyday Politics of International Intervention*. Cambridge: Cambridge University Press.

Balasubramaniam, R. Rueban. 2009. 'Judicial Politics in Authoritarian Regimes'. *University of Toronto Law Journal* 59 (3):405–15.

2012. 'Hobbism and the Problem of Authoritarian Rule in Malaysia'. *Hague Journal on the Rule of Law* 4 (2):211–34.

Batesmith, Alex, and Jake Stevens. 2019. 'In the Absence of the Rule of Law: Everyday Lawyering, Dignity and Resistance in Myanmar's "Disciplined Democracy"'. *Social & Legal Studies* 28 (5):573.

Baylis, Elena. 2008. 'Tribunal-Hopping with the Post-Conflict Justice Junkies'. *Oregon Review of International Law* 10 (361).

2015. 'What Internationals Know: Improving the Effectiveness of Post-Conflict Justice Initiatives'. *Washington University Global Studies Law Review* 14 (41):243.

BBC News. 2011. 'Burma Law to Allow Labour Unions and Strikes', 14 October.

BBC News Asia. 2015. 'Myanmar's 2015 Landmark Elections Explained', 3 December.

Beard, Jennifer. 2006. 'The Confessional Framework of Rule of Law Development: How to Offer Salvation to Willing Legal Subjects'. *Nordic Journal of International Law* 75 (3–4):409.

Becker, Howard Saul. 1973. *Outsiders: Studies in the Sociology of Deviance*. New ed. New York: Free Press.

Behrends, Andrea, Sung-Joon Park, and Richard Rottenburg, eds. 2014. *Travelling Models in African Conflict Management: Translating Technologies of Social Ordering*. Leiden/Boston: Brill.

Benton, Lauren A. 2002. *Law and Colonial Cultures: Legal Regimes in World History, 1400–1900*. Cambridge, UK: Cambridge University Press.

2018. 'Made in Empire: Finding the History of International Law in Imperial Locations: Introduction'. *Leiden Journal of International Law* 31 (3):473–8.

Benton, Lauren, and Lisa Ford. 2018. 'Island Despotism: Trinidad, the British Imperial Constitution and Global Legal Order'. *Journal of Imperial and Commonwealth History* 46 (1):21–46.

Berg, Bruce L. 1989. *Qualitative Research Methods for the Social Sciences*. Boston/London/Sydney/Toronto: Allyn and Bacon.

Berger, Tobias. 2017. *Global Norms and Local Courts: Translating the Rule of Law in Bangladesh*. Oxford: Oxford University Press.

Berger, Tobias, and Alejandro Esguerra, eds. 2017. *World Politics in Translation: Power, Relationality and Difference in Global Cooperation*. Oxford/New York: Routledge.

Bergling, Per. 2006. *Rule of Law on the International Agenda: International Support to Legal and Judicial Reform in International Administration, Transition and Development Cooperation*. Antwerp: Intersentia.

Bergling, Per, and Sophie Jin. 2015. 'The New Black on the Development Catwalk: Incorporating Rule of Law into the Sustainable Development Goals'. *Washington International Law Journal* 24 (3):435.

Bergling, Per, Jenny Ederlöf, and Veronica L. Taylor, eds. 2009. *Rule of Law Promotion: Global Perspectives, Local Applications*. Uppsala: Iustus.

Beyer, Judith. 2015. 'Finding the Law in Myanmar'. *Anthropology Today* 31 (4):3–7.

Bierschenk, Thomas, Jean-Pierre Chauveau, and Jean-Pierre Olivier de Sardan. 2002. 'Local Development Brokers in Africa: The Rise of a New Social Category'. Johannes Gutenberg University, Department of Anthropology and African Studies, Working Papers (13).

Bingham, Tom. H. 2011. *The Rule of Law*. New York/London: Penguin.

Blake, Andrew, and Meghan Bartlett. 2015. 'George Soros-Funded Groups Targeted in Russian NGO Crackdown', *Washington Times*, 30 November.

Blake, Richard Cameron. 2000. 'The World Bank's Draft Comprehensive Development Framework and the Micro-Paradigm of Law and Development'. *Yale Human Rights and Development Journal* 3 (1):158.

Bloch, Frank S. 2011. *The Global Clinical Movement: Educating Lawyers for Social Justice*. Oxford: Oxford University Press.

Boissevain, Jeremy. 1969. 'Patrons as Brokers'. *Sociologische Gids* 16:379–86.

1974. *Friends of Friends: Networks, Manipulators and Coalitions*. Oxford: Blackwell.

Booth, Melissa K. 2016. *Briefing on the Rule of Law in Myanmar*. Enlightened Myanmar Research Foundation.

Bosch, Anna. 2016. 'Local Actors in Donor-Funded Rule of Law Assistance in Indonesia: Owners, Partners, Agents?', School of Law, University of Washington.

Bourdieu, Pierre. 1986. 'The Forms of Capital'. In *Handbook of Theory and Research for the Sociology of Education*, edited by J. Richardson. New York: Greenwood.

Braithwaite, Valerie. A., and Margaret Levi. 2003. *Trust and Governance*. Vol. 2. New York: Russell Sage Foundation.

Bridges Across Borders Southeast Asia Clinical Legal Education. n.d. 'About Clinical Legal Education (CLE)'. www.babseacle.org/clinical-legal-education/.

British Council. n.d.a 'Pyoe Pin'. www.britishcouncil.org/partner/track-record/pyoe-pin.

n.d.b 'Welcome to Chevening'. www.chevening.org/.

2015. 'A New Future for Access to Justice and Legal Aid in Burma'. www.britishcouncil.org/partner/international-development/news-and-events/new-future-access-justice-legal-aid-burma.

2016. 'MyJustice'. http://myjusticemyanmar.org/about.

Broadhurst, Roderic, and Nicholas Farrelly. 2014. Organized crime control in Asia: Examples from India, China and the Golden Triangle, in L. Paoli (ed.), Oxford Handbook of Organized Crime, Oxford University Press, USA

Bureau of East Asian and Pacific Affairs. 2013. 'U.S. Relations with Burma, Fact Sheet'. www.state.gov/r/pa/ei/bgn/35910.htm.

Burke, Jason. 2012. 'Burma Releases Political Prisoners'. *The Guardian*, 13 January.

Burma Socialist Programme Party. 1963. The Philosophy of the Burma Socialist Programme Party: The System of Correlation of Man and His Environment.

Burma Tha Din Network. 2013. 'Exclusive Interview with Aung San Suu Kyi'. 23 April. http://burmathadinnetwork.blogspot.se/2013/04/.

Calavita, Kitty. 2010. *Invitation to Law & Society: An Introduction to the Study of Real Law*. Chicago: University of Chicago Press.

Calkins, Sandra, and Richard Rottenburg. 2014. 'Getting Credit for What You Write? Conventions and Techniques of Citation in German Anthropology'. *Zeitschrift für Ethnologie* 139 (1):99–129.

Call, Charles T., and Vanessa Wyeth, eds. 2008. *Building States to Build Peace*. London: Lynne Rienner Publishers.

Callahan, Mary P. 1998. 'On Time Warps and Warped Time: Lessons from Burma's "Democratic Era"'. In *Burma: Prospects for a Democratic Future*, edited by Robert I. Rotberg. Washington, DC: Brookings Institution Press.

2004. *Making Enemies: War and State Building in Burma*. Singapore: Singapore University Press.

2009. 'Myanmar's Perpetual Junta: Solving the Riddle of the Tatmadaw's Long Reign'. *New Left Review* 60.

2010. 'The Endurance of Military Rule in Burma: Not Why, but Why Not?' In *Finding Dollars, Sense and Legitimacy in Burma*, edited by Susan L. Levenstein. Washington, DC: Woodrow Wilson International Center for Scholars.

Callon, Michel. 1986. 'Some Elements of a Sociology of Translation and Domestication of the Scallops and the Fishermen of St Brieux Bay'. In *Power, Action and Belief: A New Sociology of Knowledge?*, edited by John Law. London: Routledge.

Callon, Michel, and Bruno Latour. 1981. 'Unscrewing the Big Leviathan: How Actors Macrostructure Reality and How Sociologists Help Them to Do So'. In *Advances in Social Theory and Methodology: Toward an Integration of Micro- and Macro-sociologies*, edited by K. D. Knorr-Cetina and A. V. Cicourel. Boston, MA: Routledge and Kegan Paul.

Carothers, Thomas. 1998. 'The Rule of Law Revival'. *Foreign Affairs* 77 (2):95–106.

2006a. 'The Problem of Knowledge'. In *Promoting the Rule of Law: In Search of Knowledge*, edited by Thomas Carothers. Washington, DC: Carnegie Endowment for International Peace.

2006b. 'The Rule of Law Revival'. In *Promoting the Rule of Law Abroad: In Search of Knowledge*, edited by Thomas Carothers. Washington, DC: Carnegie Endowment for International Peace.

2009. 'Democracy Assistance: Political vs. Developmental?'. *Journal of Democracy* 20 (1):5–19.

Carruthers, Bruce G., and Terence C. Halliday. 2006. 'Negotiating Globalization: Global Scripts and Intermediation in the Construction of Asian Insolvency Regimes'. *Law & Social Inquiry* 31 (3):521–84.

Carter, Nancy, Denise Bryant-Lukosius, Alba DiCenso, Jennifer Blythe, and Alan J. Neville. 2014. 'The Use of Triangulation in Qualitative Research'. *Oncology Nursing Forum* 41 (5):545–7.

Cartwright, Jan, and Joseph Truong. 2012. 'USAID Swears in First Mission Director to Burma in 24 Years'. 5 September. https://blog.usaid.gov/2012/09/usaid-swears-in-first-mission-director-to-burma-in-24-years/.

Cassrels, Deborah. 2015. 'Australians Explore Rule of Law in Myanmar through Soap Opera'. *The Australian*, 15 December.

Chalhi, Sabah, Martijn Koster, and Jeroen Vermeulen. 2018. 'Assembling the Irreconcilable: Youth Workers, Development Policies and "High Risk" Boys in the Netherlands'. *Ethnos* 83 (5):850–67.

Channell, Wade. 2006. 'Lessons Not Learned about Legal Reform'. In *Promoting the Rule of Law Abroad: in Search of Knowledge*, edited by Thomas Carothers. Washington, DC: Carnegie Endowment for International Peace.

Cheesman, Nick. 2009. 'Thin Rule of Law or Un-rule of Law in Myanmar?' *Pacific Affairs* 84 (4):597–613.

2011. 'How an Authoritarian Regime in Burma Used Special Courts to Defeat Judicial Independence'. *Law & Society Review* 45:801–30.

2012. 'Myanmar's Courts and the Sounds Money Makes'. In *Myanmar's Transition: Openings, Obstacles and Opportunities*, edited by

Nick Cheesman, Trevor Wilson, and Monique Skidmore. Singapore: ISEAS Publishing.

2013. 'Ending Forced Labour in Myanmar: Engaging a Pariah Regime'. *South East Asia Research* 21 (2):343–7.

2014a. 'Law and Order as Asymmetrical Opposite to the Rule of Law'. *Hague Journal on the Rule of Law* 6 (1):96–114.

2014b. 'What Does the Rule of Law Have to Do with Democratization (in Myanmar)?'. *South East Asia Research* 22 (2):213–32.

2015. *Opposing the Rule of Law: How Myanmar's Courts Make Law and Order.* Cambridge: Cambridge University Press.

2016. 'Rule-of-Law Lineages in Colonial and Early Post-Colonial Burma'. *Modern Asian Studies* 50 (2):564–601.

2017. 'How in Myanmar "National Races" Came to Surpass Citizenship and Exclude Rohingya'. *Journal of Contemporary Asia* 47 (3):461–83.

Cheesman, Nick, and Nicholas Farrelly. 2016. *Conflict in Myanmar: War, Politics, Religion.* Singapore: ISEAS-Yusof Ishak Institute.

Cheesman, Nick, and Kyaw Min San. 2014. 'Not Just Defending; Advocating for Law in Myanmar'. *Wisconsin International Law Journal* 31 (3):702.

Cheesman, Nick, and Kristina Simion. 2022. 'How Intermediaries Broker the Rule of Law Transnationally'. In *Routledge Handbook of the Rule of Law*, edited by Michael Sevel. London/New York: Routledge (Taylor & Francis).

Chen, Weitseng, and Hualing Fu, eds. 2020. *Authoritarian Legality in Asia: Formation, Development and Transition.* Cambridge: Cambridge University Press.

Chesterman, Simon. 2008. 'An International Rule of Law'. *New York University School of Law: Public Law & Legal Theory Research Paper Series*, Working Paper No. 08–11.

Chua, Lynette J. 2014. 'Charting Socio-legal Scholarship on Southeast Asia: Key Themes and Future Directions'. *Asian Journal of Comparative Law* 9:5–27.

2015. 'The Vernacular Mobilization of Human Rights in Myanmar's Sexual Orientation and Gender Identity Movement'. *Law & Society Review* 49 (2):299–332.

2019. *The Politics of Love in Myanmar: LGBT Mobilization and Human Rights as a Way of Life.* Stanford, CA: Stanford University Press.

Clarke, Donald C. 2007. 'What Kind of Legal System Is Necessary for Economic Development: The China Puzzle'. In *Law Reform in Developing and Transitional States*, edited by Tim Lindsey, 65–82. London/New York: Routledge.

Cohen, Anthony P., and John L. Comaroff. 1976. 'The Management of Meaning: On the Phenomenology of Political Transactions'. In *Transaction and Meaning: Directions in the Anthropology of Exchange and*

*Symbolic Behaviour*, edited by Bruce Kapferer. Philadelphia: Institute for the Study of Human Issues.

Cohen, Elin, Fandl J. Kevin, Amanda Perry Kessaris, and Veronica L. Taylor. 2011. 'Truth and Consequences in Rule of Law: Inferences, Attribution and Evaluation'. *Hague Journal on the Rule of Law* 3 (1):106–29.

Coles, Kimberley. 2007. *Democratic Designs: International Intervention and Electoral Practices in Postwar Bosnia-Herzegovina*. Ann Arbor: University of Michigan Press.

Corbin, Juliet, and Janice M. Morse. 2003. 'The Unstructured Interactive Interview: Issues of Reciprocity and Risks When Dealing with Sensitive Topics'. *Qualitative Inquiry* 9:335–54.

Creswell, John W. 2013. *Research Design: Qualitative, Quantitative, and Mixed Methods Approaches*. 4th ed. Los Angeles: Sage.

Crewe, Elizabeth, and Emma Harrison. 1998. *Whose Development? An Ethnography of Aid*. London: Zed Books.

Crewe, Emma, and Priyanthi Fernando. 2006. 'The Elephant in the Room: Racism in Representations, Relationships and Rituals'. *Progress in Development Studies* 6 (1):40–54.

Crouch, Melissa. 2013. 'Teaching Myanmar's Next Generation of Lawyers'. *East Asia Forum*, 18 September.

2014. 'Layers of Legal Development'. In *Law, Society and Transition in Myanmar*, edited by Melissa Crouch and Tim Lindsey. London: Hart Publishing.

ed. 2017. *The Business of Transition: Law Reform, Development and Economics in Myanmar*. Cambridge: Cambridge University Press.

2019. *The Constitution of Myanmar: A Contextual Analysis*: Oxford: Bloomsbury Publishing.

2020. 'Myanmar: Law as a Desirable and Dangerous Profession'. In *Lawyers in Society*, edited by Richard Abel et al. Oxford: Hart Publishing.

Crouch, Melissa, and Tim Lindsey. 2014a. 'Introduction: Myanmar, Law Reform and Asian Legal Studies'. In *Law, Society and Transition in Myanmar*, edited by Melissa Crouch and Tim Lindsey. London: Hart Publishing.

eds. 2014b. *Law, Society and Transition in Myanmar*. London: Hart Publishing.

Czarnota, Adam, Martin Krygier, and Wojciech Sadurski, eds. 2005. *Rethinking the Rule of Law after Communism: Constitutionalism, Dealing with the Past, and the Rule of Law*. Budapest: Central European University Press.

Dallara, Cristina, and Daniela Piana. 2017. *Networking the Rule of Law: How Change Agents Reshape Judicial Governance in the EU*. London/New York: Routledge.

Daniels, Ronald J, and Michael Trebilcock. 2004. 'The Political Economy of Rule of Law Reform in Developing Countries'. *Michigan Journal of International Law* 26:99.

Darian-Smith, Eve. 2013. *Laws and Societies in Global Contexts: Contemporary Approaches*. Cambridge: Cambridge University Press.

David, Roman, and Ian Holliday. 2012. 'International Sanctions or International Justice? Shaping Political Development in Myanmar'. *Australian Journal of International Affairs* 66:121–38.

2018. *Liberalism and Democracy in Myanmar*. Oxford: Oxford University Press.

Davis, Kevin E., and Michael J. Trebilcock. 2008. 'The Relationship between Law and Development: Optimists versus Skeptics'. *American Journal of Comparative Law* 56 (4):895–946.

Davis, Kevin E., Benedict Kingsbury, and Sally Engle Merry. 2012. 'Indicators as a Technology of Global Governance'. *Law and Society Review* 46 (1):71–104.

Dawkins, Alice, and Nick Cheesman. 2021. 'Political Lawyers and the Legal Occupation in Myanmar'. In *A Lawyer's Role in Access to Justice: Asian and Comparative Perspectives*, edited by Helena Whalen-Bridge. Publisher TBC.

Decker, Klaus. 2010. 'World Bank Rule-of-Law Assistance in Fragile States: Developments and Perspectives'. In *Law in the Pursuit of Development: Principles into Practice?*, edited by Amanda Perry Kessaris. London/ New York: Routledge.

Decker, Klaus, Caroline Sage, and Milena Stefanova. 2005. *Law or Justice: Building Equitable Legal Institutions*. Washington, DC: World Bank.

Décobert, Anne, and Tamas Wells. 2020. 'Interpretive Complexity and Crisis: The History of International Aid to Myanmar'. *European Journal of Development Research* 32 (2):294–315.

De Jong, Sara. 2018. 'Brokerage and Transnationalism: Present and Past Intermediaries, Social Mobility, and Mixed Loyalties'. *Identities* 25 (5):610–28.

DeLisle, Jacques. 1999. 'Lex Americana?: United States Legal Assistance, American Legal Models, and Legal Change in the Post-Communist World and Beyond'. *Journal of International Economic Law* 20 (2):179–308.

Denney, Lisa, Bennett William, and Khin Thet San. 2016. 'Making Big Cases Small & Small Cases Disappear: Experience of Local Justice in Myanmar'. MyJustice. www.myjusticemyanmar.org/sites/default/files/My-Justice_16th -Dec-2016.pdf.

Derks, Maria, and Megan Price. 2010. *EU and Rule of Law Reform in Kosovo*. Clingendael Institute. www.clingendael.org/sites/default/files/pdfs/20110 106_CRU_publication_mderks.pdf.

Desai, Deval. 2014. 'In Search of "Hire" Knowledge: Hiring Practices and the Organization of Knowledge in a Rule of Law Field'. In *The International Rule of Law Movement: A Crisis of Legitimacy and the Way Forward*, edited by David Marshall. Cambridge, MA: Harvard University Press.

2016. 'Putting Security Culture and Experimentation into Context: Towards a View from the Field(s) of Rule of Law Reform'. *Journal of Conflict and Security Law* 21 (1):135–50.

Desai, Deval, and Mareike Schomerus. 2018. '"There Was a Third Man . . .": Tales from a Global Policy Consultation on Indicators for the Sustainable Development Goals'. *Development and Change* 49 (1):89–115.

Desai, Deval, and Michael Woolcock. 2015. 'Experimental Justice Reform: Lessons from the World Bank and Beyond'. *Annual Review of Law and Social Science* 11 (1):155–74.

Desai, Deval, Deborah Isser, and Michael Woolcock. 2011. 'Rethinking Justice Reform in Fragile and Conflict-Affected States: The Capacity of Development Agencies and Lessons from Liberia and Afghanistan'. In *World Bank Legal Review, Volume 3: International Financial Institutions and Global Legal Governance*, edited by Daniel Bradlow, Hassane Cisse, and Benedict Kingsbury, 241–62. Washington, DC: World Bank.

De Sardan, Jean-Pierre Olivier. 2005. *Anthropology and Development: Understanding Contemporary Social Change*. London/New York: Zed Books.

De Soto, Hernando. 2001. *The Mystery of Capital: Why Capitalism Triumphs in the West and Fails Everywhere Else*. London: Black Swan.

D'Exelle, Ben. 2009. 'Excluded Again: Village Politics at the Aid Interface'. *Journal of Development Studies* 45 (9):1453–71.

Dezalay, Yves, and Bryant Garth. 2002. *The Internationalization of Palace Wars: Lawyers, Economists, and the Contest to Transform Latin American States*. Chicago/London: University of Chicago Press.

2010. *Asian Legal Revivals: Lawyers in the Shadow of Empire*. Chicago: University of Chicago Press.

eds. 2011. *Lawyers and the Rule of Law in an Era of Globalization*. Abingdon/New York: Routledge.

eds. 2012. *Lawyers and the Construction of Transnational Justice*. Abingdon/New York: Routledge.

Dezalay, Yves, and Mikael Rask Madsen. 2012. 'The Force of Law and Lawyers: Pierre Bourdieu and the Reflexive Sociology of Law'. *Annual Review of Law and Social Science* 8 (1):433–52.

Diallo, Amadou, and Denis Thuillier. 2005. 'The Success of International Development Projects, Trust and Communication: An African Perspective'. *International Journal of Project Management* 23 (3):237–52.

Dias, Ayesha Kadwani, and Gita Honwana Welch, eds. 2009. *Justice for the Poor: Perspectives on Accelerating Access*. Oxford: Oxford University Press.

Dicey, Albert V. 1999. *Lectures Introductory to the Study of the Law of the Constitution*. 2nd ed. Delanco, NJ: Gryphon Editions.

DiCicco-Bloom, B., and B. F. Crabtree. 2006. 'The Qualitative Research Interview'. *Medical Education* 40 (4):314–21.

Diller, Janelle M. 1997. 'The National Convention: an Impediment to the Restoration of Democracy'. In *Burma: The Challenge of Change in a Divided Society*, edited by Peter Carey. Basingstoke/London: Macmillan Press.

DiMaggio, Paul J., and W. Walter Powell. 1983. 'The Iron Cage Revisited: Institutional Isomorphism and Collective Rationality in Organizational Fields'. *American Sociological Review* 48 (2):147–60.

DLA Piper. 2013. 'New Perimeter and Bridges across Borders Southeast Asia Community Legal Education Initiative Complete'. www.dlapiper.com/ne w-perimeter-and-bridges-across-borders-southeast-asia-community-legal-education-initiative-complete-2nd-Burma-national-cle-workshop-11-25-2013/.

Dolinska, Joanna. 2017. 'The Emergence of Language Professionals in Myanmar'. *Tea Circle: An Oxford Forum for New Perspectives on Burma/Myanmar*. https://teacircleoxford.com/2017/03/23/the-emergence-of-language-professionals-in-myanmar/.

Dunlap, Bridgette. 2014. 'The Rule of Law Without Lawyers: American Legal Reformers and the Cambodian Lawyer Shortage'. SSRN Electronic Journal. 10.2139/ssrn.2424255.

Easterly, William. 2014. *The Tyranny of Experts: Economists, Dictators, and the Forgotten Rights of the Poor*. New York: Basic Books.

Edwards, Rosalind, and Janet Holland. 2013. *What Is Qualitative Interviewing?* London: Bloomsbury.

Ei Thae Thae Naing. 2013. 'Undergrads Return to Yangon University'. *Myanmar Times*, 4 August.

Elliot, Jane. 2005. *Using Narrative in Social Research. Qualitative and Quantitative Approaches* London: Sage Publications.

Elwert, Georg, and Thomas Bierschenk. 1988. 'Development Aid as an Intervention in Dynamic Systems: An Introduction'. *Sociologia Ruralis* XXVIII (2/3).

Emergency Provisions Act (No. 17 of 1950).

Equality Myanmar. 2004. Universal Declaration of Human Rights Poster.

Eslava, Luis. 2015. *Local Space, Global Life: The Everyday Operation of International Law and Development*. Cambridge: Cambridge University Press.

Esson, James, and Kevin Wang. 2016. 'Reforming a University During Political Transformation: A Case Study of Yangon University in Myanmar'. *Studies in Higher Education* 43 (7):1–12.

Evers. 2010. OSCE Efforts to Promote the Rule of Law: History, Structures, Survey. CORE Working Paper 20. Hamburg.

Ewick, Patricia, and Susan S. Silbey. 1998. *The Common Place of Law: Stories from Everyday Life*. Chicago: University of Chicago Press.

Farrall, Jeremy, and Hilary Charlesworth. 2016. *Strengthening the Rule of Law through the UN Security Council*. London: Taylor and Francis.

Farrelly, Nicholas, and Chit Win. 2016. 'Inside Myanmar's Turbulent Transformation'. *Asia & the Pacific Policy Studies* 3 (1):38–47.

Faundez, Julio. 2010. 'Rule of Law or Washington Consensus: The Evolution of the World Bank's Approach to Legal and Judicial Reform'. In *Law in the Pursuit of Development: Principles into Practice?*, edited by Amanda Perry Kessaris. London/New York: Routledge.

Fechter, Anne-Meike, and Heather Hindman. 2011. *Inside the Everyday Lives of Development Workers: The Challenges and Futures of Aidland*. Sterling, VA: Kumarian Press.

Fink, Christina. 2001. *Living Silence: Burma under Military Rule*. London/New York: Zed Books.

Finnemore, Martha, and Kathryn Sikkink. 1998. 'International Norm Dynamics and Political Change'. *International Organization* 52 (4):887–917.

Flood, John. 2005. 'Socio-legal Ethnography'. In *Theory and Method in Socio-legal Research*, edited by Reza Banakar and Max Travers. Oxford: Hart Publishing.

Foreign Economic Relations Department and the Development Partners Working Committee. n.d. 'Myanmar Aid Transparency Portal Mohinga'. http://mohinga.info/en/.

Foreign Investment Law (Pyidaungsu Hluttaw Law, No 21/2012 of 2 November 2012).

Forsyth, Miranda. 2009. *A Bird that Flies with Two Wings: The Kastom and State Justice Systems in Vanuatu*. Canberra, ACT: ANU E Press.

Fortify Rights. 2015. 'Midnight Intrusions: Ending Guest Registration and Household Inspections in Myanmar'. www.fortifyrights.org/downloads/FR_Midnight_Intrusions_March_2015.pdf.

Freedom House. 2020. 'Nations in Transit 2020: Dropping the Democratic Facade'. https://freedomhouse.org/sites/default/files/2020-04/05062020_FH_NIT2020_vfinal.pdf.

Friedman, Lawrence M. 1975. *The Legal System: A Social Science Perspective*. New York: Russell Sage Foundation.

Friedrich Naumann Stiftung für die Freiheit. n.d. 'What We Do'. http://myanmar-en.fnst.org/content/what-we-do-1.

Fukuyama, Francis. 1995. *Trust: The Social Virtues and the Creation of Prosperity*. London: Hamish Hamilton.

2000. *Social Capital and Civil Society*. Washington, DC: International Monetary Fund.

Fuller, Lon L. 1964. *The Morality of Law*. New Haven, CT/London: Yale University Press.

Fuller, Thomas. 2015a. 'Those Who Would Remake Myanmar Find That Words Fail Them'. *New York Times*, 19 July.

2015b. 'Myanmar Military Still Big Power Despite Opposition Victory'. *New York Times*, 10 November.

Funakoshi, Minami. 2016. 'Suu Kyi Says "Delicate" Myanmar Conflict Handled by Rule of Law'. *Reuters*, 3 November.

Furnivall, John S. 1948. *Colonial Policy and Practice: A Comparative Study of Burma and Netherlands India*. New York: Cambridge University Press.

Ganesan, Narayanan, and Kyaw Yin Hlaing, eds. 2007. *Myanmar: State, Society, and Ethnicity*. Hiroshima, Japan, Singapore: Institute of Southeast Asian Studies.

Gardner, James. 1980. *Legal Imperialism: American Lawyers and Foreign Aid in Latin America*. Madison: University of Wisconsin Press.

Geertz, Clifford. 1960. 'The Javanese Kijaji: The Changing Role of a Cultural Broker'. *Comparative Studies in Society and History* 2 (2):228–49

1973. *The Interpretation of Cultures: Selected Essays*. New York: Basic Books.

Gibson, Clark C., Krister Andersson, Elinor Ostrom, and Sujai Shivakumar. 2005. *The Samaritan's Dilemma: The Political Economy of Development Aid*. Oxford: Oxford University Press.

Gil, Sylwia. 2008. *The Role of Monkhood in Contemporary Myanmar Society*. Bonn: Friedrich-Ebert-Stiftung.

Gillespie, John. 2004. 'Concept of Law in Vietnam: Transforming Statist Socialism'. In *Asian Discourses of Rule of Law: Theories and Implementation of Rule of Law in Twelve Asian Countries, France and the U.S.*, edited by Randall Peerenboom. London: Routledge.

2017. 'Transforming Land Taking Disputes in Socialist Asia: Engaging an Authoritarian State'. *Law & Policy* 39 (3):280–303.

Ginsburg, Tom. 2000. 'Does Law Matter for Economic Development? Evidence from East Asia'. *Law & Society Review* 34 (3):829–56.

2011. 'Pitfalls of Measuring the Rule of Law'. *Hague Journal on the Rule of Law* 3 (2):269–80.

Ginsburg, Tom, and Tamir Moustafa, eds. 2008. *Rule by Law: The Politics of Courts in Authoritarian Regimes*. New York: Cambridge University Press.

Global Goals for Sustainable Development. n.d. '16 Peace, Justice and Strong Institutions'. www.globalgoals.org/global-goals/peace-and-justice.

Gluckman, Max, J. C. Mitchell, and J. A. Barnes. 1949. 'The Village Headman in British Central Africa'. *Africa: Journal of the International African Institute* 19 (2):89–106.

Golub, Stephen. 2006. 'The Legal Empowerment Alternative'. In *Promoting the Rule of Law Abroad: In Search of Knowledge*, edited by Thomas Carothers. Washington, DC: Carnegie Endowment for International Peace.

Gonzalez, Nancy. 1972. 'Patron-Client Relationships at the International Level'. In *Structure and Process in Latin America: Patronage, Clientage, and Power Systems*, edited by Arnold Strickon and Sidney M. Greenfield. Albuquerque: University of New Mexico Press.

Gonzalez, Susan. 2012. 'Establishing Rule of Law Is First Step toward a Democratic Burma, Says Nobel Laureate'. *Yale News*, 27 September.

Government of Myanmar. 2012. Framework for Economic and Social Reforms: Policy Priorities for 2012–15 towards the Long-Term Goals of the National Comprehensive Development Plan.

Government of the Republic of the Union of Myanmar. 2013. Nay Pyi Taw Accord for Effective Development Cooperation.

Gowder, P. 2016. *The Rule of Law in the Real World*. Cambridge: Cambridge University Press.

Grasten, Maj Lervad. 2016. 'Whose Legality?: Rule of Law Missions and the Case of Kosovo'. In *The Power of Legality: Practices of International Law and Their Politics*, edited by N. M. Rajkovic, T. Aalberts, and T. Gammeltoft-Hansen, 320–42. Cambridge: Cambridge University Press.

Gray, David E. 2009. *Doing Research in the Real World*. 2nd ed. Thousand Oaks, CA: Sage Publications.

Gretchen, Helmke. 2005. *Courts under Constraints: Judges, Generals, and Presidents in Argentina* Cambridge: Cambridge University Press.

Guilfoyle, Douglas. 2019. 'The ICC Pre-Trial Chamber Decision on Jurisdiction Over the Situation in Myanmar'. *Australian Journal of International Affairs* 73 (1):2–8.

Guilloux, Alain. 2010. 'Myanmar: Analyzing Problems of Transition and Intervention'. *Contemporary Politics* 16:383–401.

Hale, Kip, and Melinda Rankin. 2019. 'Extending the "System" of International Criminal Law? The ICC's Decision on Jurisdiction over Alleged Deportations of Rohingya People'. *Australian Journal of International Affairs* 73 (1):22–8.

Halliday, Terence C., and Bruce G. Carruthers. 2007. 'The Recursivity of Law: Global Norm Making and National Lawmaking in the Globalization of Corporate Insolvency Regimes'. *American Journal of Sociology* 112 (4):1135–1202.

  2009. *Bankrupt: Global Lawmaking and Systemic Financial Crisis*. Stanford, CA: Stanford University Press.

Halliday, Terence C., and Pavel Osinsky. 2006. 'Globalization of Law'. *Annual Review of Sociology* 32:447–70.

Halliday, Terence C., and Gregory C. Shaffer. 2014. *Transnational Legal Orders*. New York: Cambridge University Press.

Halliday, Terence C., Lucien Karpik, and Malcolm Feeley, eds. 2007. *Fighting for Political Freedom: Comparative Studies of the Legal Complex and Political Liberalism*. Oxford: Hart Publishing.

Hammerslev, Ole. 2006. 'The Construction of a Dominant Position in an International Field of Legal Assistance'. *RETFAERD* 29 (3/114):1–6.

Hancock, Graham. 1989. *Lords of Poverty: The Power, Prestige, and Corruption of the International Aid Business*. New York: Atlantic Monthly Press.

Hanks, William F., and Carlo Severi. 2014. 'Translating Worlds: The Epistemological Space of Translation'. *Journal of Ethnographic Theory* 4 (2):1–16.

Hardin, R. 2001. 'Conceptions and Explanations of Trust'. In *Trust in Society*, edited by K. S. Cook, 3–39. New York: Russell Sage Foundation.

Harding, Andrew. 2014. 'Law and Development in Its Burmese Moment: Legal Reform in an Emerging Democracy'. In *Law, Society and Transition in Myanmar*, edited by Melissa Crouch and Tim Lindsey. London: Hart Publishing.

⎯⎯ 2017. 'Irresistible Forces and Immovable Objects: Constitutional Change in Myanmar'. In *Constitutionalism and Legal Change in Myanmar*, edited by Andrew Harding and Khin Khin Oo. Oxford/Portland, OR: Hart Publishing.

Hart, Herbert L. A. 2012. *The Concept of Law*. 3rd ed. Oxford: Oxford University Press.

Harvard Kennedy School. 2012. 'Aung San Suu Kyi: "The Basics of Democratic Practice"'. *Harvard Magazine*, 28 September.

Hasegawa, Ko. 2009. 'Incorporating Foreign Legal Ideas through Translation'. In *Theorising the Global Legal Order*, edited by Andrew Halpin and Roeben Volker. Oxford/Portland, OR: Hart Publishing.

Hayek, Friedrich A. 1944 (repr. 2006) *The Road to Serfdom*. London/ New York: Routledge.

⎯⎯ 1955. *The Political Ideal of the Rule of Law*. National Bank of Egypt Fiftieth Anniversary Commemoration Lectures.

Heike Gramckow, P., and Valerie Nussenblatt. 2013. 'Caseflow Management: Key Principles and the Systems to Support Them'. Justice and Development Working Paper Series, 23/2013. Washington, DC: World Bank.

Hilbink, Lisa. 2007. *Judges beyond Politics in Democracy and Dictatorship: Lessons from Chile*. Cambridge/New York: Cambridge University Press.

Hilhorst, Dorothea, and Bram Jansen. 2003. 'For Better or for Worse … Partnership between Dutch Humanitarian NGOs and Implementing Local Partners'. Cooperation with Implementing Partners in Humanitarian Assistance.

Hobbs, Cecil. 1947. 'Nationalism in British Colonial Burma'. *Far Eastern Quarterly* 6 (2):113–21.

Holliday, Ian. 2010. 'Ethnicity and Democratization in Myanmar'. *Asian Journal of Political Science* 18 (2):111–28.

 2011. *Burma Redux: Global Justice and the Quest for Political Reform in Myanmar*. New York/Chichester: Columbia University Press.

 2013. 'Myanmar in 2012: Toward a Normal State'. *Asian Survey* 53:93–100.

 2014. 'Thinking about Transitional Justice in Myanmar'. *South East Asia Research* 22 (2):183–200.

Homans, George Caspar. 1950. *The Human Group*. New York: Harcourt, Brace & Company.

Hookway, James. 2012. 'Myanmar Passes Investment Law'. *Wall Street Journal*, 7 September.

Horsey, Richard. 2011. *Ending Forced Labour in Myanmar: Engaging a Pariah Regime*. Vol. 31. Abingdon/New York: Routledge.

 2015. 'New Religious Legislation in Myanmar'. Conflict Prevention and Peace Forum.

Huang, Roger Lee. 2020. *The Paradox of Myanmar's Regime Change*. London: Routledge.

Humphreys, Stephen. 2010. *Theatre of the Rule of Law: Transnational Legal Intervention in Theory and Practice* New York: Cambridge University Press.

Hurst, William. 2018. *Ruling Before the Law: The Politics of Legal Regimes in China and Indonesia*. Cambridge: Cambridge University Press.

Huxley, Andrew. 1987. 'Burma: It Works, But Is It Law?' *Journal of Family Law* 27:23–34.

 1998. 'The Last Fifty Years of Burmese Law: E Maung and Maung Maung'. LAWASIA 9–20.

Ichihara, Maiko. 2017. *Japan's International Democracy Assistance as Soft Power: Neoclassical Realist Analysis*. Abingdon: Taylor and Francis.

Institute for Democracy and Electoral Assistance (International IDEA), and Local Resource Centre. 2015. English-Myanmar Glossary of Democratic Terms.

International Bar Association's Human Rights Institute. 2012. 'The Rule of Law in Myanmar: Challenges and Prospects'.

 2014. 'Laws Regulating the Legal Profession: A Comparative Review from Around the World'. Hotel Max, Nay Pyi Taw, Myanmar, 28–30 October.

International Commission of Jurists. 2013. 'Right to Counsel: The Independence of Lawyers in Myanmar'.

 2014. 'Myanmar's Court Officials Discuss Judicial Independence and Integrity with International Experts', 11 February.

International Council on Human Rights. 2000. 'Local Perspectives: Foreign Aid to the Justice Sector'.

International Development Law Organization. 2016. 'Rule of Law Centres: Building Trust in Myanmar's Justice System'. www.idlo.int/what-we-do /initiatives/building-trust-myanmays-justice-system-rule-law-centres.

James, Deborah. 2011. 'The Return of the Broker: Consensus, Hierarchy, and Choice in South African Land Reform'. *Journal of the Royal Anthropological Institute* 17 (2):318–38.

2018. 'Mediating Indebtedness in South Africa'. *Ethnos* 83 (5):814–31.

Jayasuriya, Kanishka, ed. 1999. *Law, Capitalism and Power in Asia: The Rule of Law and Legal Institutions*. New York: Routledge.

JBI Human Rights. 2013. 'Burma: New Publication Outlines Needed Law Reforms'. 25 March. www.jbi-humanrights.org/jacob-blaustein-institute/2013/03/burma-needed-law-reforms.html.

Jensen, Erik G. 2003. 'The Rule of Law and Judicial Reform: The Political Economy of Diverse Institutional Patterns and Reformers' Responses'. In *Beyond Common Knowledge: Empirical Approaches to the Rule of Law*, edited by Erik G. Jensen and Thomas C. Heller. Stanford, CA: Stanford University Press.

Johannesburg Declaration (2014) on the Implementation of the United Nations Principles and Guidelines on Access to Legal Aid in Criminal Justice Systems.

Justice Reform Practice Group of the World Bank's Legal Vice Presidency. 2012. 'Law and Justice Institutions'. http://go.worldbank.org/LE354RG990.

Kamarul, Bahrin, and Roman Tomasic. 1999. 'The Rule of Law and Corporate Insolvency in Six Asian Legal Systems'. In *Law, Capitalism and Power in Asia: The Rule of Law and Legal Institutions*, edited by Kanishka Jayasuriya. New York: Routledge.

Kellogg, Thomas E. 2020. 'The Foreign NGO Law and the Closing of China'. In *Authoritarian Legality in Asia: Formation, Development and Transition*, edited by Weitseng Chen and Hualing Fu. Cambridge: Cambridge University Press.

Khan, Mish, and Nick Cheesman. 2020. 'Law, Lawyers and Legal Institutions'. In *Myanmar: Politics, Economy & Society*, edited by Adam Simpson and Nicholas Farrelly. London: Routledge.

Khin Khin Oo. 2017. 'Judicial Power and the Constitutional Tribunal: Some Suggestions for Better Legislation Relating to the Tribunal and Its Role'. In *Constitutionalism and Legal Change in Myanmar*, edited by Andrew Harding and Khin Khin Oo. Oxford/Portland, OR: Hart Publishing.

Khodyakov, Dmitry. 2007. 'Trust as a Process: A Three-Dimensional Approach'. *Sociology* 41 (1):115–32.

Kingsbury, Benedict, Nico Krisch, and Richard B. Stewart. 2005. 'The Emergence of Global Administrative Law'. *Law and Contemporary Problems* 68 (3/4):15–61.

Kisilowski, Maciej. 2015. 'The Middlemen: The Legal Profession, the Rule of Law, and Authoritarian Regimes'. *Law & Social Inquiry* 40 (3):700–22.

Kleinfeld, Rachel. 2005. 'Competing Definitions of the Rule of Law: Implications for Practitioners'. Democracy and Rule of Law Project. Washington, DC: Carnegie Endowment for International Peace: 55.

2012. *Advancing the Rule of Law Abroad: Next Generation Reform*. Washington, DC: Carnegie Endowment for International Peace.

Koster, Martijn, and Yves van Leynseele. 2018. 'Brokers as Assemblers: Studying Development through the Lens of Brokerage'. *Ethnos* 83 (5):803–13.

Krieger, Heike, and Georg Nolte. 2016. 'The International Rule of Law – Rise or Decline? Points of Departure'. KFG Working Paper Series, No. 1, October. https://publishup.uni-potsdam.de/opus4-ubp/frontdoor/deliver/index/docId/41952/file/kfg_wps01.pdf.

Krisch, Nico, and Benedict Kingsbury. 2006. 'Introduction: Global Governance and Global Administrative Law in the International Legal Order'. *European Journal of International Law* 17 (1):1–13.

Krygier, Martin. 2006. 'The Rule of Law: An Abuser's Guide'. In *Abuse: The Dark Side of Fundamental Rights*, edited by András Sajó. Utrecht: Eleven International Publishing.

2009a. 'The Rule of Law and "the Three Integrations"'. *Hague Journal on the Rule of Law* 1 (1):21–7.

2009b. 'The Rule of Law: Legality, Teleology, Sociology'. In *Relocating the Rule of Law*, edited by Gianluigi Palombella and Neil Walker, 45–69. Oxford: Hart Publishing.

2017a. 'The Rule of Law and Its Rivals: Commentary on Opposing the Rule of Law: How Myanmar's Courts Make Law and Order by Nick Cheesman'. *Hague Journal on the Rule of Law* 9 (1):19–27.

2017b. 'Why Rule of Law Promotion Is Too Important to Be Left to Lawyers'. In *Who's Afraid of International Law?*, edited by Raimond Gaita and Gerry Simpson, 133–68. Monash: Monash University Publishing.

Krygier, Martin, and Adam Czarnota, eds. 1999. *The Rule of Law After Communism*. Aldershot: Ashgate.

Kublin, Hyman. 1959. 'The Evolution of Japanese Colonialism'. *Comparative Studies in Society and History* 2 (1):67–84.

Kuhn, Thomas S. 2012. *The Structure of Scientific Revolutions*, 4th ed. Chicago: University of Chicago Press.

Kuper, Adam. 1970. 'Gluckman's Village Headman'. *American Anthropologist* 72:355–8.

Kutateladze, Besiki, and Jim Parsons. 2014. *Why, What and How to Measure? A User's Guide to Measuring Rule of Law, Justice and Security Programmes*. United Nations Development Programme.

Kyed, Helene Maria. 2017. Justice Provision in Myanmar. DIIS Policy Brief.

Lamont-Brown, Raymond. 1998. *Kempeitai: Japan's Dreaded Military Police*. Stroud: Sutton Publishing.

Law to Protect National Solidarity (1964).

Latour, Bruno. 1987. *Science in Action: How to Follow Scientists and Engineers through Society*. Milton Keynes: Open University Press.

Latusek, Dominika, and Karen S. Cook. 2012. 'Trust in Transitions'. *Kyklos* 65 (4):512–25.

Latusek, Dominika, and Tomasz Olejniczak. 2016. 'Development of Trust in Low-Trust Societies'. *Polish Sociological Review* 195 (3):309–26.

Lawrance, Benjamin N., Emily Lynn Osborn, and Richard L. Roberts. 2015. *Intermediaries, Interpreters, and Clerks: African Employees in the Making of Colonial Africa*. Wisconsin: University of Wisconsin Press.

Lee, Raymond M., and Claire M. Renzetti. 1990. 'The Problems of Researching Sensitive Topics'. *American Behavioral Scientist* 33 (5):510–28.

Legal Vice Presidency/World Bank. 2003. *Legal and Judicial Reform: Strategic Directions*. Washington, DC: World Bank. http://documents1 .worldbank.org/curated/en/218071468779992785/pdf/269160Legal0101 e0also0250780SCODE09.pdf.

Lewis, David. 2005. 'Anthropology and Development: The Uneasy Relationship'. LSE Research Online. http://eprints.lse.ac.uk/archive/ 00000253.

Lewis, David, and David Mosse, eds. 2006. *Development Brokers and Translators: The Ethnography of Aid and Agencies*. Bloomfield, CT: Kumarian Press.

Levitt, Peggy, and Sally Merry. 2009. 'Vernacularization on the Ground: Local Uses of Global Women's Rights in Peru, China, India and the United States'. *Global Networks* 9 (4):441–61.

Liamputtong, Pranee. 2009. 'Qualitative Data Analysis: Conceptual and Practical Considerations'. *Health Promotion Journal of Australia* 20 (2):133–9.

Liddell, Zunetta. 1997. 'No Room to Move: Legal Constraints on Civil Society in Burma'. One of Four Papers Presented at the Conference 'Strengthening Civil Society in Burma: Possibilities and Dilemmas for International NGOs' organised by the Transnational Institute and the Burma Centrum Nederland, 4–5 December, Royal Tropical Institute, Amsterdam. www .burmalibrary.org/sites/burmalibrary.org/files/obl/docs3/liddellpaper.htm.

Lidholm, Charles. 2018. 'Charisma'. In *International Encyclopedia of Anthropology*, 1–3.

Liljeblad, Jonathan. 2016a. 'The 2014 Enabling Law of the Myanmar National Human Rights Commission and the United Nations Paris Principles: A Critical Evaluation'. *Journal of East Asia and International Law* 9 (2):427–47.

2016b. 'Transnational Support and Legal Education Reform in Developing Countries: Findings and Lessons from Burma/Myanmar'. *Loyola University Chicago International Law Review* 14:133.

2019. 'The Independent Lawyers' Association of Myanmar (ILAM): Challenges Facing the Legal Transplant of International Expectations for a Bar Association into a Local Context'. *Fordham International Law Journal* 43:1133.

Lin, Nan. 2001. *Social Capital: A Theory of Social Structure and Action*. Vol. 19. Cambridge/New York: Cambridge University Press.

Lindquist, Johan. 2015a. 'Brokers and Brokerage, Anthropology of'. In *International Encyclopedia of Social and Behavioral Science*. Amsterdam: Elsevier.

2015b. 'Of Figures and Types: Brokering Knowledge and Migration in Indonesia and Beyond'. *Journal of the Royal Anthropological Institute* 21 (S1):162–77.

Lindsey, Tim. 2007. 'Legal Infrastructure and Governance Reform in Post-Crisis Asia: The Case of Indonesia'. In *Law Reform in Developing and Transitional States*, edited by Tim Lindsey. London/New York: Routledge.

Lintner, Bertil. 1989. *Outrage: Burma's Struggle for Democracy*. Hong Kong: Review Publishing Company Limited.

Linz, Juan J. 2000. *Totalitarian and Authoritarian Regimes*. Colorado/London: Lynne Rienner Publishers.

2012. 'Bridging the Gap Between Donor Community and Local Organizations in Myanmar'. www.academia.edu/4446401/Bridging_the_Gap_between_D onor_Community_and_Local_Organizations_in_Myanmar.

Loka Ahlinn. n.d. 'Loka Ahlinn Social Development Project'. www .lokaahlinn.com/.

London School of Economics and Political Science. 2012. The Rule of Law, 12 June.

Long, Norman. 1975. 'Structural Dependency, Modes of Production and Economic Brokerage in Rural Peru'. In *Beyond the Sociology of Development: Economy and Society in Latin America and Africa*, edited by Ivar Oxaal, Tony Barnett and David Booth, 253–82. London/Boston/ Henley: Routledge & Kegan Paul.

2001. *Development Sociology: Actor Perspectives*. London/New York: Routledge.

Looi, Florence. 2015. 'Myanmar Bill Limits Women's Right to Wed Non-Buddhists'. *Al Jazeera*.

Luhmann, Niklas. 1979. *Trust and Power*. Chichester: Wiley.

Macdonald, Adam P. 2013. 'From Military Rule to Electoral Authoritarianism: The Reconfiguration of Power in Myanmar and Its Future'. *Asian Affairs: An American Review* 40:20–36.

Madden, Raymond. 2010. *Being Ethnographic: A Guide to the Theory and Practice of Ethnography*. London: Sage.

Magen, Amichai, and Leonardo Morlino, eds. 2009. *International Actors, Democratization and the Rule of Law: Anchoring Democracy?* New York/ London: Routledge.

Manji, Ambreena. 2006. *The Politics of Land Reform in Africa: From Communal Tenure to Free Markets*. London/New York: Zed Books.

Marcus, George E. 1995. 'Ethnography in/of the World System: The Emergence of Multi-sited Ethnography'. *Annual Review of Anthropology* 24:95–117.

Massoud, Mark Fathi. 2011. 'Do Victims of War Need International Law? Human Rights Education Programs in Authoritarian Sudan'. *Law & Society Review* 45 (1):1–32.

   2013. *Law's Fragile State: Colonial, Authoritarian, and Humanitarian Legacies in Sudan*. Cambridge: Cambridge University Press.

   2015. 'Work Rules: How International NGOs Build Law in War-Torn Societies: Work Rules'. *Law & Society Review* 49 (2):333–64.

Maung Maung, U. 1989. *Burmese Nationalist Movements 1940–1948*. Honolulu: University of Hawai'i Press.

Mawdsley, Emma, Janet G. Townsend, and Gina Porter. 2005. 'Trust, Accountability, and Face-to-Face Interaction in North–South NGO Relations'. *Development in Practice* 15 (1):77–82.

Mayall, James. 1996. *The New Interventionism, 1991–1994: United Nations Experience in Cambodia, Former Yugoslavia and Somalia*. Cambridge/New York: Cambridge University Press.

McAlinn, Gerald Paul, and Caslav Pejovic, eds. 2012. *Law and Development in Asia*. Abingdon/New York: Routledge.

McBride, Keally D. 2016. *Mr. Mothercountry: The Man Who Made the Rule of Law*. Oxford/New York: Oxford University Press.

McWha, Ishbel. 2011. 'The Roles of, and Relationships between, Expatriates, Volunteers, and Local Development Workers'. *Development in Practice* 21 (1):29–40.

Meehan, Patrick, and Sharri Plonsky. 2017. 'Brokering the Margins: A Review of Concepts and Methods'. Working Paper No.1. SOAS and the University of Bath.

Meetings Coverage: United Nations General Assembly. 2012. World Leaders Adopt Declaration Reaffirming Rule of Law as Foundation for Building Equitable State Relations, Just Societies, 24 September.

Meierhenrich, Jens. 2008. *The Legacies of Law: Long-Run Consequences of Legal Development in South Africa, 1652–2000*. Cambridge: Cambridge University Press.

Mendras, Henri, and Ioan Mihailescu, eds. 1982. *Theories and Methods in Rural Community Studies*. Oxford: Pergamon Press.

Merry, Sally Engle. 1988. 'Legal Pluralism'. *Law & Society Review* 22 (5):869–96.

   2006a. 'Transnational Human Rights and Local Activism: Mapping the Middle'. *American Anthropologist* 108:38–51.

   2006b. *Human Rights and Gender Violence*. Chicago: University of Chicago Press.

2010. 'Colonial Law and Its Uncertainties'. *Law and History Review* 28 (4):1067–71.

2015. 'Ethnography of the Global' [podcast]. Regulatory Institutions Network Key Thinkers Series, 17 March, Australian National University, Canberra. http://regnet.anu.edu.au/news-events/podcasts/56 1/sally-engle-merry-ethnography-global.

2016. 'The Rule of Law and Authoritarian Rule: Legal Politics in Sudan'. *Law & Social Inquiry* 41 (2):465–70. doi: 10.1111/lsi.12197.

Merry, Sally Engle, and Susan Bibler Coutin. 2014. 'Technologies of Truth in the Anthropology of Conflict: AES/APLA Presidential Address, 2013'. *American Ethnologist* 41 (1):1–16.

Merry, Sally Engle, Kevin E. Davis, and Benedict Kingsbury, eds. 2015. *The Quiet Power of Indicators: Measuring Governance, Corruption, and Rule of Law*. Cambridge: Cambridge University Press.

Merryman, John. H. 1977. 'Comparative Law and Social Change: On the Origins, Style, Decline & Revival of the Law and Development Movement'. *American Journal of Comparative Law* 25:457–83.

Meyer, John W. 1996. 'Otherhood: The Promulgation and Transmission of Ideas in the Modern Organizational Environment'. In *Translating Organizational Change*, edited by Barbara Czarniawska and Guje Sevón. Berlin/New York: Walter de Gruyter.

Michael, Sarah. 2004. *Undermining Development: The Absence of Power among Local NGOs in Africa*. Bloomington/Indianapolis: Indiana University Press.

Milbrandt, Jay. 2012. 'Tracking Genocide: Persecution of the Karen in Burma'. *Texas International Law Journal* 48 (1):63.

Mishler, William, and Richard Rose. 2001. 'What Are the Origins of Political Trust? Testing Institutional and Cultural Theories in Post-Communist Societies'. *Comparative Political Studies* 34 (1):30–62.

Mizzima News. 2013. 'UNODC to Assist Efforts to Transform Myanmar Police'. 17 September.

2014. 'Myanmar, UNODC Sign "Landmark" Collaboration Agreement'. 19 August.

Moore, Adam. 2013. *Peacebuilding in Practice: Local Experience in Two Bosnian Towns*. Ithaca, NY: Cornell University Press.

Moore, Sally Falk. 1973. 'Law and Social Change: The Semi-autonomous Social Field as an Appropriate Subject of Study'. *Law & Society Review* 7:719–46.

Mosse, David. 1994. 'Authority, Gender and Knowledge: Theoretical Reflections on the Practice of Participatory Rural Appraisal'. *Development and Change* 25 (3):497–526.

2004. *Cultivating Development: An Ethnography of Aid Policy and Practice*. London: Pluto Press.

Moustafa, Tamir. 2008. 'The Political Origins of "Rule-by-Law" Regimes'. Yale University Workshop on the Rule of Law.

2014. 'Law and Courts in Authoritarian Regimes'. *Annual Review of Law and Social Science* 10:281–99.

Mullen, Matthew. 2016. *Pathways that Changed Myanmar*. London: Zed Books.

Munger, Frank. 2012a. 'Constructing Law from Development: Cause Lawyers, Generational Narratives, and the Rule of Law in Thailand'. In *Law and Development and the Global Discourses of Legal Transfers*, edited by John Gillespie and Pip Nicholson. Cambridge: Cambridge University Press.

2012b. 'Globalization through the Lens of Palace Wars: What Elite Lawyers' Careers Can and Cannot Tell Us about Globalization of Law'. *Law & Social Inquiry* 37 (2):476–99.

2014. 'Revolution Imagined: Cause Advocacy, Consumer Rights, and the Evolving Role of NGOs in Thailand'. *Asian Journal of Comparative Law* 9 (1):29–64.

2017. 'Rule of Law Inside Out in Myanmar: Commentary on Opposing the Rule of Law: How Myanmar's Courts Make Law and Order by Nick Cheesman'. *Hague Journal on the Rule of Law* 9 (1):3 10.

Myanmar Ministry of Hotels and Tourism. n.d. 'Permitted Area'. tourism.gov.mm/en_US/information/permitted-area/.

Myers, Ramon H., and Mark R. Peattie, eds. 1984. *The Japanese Colonial Empire, 1895–1945*. Princeton, NJ: Princeton University Press.

Myint Zan. 2000a. 'Judicial Independence in Burma: Constitutional History, Actual Practice and Future Prospects'. *Southern Cross University Law Review* 4 (December):17–59.

2000b. 'Judicial Independence in Burma: No March Backwards towards the Past'. *Asian-Pacific Law & Policy Journal* 1 (5):1–38.

2008. 'Legal Education in Burma since the Mid-1960s'. *Journal of Burma Studies* 12:63–107.

2014. 'Of Consummation, Matrimonial Promises, Fault, and Parallel Wives: The Role of Original Texts, Interpretation, Ideology and Policy in Pre- and Post-1962 Burmese Case Law'. *Columbia Journal of Asian Law* 14:153–212.

2017. 'Rule of Law Concepts in Burma's Constitutions and Actual Practice: No Ground for Optimism'. In *Constitutionalism and Legal Change in Myanmar*, edited by Andrew Harding and Khin Khin Oo, chapter 2. Oxford/Portland, OR: Hart Publishing.

MyJustice. 2018. *Searching for Justice in the Law: Understanding Access to Justice in Myanmar*. London: British Council.

Nader, Laura. 2007. 'Promise or Plunder? A Past and Future Look at Law and Development'. *Global Jurist* 7 (2):1.

Nagoya University. 2013. 'Myanmar-Japan Legal Research Center'. www
.iech.provost.nagoya-u.ac.jp/en/cooperation_center.html.
Namati: Innovations in Legal Empowerment. n.d. 'Loka Ahlinn Social
Development Network'. http://namati.org/network/organization/loka-
ahlinn-social-development-network/.
Nardi, Dominic J. Jr. 2014. 'Finding Justice Scalia in Burma: Constitutional
Interpretation and the Impeachment of Myanmar's Constitutional
Tribunal'. *Pacific Rim Law & Policy Journal* 23 (3):633–82.
    2017. 'How the Constitutional Tribunal's Jurisprudence Sparked a Crisis'.
In *Constitutionalism and Legal Change in Myanmar*, edited by
Andrew Harding and Khin Khin Oo, chapter 9. Oxford/Portland, OR:
Hart Publishing.
Nardi, Dominic J. Jr., and Lwin Moe. 2014. 'Understanding the Myanmar
Supreme Court's Docket: An Analysis of Case Topics from 2007 to 2011'.
In *Law, Society and Transition in Myanmar*, edited by Melissa Crouch and
Tim Lindsey, 95–115. London: Hart Publishing.
Network for Human Rights Documentation. n.d. 'About Us'. http://nd-
burma.org/about-us/.
New Light of Myanmar. 31 March 2011. President U Thein Sein Delivers
Inaugural Address to Pyidaungsu Hluttaw.
    22 August 2011. Translation of the Speech Delivered by President of the
Republic of the Union of Myanmar U Thein Sein at the First Pyidaungsu
Hluttaw Second Regular Session Today.
New Perimeter, Perseus Strategies, and Jacob Blaustein Institute for the
Advancement of Human Rights. 2013. Myanmar Rule of Law
Assessment.
Newton, Scott. 2006. 'The Dialectics of Law and Development'. In *The New
Law and Economic Development: A Critical Appraisal*, edited by David
M. Trubek and Alvaro Santos, 174–202. Cambridge/New York:
Cambridge University Press.
Ng, Kwai Hang, and Xin He. 2017. *Embedded Courts: Judicial Decision-Making
in China*. New York: Cambridge University Press.
Nicholson, Pip, and Samantha Hinderling. 2013. 'Japanese Aid in
Comparative Perspective'. *Hague Journal on the Rule of Law* 5
(2):274–309.
Nicholson, Pip, and Teilee Kuong. 2014. 'Japanese Legal Assistance: An East
Asian Model of Legal Assistance and Rule of Law?' *Hague Journal on the
Rule of Law* 6 (2):141–77.
Nicholson, Pip, and Sally Low. 2013. 'Local Accounts of Rule of Law Aid:
Implications for Donors'. *Hague Journal on the Rule of Law* 5 (1):1–43.
Nirmal, Ghosh. 2012. 'Myanmar Eases Media Censorship: Reporters Cheer
Move, but Are Wary about Shape of New Media Law'. *Straits Times*.

Nouwen, Sarah M. H. 2012. 'The ICC's Intervention in Uganda'. In *Rule of Law Dynamics: In an Era of International and Transnational Governance*, edited by Michael Zürn, André Nollkaemper, and Randall Peerenboom, 278. New York: Cambridge University Press.

Noy, Chaim. 2008. 'Sampling Knowledge: The Hermeneutics of Snowball Sampling in Qualitative Research'. *International Journal of Social Research Methodology* 11 (4):327–44.

Nyein Nyein. 2012a. 'Hardliners Will Be Left Behind: Thein Sein'. *The Irrawaddy*, 14 May.

2012b. 'Suu Kyi to Head "Rule of Law" Committee'. *The Irrawaddy*, 7 August.

Orrick Lawyers. n.d. 'Robert S. Pe, Partner, Commercial Litigation'. www.orrick.com/lawyers/robert-pe/Pages/default.aspx.

Owen, Richard. 2011. 'Developments in International Clinical Legal Education: Bridges across Borders Southeast Asia Community Legal Education (BABSEA CLE) Legal Studies Internship Program'. *The Law Teacher* 45 (2):240–2.

Paine, Robert. 1971. 'A Theory of Patronage and Brokerage'. In *Patrons and Brokers in the East Arctic*, edited by Robert Paine, 8–22. Canada: University of Toronto Press.

Parfitt, Rose. 2019. *The Process of International Legal Reproduction: Inequality, Historiography, Resistance*. Cambridge: Cambridge University Press.

Park, C. 2012. 'Associations, Social Networks, and Democratic Citizenship: Evidence from East Asia'. *Taiwan Journal of Democracy* 8 (2):35–50.

Parsons, Jim, Besiki Kutateladze, Monica Thornton, April Bang, and Aminou Yaya. 2010. 'Justice Indicators for Post-Conflict Settings: A Review'. *Hague Journal on the Rule of Law* 2 (2):203–17.

Patton, Michael Quinn. 2002. *Qualitative Research and Evaluation Method*, 3rd ed. Thousand Oaks, CA: Sage.

Pedersen, Morten B. 2008. *Promoting Human Rights in Burma: A Critique of Western Sanctions Policy*. Plymouth: Rowman & Littlefield.

2014. 'Myanmar's Democratic Opening: The Process and Prospect of Reform'. In *Debating Democratization in Myanmar*, edited by Nick Cheesman, Nicholas Farrelly and Trevor Wilson, 19–40. Singapore: ISEAS Publishing.

2019. 'The ICC, the Rohingya and the Limitations of Retributive Justice'. *Australian Journal of International Affairs* 73 (1):9–15.

Peerenboom, Randall, ed. 2004. *Asian Discourses of Rule of Law: Theories and Implementation of Rule of Law in Twelve Asian Countries, France and the U.S.* London: Routledge.

2009. 'The Future of Rule of Law: Challenges and Prospects for the Field'. *Hague Journal on the Rule of Law* 1 (6 September). http://dx.doi.org/10.2139/ssrn.1673031.

Pereira, Anthony. 2005. *Political (In)Justice: Authoritarianism and the Rule of Law in Brazil, Chile, and Argentina.* Pittsburgh: University of Pittsburgh Press.

Permanent Mission of Pakistan and the United Nations System through the Rule of Law Coordination and Resource Group (RoLCRG1). 2014. 'Measuring Rule of Law and the Post-2015 Agenda'. Side Event to the Eighth Session of the Open Working Group on Sustainable Development Goals, Trusteeship Council Chamber, Friday 7 February, 1.15 p.m.

Perry-Kessaris, Amanda. 2014. 'The Case for a Visualized Economic Sociology of Legal Development'. *Current Legal Problems* 67 (1):169–98.

Phillips, Tom. 2016. 'China Passes Law Imposing Security Controls on Foreign NGOs'. *The Guardian*, 28 April.

Pompe, Sebastiaan. 2005. *The Indonesian Supreme Court: A Study of Institutional Collapse.* Ithaca, NY: Southeast Asia Program Publications.

Prasse-Freeman, Elliott. 2015. 'Conceptions of Justice and the Rule of Law in Burma'. In *Myanmar: The Dynamics of an Evolving Polity*, edited by David I. Steinberg, chapter 5. Boulder, CO: Lynne Rienner Publishers.

2019. 'Of Punishment, Protest, and Press Conferences'. In *Criminal Legalities in the Global South: Cultural Dynamics, Political Tensions, and Institutional Practices*, edited by Pablo Ciocchini and George Radics, chapter 7. London: Routledge.

Pritchard, Ashley. 2016. *A Wolf in Sheep's Clothing: 'Post-Junta' Judicial Reform in Myanmar (2010–2015).* University of Windsor, Universiti Sains Malaysia, and Berghof Foundation.

Pritchett, Lant, Michael Woolcock, and Matt Andrews. 2012. 'Looking Like a State: Techniques of Persistent Failure in State Capability for Implementation'. CID Working Paper No. 239, June. Center for International Development at Harvard University. https://bsc .cid.harvard.edu/files/bsc/files/239.pdf.

Pyae Thet Phyo. 2016. 'NLD Plans End to Rules on Overnight Visitors'. *Myanmar Times*, 31 August.

Rajagopal, Balakrishnan. 2007. 'Invoking the Rule of Law in Post-Conflict Rebuilding: A Critical Examination'. *William & Mary Law Review* 49:1347.

Rajah, Jothie. 2012. *Authoritarian Rule of Law: Legislation, Discourse and Legitimacy in Singapore.* Cambridge: Cambridge University Press.

2014. '"Rule of Law" as Transnational Legal Order'. In *Transnational Legal Orders*, edited by Terence C. Halliday and Gregory C. Shaffer. New York: Cambridge University Press.

Registration of Organizations Law (Pyidaungsu Hluttaw Law No. 31/2014).

Reilly, James. 2013. 'China and Japan in Myanmar: Aid, Natural Resources and Influence'. *Asian Studies Review* 37 (2):141–57.

Remadji, Hoinathy, and Andrea Behrends. 2014. 'Does Rationality Travel? Translations of a World Bank Model for Fair Oil Revenue Distribution in Chad'. In *Travelling Models in African Conflict Management: Translating Technologies of Social Ordering*, edited by Andrea Behrends, Sung-Joon Park, and Richard Rottenburg. Leiden/Boston: Brill.

Restrepo Amariles, David. 2015. 'Legal Indicators, Global Law and Legal Pluralism: An Introduction'. *Journal of Legal Pluralism and Unofficial Law* 47 (1):9–21.

Revolutionary Council of the Union of Burma. 1962. *The Burmese Way to Socialism*. Rangoon: Information Department for the Revolutionary Council.

Richter, Daniel K. 1988. 'Cultural Brokers and Intercultural Politics: New York-Iroquois Relations, 1664–1701'. *Journal of American History* 75 (1):40–67.

Rieffel, Lex, and James W. Fox. 2013. 'Too Much, Too Soon? The Dilemma of Foreign Aid to Myanmar/Burma'. Arlington, VA: Nathan Associates Inc.

Riles, Annelise. 2005. 'A New Agenda for the Cultural Study of Law: Taking on the Technicalities'. *Buffalo Law Review* 53:973.

Risse, Nathalie. 2017. 'Scientists Provide Update on GSDR 2019'. Murphy International, SDG Knowledge Hub https://murphyintldev.com/website/publish/newsroom/newsDetail.php?Scientists-Provide-Update-on-GSDR-2019-344.

Risse, Thomas, and Nelli Babayan. 2015. 'Democracy Promotion and the Challenges of Illiberal Regional Powers: Introduction to the Special Issue'. *Democratization* 22 (3):381–99.

Risse-Kappen, Thomas, Steve C. Ropp, and Kathryn Sikkink. 1999. *The Power of Human Rights: International Norms and Domestic Change*. Vol. 66. Cambridge: Cambridge University Press.

Rittich, Kerry. 2006. 'The Future of Law and Development: Second-Generation Reforms and the Incorporation of the Social'. In *The New Law and Economic Development: A Critical Appraisal*, edited by David M. Trubek and Alvaro Santos. New York: Cambridge University Press.

Rodriguez-Garavito, Cesar. 2011. 'Judicial Reform and the Transnational Construction of the Rule of Law in Latin America: The Return of Law and Development'. In *Lawyers and the Rule of Law in an Era of Globalization*, edited by Yves Dezalay and Bryant G. Garth. Abingdon/New York: Routledge.

Roe, Emery M. 1989. 'Folktale Development'. *American Journal of Semiotics* 6 (2/3):277.

——— 1991. 'Development Narratives, or Making the Best of Blueprint Development'. *World Development* 19 (4):287–300.

Rossi, Benedetta. 2006. 'Aid Policies and Recipient Strategies in Niger: Why Donors and Recipients Should Not Be Compartmentalized into Separate "Worlds of Knowledge"'. In *Development Brokers and Translators: The*

*Ethnography of Aid and Agencies*, edited by David Lewis and David Mosse, 27–50. Bloomfield, CT: Kumarian Press.

Roth, Silke. 2012. 'Professionalisation Trends and Inequality: Experiences and Practices in Aid Relationships'. *Third World Quarterly* 33 (8):1459–74.

——— 2015. *The Paradoxes of Aid Work: Passionate Professionals*. New York: Routledge.

——— 2019. 'Linguistic Capital and Inequality in Aid Relations'. *Sociological Research Online* 24 (1):38–54.

Rottenburg, Richard. 2005. 'Code-Switching, or Why a Metacode Is Good to Have'. In *Global Ideas: How Ideas, Objects and Practices Travel in the Global Economy*, edited by Barbara Czarniawska and Guje Sevon, 259–74. Malmö, Sweden: Författarna och Liber AB.

——— 2009. *Far-Fetched Facts: A Parable of Development Aid*. Translated by Allison Brown and Tom Lampert. Cambridge, MA/London: MIT Press.

——— 2013. 'Ethnologie und Kritik'. In *Ethnologie im 21. Jahrhundert*, edited by Thomas Bierschenk, Matthias Krings and Carola Lentz, 55–76. Berlin: Reimer.

Rottenburg, Richard, Sally Engle Merry, Sung-Joon Park, and Johanna Mugler, eds. 2015. *The World of Indicators: The Making of Governmental Knowledge through Quantification*. Cambridge: Cambridge University Press.

S/2004/616 23 August 2004. UN Doc. 'Rule of law and Transitional Justice in Conflict and Post-Conflict Societies'.

Saha, Jonathan. 2012. 'A Mockery of Justice? Colonial Law, the Everyday State and Village Politics in the Burma Delta, c.1890–1910'. *Past & Present* 217 (1):187–212.

Said, Edward W. 2003. *Orientalism*. London: Penguin.

Saisana, Michaela, and Andrea Saltelli. 2012. 'Statistical Audit'. World Justice Project. https://worldjusticeproject.org/sites/default/files/statistical_audit.pdf.

Samet, Oren. 2018. 'Inside Myanmar's Dangerous Media Repression Campaign'. *Pacific Standard*, 19 January.

Samuels, Kirsti. 2006. 'RoL Reform in Post Conflict Countries: Operational Initiatives and Lessons Learnt'. World Bank Social Development Papers Series.

Sannerholm, Richard. 2012. *Rule of Law After War and Crisis*. Cambridge: Intersentia.

Sannerholm, Richard, Frida Möller, Kristina Simion, and Hanna Hallonsten. 2012. 'Looking Back, Moving Forward: UN Peace Operations and Rule of Law Assistance in Africa, 1989–2010'. *Hague Journal on the Rule of Law* 4 (2):359–73.

San Pe, Robert. 2014. 'Burma/Myanmar: Prospects for Democracy and Rule of Law'. Bingham Centre for the Rule of Law. www.biicl.org/files/6839_robert_pe_burma_myanmar_rule_of_law_paper_10_feb_14.pdf.

Santos, Alvaro. 2006. 'The World Bank's Uses of the "Rule of Law" Promise in Economic Development'. In *The New Law and Economic Development: A Critical Appraisal*, edited by David Trubek and Alvaro Santos, 253–300. Cambridge: Cambridge University Press.

Sarat, Austin, and Stuart A. Scheingold. 2008. *The Cultural Lives of Cause Lawyers*. Cambridge/New York: Cambridge University Press.

Schaffer, Frederic Charles. 1998. *Democracy in Translation: Understanding Politics in an Unfamiliar Culture*. Ithaca, NY: Cornell University Press.

Scribner, Druscilla, and Tracy Slagter. 2017. 'Recursive Norm Development: The Role of Supranational Courts'. *Global Policy* 8 (3):322–32.

SDG 16 Data Initiative. n.d. www.sdg16.org/.

Seekins, Donald M. 2006. *Historical Dictionary of Burma (Myanmar)*. Maryland: Scarecrow Press.

2009. 'State, Society and Natural Disaster: Cyclone Nargis in Myanmar (Burma)'. *Asian Journal of Social Science* 37 (5):717–37.

Seeley, Janet. 1985. 'Praise, Prestige and Power: The Organisation of Social Welfare in a Developing Kenyan Town'. Jesus College, University of Cambridge.

Seidel, Katrin. 2017. 'Rule of Law Promotion in Translation: Technologies of Normative Knowledge Transfer in South Sudan's Constitution Making'. In *World Politics in Translation: Power, Relationality and Difference in Global Cooperation*, edited by Tobias Berger and Alejandro Esguerra, 76–91. Routledge.

Selth, Andrew. 1998. 'Burma's Intelligence Apparatus'. *Intelligence and National Security* 13 (4):33–70.

2010. 'Modern Burma Studies: A Survey of the Field'. *Modern Asian Studies* 44 (2):401–40.

2013. 'Police Reform in Burma (Myanmar): Aims, Obstacles and Outcomes'. Regional Outlook Paper No. 44. Brisbane: Griffith Asia Institute.

Sen, Amartya. 2000. 'What Is the Role of Legal and Judicial Reform in the Development Process?' World Bank Legal Conference, Washington DC.

2009. *The Idea of Justice*. Boston, MA: Harvard University Press.

Shigetomi, Shin'ichi. 2002. *The State and NGOs: Perspective from Asia*. Singapore: Institute of Southeast Asian Studies.

Shklar, N. Judith. 1998. *Political Thought and Political Thinkers*. Chicago: University of Chicago Press.

Shwe Lu Maung. 1989. *Burma, Nationalism and Ideology: An Analysis of Society, Culture, and Politics*. Dhaka: University Press Limited.

Silverman, Sydel F. 1965. 'Patronage and Community-Nation Relationships in Central Italy'. *Ethnology* 4 (2):172–89.

Silverstein, Josef. 1977. *Burma: Military Rule and the Politics of Stagnation*. Ithaca, NY/London: Cornell University Press.

1997. 'The Civil War, the Minorities and Burma's New Politics'. In *Burma: The Challenge of Change in a Divided Society*, edited by Peter Carey. Basingstoke/London: Macmillan Press.

Simion, Kristina. 2018. 'Research Access and Ethics in Myanmar'. *Journal of the Oxford Centre for Socio-legal Studies*. https://joxcsls.com/2018/12/09/research-access-and-ethics-in-myanmar/.

2019. 'Bottom-Up Explorations: Locating Rule of Law Intermediaries after Transition in Myanmar'. *Journal of Burma Studies* 23 (1):125–41. doi: 10.1353/jbs.2019.0004.

Simion, Kristina, and Veronica L. Taylor. 2015. Professionalizing Rule of Law: Issues and Directions. Folke Bernadotte Academy. RegNet Research Paper No. 2015/81. https://ssrn.com/abstract=2635323.

Singh, Udai Bhanu. 2013. 'Do the Changes in Myanmar Signify a Real Transition?' *Strategic Analysis* 37:101–4.

Skidmore, Monique. 2003. 'Darker than Midnight: Fear, Vulnerability, and Terror Making in Urban Burma (Myanmar)'. *American Ethnologist* 30 (1):5–21.

Skidmore, Monique, and Trevor Wilson. 2010. 'Perspectives on a Transitional Situation'. In *Ruling Myanmar: From Cyclone Nargis to National Elections*, edited by Nick Cheesman, Monique Skidmore, and Trevor Wilson. Singapore: ISEAS Publishing.

South, Ashley. 2008. *Civil Society in Burma: The Development of Democracy amidst Conflict*, Vol. 51. Washington, DC: East-West Center; Singapore: Institute of Southeast Asian Studies.

Sperfeldt, Cristoph. 2013. 'From the Margins of Internationalized Criminal Justice: Lessons Learned at the Extraordinary Chambers in the Courts of Cambodia'. *Journal of International Criminal Justice* 11 (5):1111–37.

Spillius, Alex. 2012. 'Aung San Suu Kyi in First Foreign Trip in 24 Years'. *The Telegraph*, 29 May.

Spivak, Gayatri Chakravorty. 2007. *Other Asias*. Malden, MA: Blackwell Publishing.

Steinberg, David I. 2001. *Burma: The State of Myanmar*. Washington, DC: Georgetown University Press.

2013. *Burma/Myanmar: What Everyone Needs to Know*. 2nd ed. New York: Oxford University Press.

Stern, Marc J. 2008. 'The Power of Trust: Toward a Theory of Local Opposition to Neighboring Protected Areas'. *Society & Natural Resources* 21 (10):859–75.

Stokke, Kristian, and Soe Myint Aung. 2020. 'Transition to Democracy or Hybrid Regime? The Dynamics and Outcomes of Democratization in Myanmar'. *European Journal of Development Research* 32 (2):274–93.

Stovel, Katherine, and Lynette Shaw. 2012. 'Brokerage'. *Annual Review of Sociology* 38 (1):139–58.

Stromseth, Jane, David Wippman, and Rosa Brooks. 2006. *Can Might Make Rights? Building the Rule of Law after Military Interventions*. Cambridge: Cambridge University Press.

Supreme Court of the Republic of the Union of Myanmar. 2017. www .myjusticemyanmar.org/code-judicial-ethics-myanmar-judges.

Supreme Court of the Union of Myanmar. 2014. *Advancing Justice Together (Judiciary Strategic Plan 2015–2017)*. Nay Pyi Taw, Myanmar.

    2016. *Advancing Justice Together (Judiciary Strategic Plan 2015–2017): Year 2 Action Plan*. Nay Pyi Taw, Myanmar.

Szasz, Margaret Connell. 1994. 'Introduction'. In *Between Indian and White Worlds: The Cultural Broker*, edited by Margaret Connell Szasz. Oklahoma: University of Oklahoma Press.

Tamanaha, Brian Z. 2004. *On the Rule of Law: Politics, History, Theory*. Cambridge: Cambridge University Press.

    2008. 'Understanding Legal Pluralism: Past to Present, Local to Global'. *Sydney Law Review* 30 (3):375–411.

    2011. 'The Rule of Law and Legal Pluralism in Development'. *Hague Journal on the Rule of Law* 3 (1):1–17.

Tamanaha, Brian Z., and Martin Krygier. 2005. 'On the Rule of Law: History, Politics, Theory'. *Journal of Law and Society* 32 (4):657–66.

Taylor, Robert H. 2009. *The State in Myanmar*. London: Hurst & Company.

    2012. 'Myanmar: from Army Rule to Constitutional Rule?' *Asian Affairs* 43 (2):221–36.

Taylor, Veronica L. 2007. 'The Law Reform Olympics: Measuring the Effects of Law Reform in Transition Economies'. In *Law Reform in Developing and Transitional States*, edited by Tim Lindsey, chapter 4. Abingdon: Routledge.

    2009. 'Frequently Asked Questions about Rule of Law Assistance (And Why Better Answers Matter)'. *Hague Journal on the Rule of Law* 1 (1):46.

    2010a. 'Legal Education as Development'. In *Legal Education in Asia: Globalization, Change and Contexts*, edited by Stacey Steele and Kathryn Taylor, 215–40. Abingdon/New York: Routledge.

    2010b. 'Rule-of-Law Assistance Discourse and Practice: Japanese Inflections'. In *Law in the Pursuit of Development: Principles into Practice?*, edited by Amanda Perry Kessaris. Abingdon/New York: Routledge.

    2016. 'Big Rule of Law ©®ᔆᴹ™ (pat.pending): Branding and Certifying the Business of the Rule of Law'. In *Strengthening the Rule of Law through the UN Security Council*, edited by Jeremy Matam Farrall and Hilary Charlesworth, chapter 3. Abingdon/New York: Routledge.

Tetra Tech. n.d. 'Promoting the Rule of Law in Myanmar'. www.tetratech.com /en/projects/promoting-the-rule-of-law-in-myanmar.

Than, Tharaphi. 2015. 'Nationalism, Religion, and Violence: Old and New Wunthanu Movements in Myanmar'. *Review of Faith & International Affairs* 13 (4):12–24.

Thant Myint-U. 2004. *The Making of Modern Burma*. Cambridge: Cambridge University Press.

Thomas, Melissa. 2005. 'The Rule of Law in Western Thought'. World Bank Factsheet. Washington, DC: World Bank.

Thomson Reuters Foundation. 2013. 'Myanmar Seeks Inspiration from South Africa for Nascent Legal Aid Movement'. https://news.trust.org/item/20130516125223-i4za9/.

Tommasoli, Massimo. 2017. "People-Centred Monitoring of SDG16: Peace, Justice and Strong Inclusive Institutions." Roundtable with Massimo Tommasoli, Permanent Observer for International IDEA to the United Nations and Alexandra Wilde, Senior Research and Policy Advisor of the UNDP Oslo Governance Centre'. www.idea.int/news-media/events/people-centred-monitoring-sdg16-peace-justice-and-strong-inclusive-institutions.

Trager, Frank N. 1959. *Marxism in Southeast Asia: A Study of Four Countries*. Stanford, CA: Stanford University Press.

Trebilcock, Michael J., and Mariana Mota Prado. 2011. *What Makes Poor Countries Poor? Institutional Determinants of Development*. Cheltenham: Edward Elgar.

Trubek, David M. 1972. 'Toward a Social Theory of Law: An Essay on the Study of Law and Development'. *Yale Law Journal* 82 (1):1–50.

   2006. 'The "Rule of Law" in Development Assistance: Past, Present, and Future'. In *The New Law and Economic Development: A Critical Appraisal*, edited by David M. Trubek and Alvaro Santos, 74–94. Cambridge: Cambridge University Press.

Trubek, David M., and Marc Galanter. 1974. 'Scholars in Self-Estrangement: Some Reflections on the Crisis in Law and Development Studies'. *Wisconsin Law Review* 4 (4):1062–1102.

Trubek, David M., and Alvaro Santos, eds. 2006. *The New Law and Economic Development: A Critical Appraisal*. Cambridge: Cambridge University Press.

Tun, Melinda. 2014. 'A Principled Approach to Company Law Reform in Myanmar'. In *Law, Society and Transition in Myanmar*, edited by Melissa Crouch and Tim Lindsey. London: Hart Publishing.

Tungnirun, Arm. 2017. 'Filling the Void with Lawyers: Globalization and Foreign Corporate Lawyers in Myanmar'. PhD thesis, Stanford Law School.

   2018. 'Practising on the Moon: Globalization and Legal Consciousness of Foreign Corporate Lawyers in Myanmar'. *Asian Journal of Law and Society* 5 (1):49–67.

Tun Lin Moe. 2008. 'An Empirical Investigation of Relationships between Official Development Assistance (ODA) and Human and Educational Development'. *International Journal of Social Economics* 35 (3):202–21.

Tun Zaw Mra. 2014. 'The Securities Exchange Law and Prospectus Regulation: Early Sketches of Equity Capital Market Law and Regulation in Myanmar'. In *Law, Society and Transition in Myanmar*, edited by Melissa Crouch and Tim Lindsey, 245–69. London: Hart Publishing.

Turku, Helga. 2009. *Isolationist States in an Interdependent World*. Farnham: Ashgate.

Turnell, Sean. 2011. 'Myanmar's Fifty-Year Authoritarian Trap'. *Journal of International Affairs* 65 (1):79–92.

——— 2014. 'Legislative Foundations of Myanmar's Economic Reforms'. In *Law, Society and Transition in Myanmar*, edited by Melissa Crouch and Tim Lindsey, 183–200. London: Hart Publishing.

Union Attorney General's Office. 2015. *Moving Forward to the Rule of Law (Strategic Plan 2015–2017)*. Nay Pyi Taw, Myanmar.

United Nations. 1985. 'Basic Principles on the Independence of the Judiciary'. www.un.org/ruleoflaw/blog/document/basic-principles-on-the-independence-of-the-judiciary/.

——— 1990a. 'Basic Principles on the Role of Lawyers'. www.un.org/ruleoflaw/blog/document/basic-principles-on-the-role-of-lawyers/.

——— 1990b. 'Guidelines on the Role of Prosecutors'. www.un.org/ruleoflaw/blog/document/guidelines-on-the-role-of-prosecutors/.

——— 2008. 'Guidance Note of the Secretary-General: UN Approach to Rule of Law Assistance'. www.un.org/ruleoflaw/blog/document/guidance-note-of-the-secretary-general-un-approach-to-rule-of-law-assistance/.

——— 2011. 'The United Nations Rule of Law Indicators: Implementation Guide and Project Tools'. www.un.org/ruleoflaw/blog/document/the-united-nations-rule-of-law-indicators-implementation-guide-and-project-tools/.

——— 2013. 'The United Nations Guidelines and Principles on Access to Legal Aid in Criminal Justice Systems'.

——— n.d. 'The Rule of Law in the UN's Intergovernmental Work'. www.un.org/ruleoflaw/what-is-the-rule-of-law/the-rule-of-law-in-un-work/.

United Nations Department of Peacekeeping Operations (DPKO) and the Office of the United Nations High Commissioner for Human Rights (OHCHR). 2011. 'The United Nations Rule of Law Indicators: Implementation Guide and Project Tools'.

United Nations Department of Peacekeeping Operations Department of Field Support. 2009. 'Methodology for Review of Justice and Corrections Components in United Nations Peace Operations'. www.un.org/ruleoflaw/blog/document/guidelines-on-the-methodology-for-review-of-justice-and-corrections-components-in-united-nations-peace-operations/.

United Nations Development Policy and Analysis Division. 2015. 'Least Developed Countries Factsheet: Myanmar'. www.un.org/en/development/desa/policy/cdp/ldc/profile/country_129.shtml.

n.d. 'Support to Democratic Governance in Myanmar'. www.mm.undp.org /content/myanmar/en/home/operations/projects/democratic_gover nance/Support_to_Democratic_Governance/.

2011. 'New Voices: National Perspectives on Rule of Law Assistance'. www .un.org/ruleoflaw/blog/document/new-voices-national-perspectives-on-rule-of-law-assistance/.

United Nations Development Programme. 2014. Summary Report of Rule of Law and Access to Justice Mapping in Myanmar. (On file with the author.)

United Nations Development Programme. 2014. 'Bridges to Justice: Rule of Law Centres for Myanmar'. www.mm.undp.org/content/myanmar/en/ho me/library/democratic_governance/bridges-to-justice.html.

United Nations Development Programme and United Nations Office on Drugs and Crime. 2016. Global Study on Legal Aid.

United Nations Development Programme and others. 2014. 'International Conference on Access to Legal Aid in Criminal Justice Systems'. www .un.org/ruleoflaw/blog/2015/03/event-on-enhancing-access-to-legal-aid-in-criminal-justice-systems-on-thursday-13-november-2014/.

United Nations Economic and Social Council. 2017. 'Progress towards the Sustainable Development Goals: Report of the Secretary-General'. http s://digitallibrary.un.org/record/1288024?ln=en.

United Nations General Assembly. 2012. 'Declaration of the High-level Meeting of the General Assembly on the Rule of Law at the National and International Levels, 19 September'. (On file with the author.)

2005. 'Resolution adopted by the General Assembly: 2005 World Summit Outcome'. www.un.org/en/development/desa/population/migration/gen eralassembly/docs/globalcompact/A_RES_60_1.pdf.

United Nations Human Rights Office of the High Commissioner. 2017. Treaty Body Database.

United Nations Office of the High Commissioner for Human Rights. 2015. 'Myanmar: UN Rights Experts Express Alarm at Adoption of First of Four "Protection of Race and Religion" Bills'. www.ohchr.org/EN/NewsEven ts/Pages/DisplayNews.aspx?NewsID=16015&LangID=E.

United Nations Office on Drugs and Crime. n.d. 'UNODC's History in Myanmar'.

2006. 'Access to Justice: The Independence, Impartiality and Integrity of the Judiciary'. Criminal Justice Assessment Toolkit. New York: United Nations. www.unodc.org/documents/justice-and-prison-reform/cjat_eng/ 2_Independence_Impartiality_Integrity_of_Judiciary.pdf.

2010/2011. 'Criteria for the Design and Evaluation of Juvenile Justice Reform Programmes'. Interagency Panel on Juvenile Justice. New York: United Nations. www.unodc.org/pdf/criminal_justice/Criteria_for_the_ Design_and_Evaluation_of_Juvenile_Justice_Reform_Programmes.pdf.

2012. 'UNODC Executive Director Meets Daw Aung San Suu Kyi, 3 December'. www.unodc.org/unodc/en/press/releases/2012/December/u nodcs-executive-director-meets-daw-aung-san-suu-kyi.html.

2017. 'Criminal Justice Reform'. www.unodc.org/unodc/en/justice-and-prison-reform/criminaljusticereform.html.

United Nations Office on Drugs and Crime, and United Nations Development Programme. 2014. 'Early Access to Legal Aid in Criminal Justice Processes: A Handbook for Policymakers and Practitioners'. www.unodc.org/docu ments/justice-and-prison-reform/eBook-early_access_to_legal_aid.pdf.

United Nations Report of the UN Secretary-General. 6 August 2008. 'Strengthening and Coordinating United Nations Rule of Law Activities'. www.refworld.org/docid/4a54bbf8d.html.

United Nations Secretary General. 2012. Background Note: High-Level Meeting of the General Assembly on the Rule of Law: 'Delivering Justice: Programme of Action to Strengthen the Rule of Law at the National and International Levels', 24 September. www.un.org/ruleoflaw/ files/74077_ROL%20GA%20High-Level%20meeting_Background_Engli sh.pdf.

United Nations Security Council. 24 September 2003. 'Statement by the President of the Security Council'. https://undocs.org/S/PRST/2003/ 15.

United States Agency for International Development. 2013. International Rule of Law (ROL) Technical Assistance Services. Section A – Request for Task Order Proposal (RFTOP): Promoting the Rule of Law in Burma. (On file with the author.)

2016a. 'Democracy, Human Rights, and Rule of Law'. www.usaid.gov/bur ma/our-work/democracy-human-rights-and-rule-law.

2016b. 'Democratic Governance Fact Sheet, Democratic Governance: Inclusive, Accountable, Transparent'. www.usaid.gov/burma/docu ments/democratic-governance-fact-sheet.

United States Institute of Peace. 2013. 'USIP Burma/Myanmar Rule of Law Trip Report: Working Document for Discussion'. https://themimu.info/ sites/themimu.info/files/documents/Report_Burma-Myanmar_Rule_of_L aw_Trip_US_Institute_of_Peace_June2013.pdf.

Upham, Frank. 2002. 'Mythmaking in the Rule of Law Orthodoxy'. Rule of Law Series, Democracy and Rule of Law Project, Carnegie Working Papers.

2006. 'Mythmaking in the Rule-of-Law Orthodoxy'. In Promoting the Rule of Law Abroad: In Search of Knowledge, edited by Thomas Carothers. Washington, DC: Carnegie Endowment for International Peace.

Van de Meene, Ineke, and Benjamin van Rooij, eds. 2008. Access to Justice and Legal Empowerment: Making the Poor Central in Legal Development Co-operation. Leiden: Leiden University Press.

Van Leynseele, Yves. 2018. 'White Belonging and Brokerage at a South African Rural Frontier'. *Ethnos* 83 (5):868–87.

Van Rooij, Benjamin. 2009. 'Bringing Justice to the Poor: Bottom-Up Legal Development Cooperation'. Working Paper.

Venice Commission. 2006. The Rule of Law Checklist. www.venice.coe.int /images/SITE%20IMAGES/Publications/Rule_of_Law_Check_List.pdf.

Verma, Ritu. 2011. 'Intercultural Encounters, Colonial Continuities and Contemporary Disconnects in Rural Aid'. In *Inside the Everyday Lives of Development Workers: The Challenges and Futures of Aidland*, edited by Anne-Meike Fechter and Heather Hindman. Sterling, VA: Kumarian Press.

Von Benda-Beckmann, Franz. 2002. 'Who's Afraid of Legal Pluralism?' *Journal of Legal Pluralism and Unofficial Law* 34 (47):37–82.

Walton, Matthew J. 2013. 'The "Wages of Burman-ness": Ethnicity and Burman Privilege in Contemporary Myanmar'. *Journal of Contemporary Asia* 43 (1):1–27.

2016. *Buddhism, Politics and Political Thought in Myanmar*. Cambridge: Cambridge University Press.

Walton, Matthew J., and Susan Hayward. 2014. *Contesting Buddhist Narratives: Democratization, Nationalism, and Communal Violence in Myanmar*. Vol. 71. Honolulu, HI: East-West Center.

Wang, Yuhua. 2015. *Tying the Autocrat's Hands: The Rise of the Rule of Law in China*. New York: Cambridge University Press.

Wanvoeke, Jonas, Jean-Philippe Venot, Charlotte de Fraiture, and Margreet Zwarteveen. 2016. 'Smallholder Drip Irrigation in Burkina Faso: The Role of Development Brokers'. *Journal of Development Studies* 52 (7):1019–33.

Ward and Village Tract Administration Law (Pyidaungsu Hluttaw Law No. 1/ 2012).

Ware, Anthony. 2012a. *Context-Sensitive Development: How International NGOs Operate in Myanmar*. Sterling, VA: Kumarian Press.

2012b. 'Context Sensitivity by Development INGOs in Myanmar'. In *Myanmar's Transition: Openings, Obstacles and Opportunities*, edited by Nick Cheesman, Monique Skidmore, and Trevor Wilson, 323–47. Singapore: Institute of Southeast Asian Studies.

2013. 'Supporting National Transition in Myanmar with Development Assistance'. *Journal of International Studies* 9 (1):47–57.

Wells, Tamas, and Matthew J. Walton. 2015. 'Is Democracy Really Lost in Translation?' *The Myanmar Times*, 1 September.

Wiener, Antje. 2008. *The Invisible Constitution of Politics: Contested Norms and International Encounters*. Cambridge: Cambridge University Press.

Williams, David C. 2012. 'Changing Burma from Without: Political Activism among the Burmese Diaspora'. *Indiana Journal of Global Legal Studies* 19 (1):121–42.

2014. 'What's So Bad about Burma's 2008 Constitution? A Guide for the Perplexed'. In *Law, Society and Transition in Myanmar*, edited by Melissa Crouch and Tim Lindsey, 117–40. London: Hart Publishing.

2017. 'A Second Panglong Agreement: Burmese Federalism for the Twenty-First Century'. In *Constitutionalism and Legal Change in Myanmar*, edited by Andrew Harding and Khin Khin Oo. Oxford/Portland, OR: Hart Publishing.

Wolf, Eric R. 1956. 'Aspects of Group Relations in a Complex Society: Mexico'. *American Anthropologist* 58 (6):1065–78.

Wolfensohn, James D. 1999. 'A Proposal for a Comprehensive Development Framework (A Discussion Draft)'. Washington, DC: World Bank, Office of the President.

Wong, Edward. 2016. 'Clampdown in China Restricts 7,000 Foreign Organizations'. *New York Times*, 28 April.

World Bank. 2007. *A Decade of Measuring the Quality of Governance: Governance Matters 2007*. Washington, DC: World Bank.

2011. 'Justice for the Poor'. http://go.worldbank.org/IMMQE3ET20.

2012. *New Directions in Justice Reform: A Companion Piece to the Updated Strategy and Implementation Plan on Strengthening Governance, Tackling Corruption*. Washington, DC: World Bank. http://documents1.worldbank.org/curated/en/928641468338516754/pdf/706400REPLACEM0Justice0Reform0Final.pdf.

2015. 'Justice and Rule of Law'. Last Modified 28 April 2015.

2017. World Development Report 2017: Governance and the Law. www.worldbank.org/en/publication/wdr2017.

World Bank Legal Vice Presidency. 2009. *Initiatives in Justice Reform*. World Bank.

World Economic Forum. 2012. 'Suu Kyi Calls on Investors to Focus on How to Help Myanmar'. 1 June. www.ebcworldnews.com/index.php/world/85-asia-pacific/june-2012/98-suu-kyi-calls-to-focus-on-how-to-help-myanmar.

World Justice Project. 2014. Rule of Law Index 2014. https://worldjusticeproject.org/our-work/publications/rule-law-index-reports/wjp-rule-law-index-2014-report#:~:text=The%20WJP%20Rule%20of%20Law,to%20the%20rule%20of%20law.

Yin, Robert K. 2003. *Case Study Research: Design and Methods*, 3rd ed. Applied Social Research Methods Series. Thousand Oaks, CA/London/New Delhi: Sage.

Young, Robert J. C. 2003. *Postcolonialism: A Very Short Introduction*. Oxford: Oxford University Press.

Zimmermann, Lisbeth. 2017. *Global Norms with a Local Face: Rule-of-Law Promotion and Norm Translation*. Cambridge: Cambridge University Press.

Zürn, Michael, André Nollkaemper, and Randall Peerenboom, eds. 2012. *Rule of Law Dynamics in an Era of International and Transnational Governance*. New York: Cambridge University Press.

# INDEX

CAMBRIDGE STUDIES IN LAW AND SOCIETY

Chris Thornhill

*A Sociology of Transnational Constitutions: Social Foundations of the Post-National Legal Structure*
Chris Thornhill

*Genocide Never Sleeps: Living Law at the International Criminal Tribunal for Rwanda*
Nigel Eltringham

*Shifting Legal Visions: Judicial Change and Human Rights Trials in Latin America*
Ezequiel A. González-Ocantos

*The Demographic Transformations of Citizenship*
Heli Askola

*Criminal Defense in China: The Politics of Lawyers at Work*
Sida Liu and Terence C. Halliday

*Contesting Economic and Social Rights in Ireland: Constitution, State and Society, 1848–2016*
Thomas Murray

*Buried in the Heart: Women, Complex Victimhood and the War in Northern Uganda*
Erin Baines

*Palaces of Hope: The Anthropology of Global Organizations*
Edited by
Ronald Niezen and Maria Sapignoli

*The Politics of Bureaucratic Corruption in Post-Transitional Eastern Europe*
Marina Zaloznaya

*Revisiting the Law and Governance of Trafficking, Forced Labor and Modern Slavery*
Edited by
Prabha Kotiswaran

*Incitement on Trial: Prosecuting International Speech Crimes*
Richard Ashby Wilson

*Criminalizing Children: Welfare and the State in Australia*
David McCallum

*Global Lawmakers: International Organizations in the Crafting of World Markets*
Susan Block-Lieb and Terence C. Halliday

For EU product safety concerns, contact us at Calle de José Abascal, 56–1°, 28003 Madrid, Spain or eugpsr@cambridge.org.

www.ingramcontent.com/pod-product-compliance
Ingram Content Group UK Ltd.
Pitfield, Milton Keynes, MK11 3LW, UK
UKHW020355140625
459647UK00020B/2490

* 9 7 8 1 1 0 8 8 2 9 8 5 4 *